Henry & Nitza,

I hope you will find this
interesting.

Best Regards
Elias

May 22' 96

THE PERSISTENCE OF ECONOMIC DISCRIMINATION

THE PERSISTENCE OF
ECONOMIC
DISCRIMINATION:
Race, Ethnicity, and Gender

A Comparative Analysis

Elias H. Tuma

PACIFIC BOOKS, PUBLISHERS
Palo Alto, California

Library of Congress Cataloging-in-Publication Data

Tuma, Elias H.
    The persistence of economic discrimination: race, ethnicity, and
gender: a comparative analysis / Elias H. Tuma.
        p.   cm.
    Includes bibliographical references and index.
    ISBN 0-87015-265-3
    1. Discrimination – Economic aspects. 2. Discrimination – Cost
Effectiveness. I. Title
JC575. T85 1995
305 – dc20   95-33202
                                                                              CIP

PACIFIC BOOKS, PUBLISHERS
P.O. Box 558, Palo Alto, California 94302-0558, U.S.A.

To all who feel victimized because of physical and ethnic features over which they have no control

Preface

It is not by affirmative action that discrimination will go away, as the reformists say, nor by forces of the market, as the free-market economists say, nor by love and harmony, as the idealists hope, nor by cruelty and repression, as the supremacists and bigots say. None of these will do, for we are brought up to believe in material gain, accumulation, and rule over others. It is by ensuring the availability of work for all that racial, ethnic, and gender conflict in the market place can be minimized, and by establishing equal opportunity for all from the time of birth that mutual respect and fair play can be achieved. Only then will equality before the law and affirmative action be effective, and only then can discrimination be tamed and rendered (almost) harmless.

This study had its seeds in two quarters of a freshman seminar on economic discrimination I conducted in 1989-90. Each student had to address the topic "My Experiences with Discrimination." After finishing his paper, one of the students proudly came to tell me that now he could understand why his mother was anxious to leave the South, even though in doing so she made him leave behind his friends and the security of the home in which he grew up. In the process I also addressed my own experiences with discrimination, going back to my growing up in Palestine. I remember how the British government of Palestine favored Christians over Muslims, Jews over Arabs, and the British residents above all. I also remember how among the Arabs ethnic origin, color of the skin, eyes, and hair, and the gender of a person made so much difference in how one was treated. But I also recalled my early experiences in this country. One in particular had a great impression on me in Berkeley when a young black student could not rent a room in the house I had a room in just because he was black.

However, there is also an intellectual, inquisitive basis for the study. I have created a challenge for myself by asking why problems do not go away. Discrimination is a problem; why does it not go away, even when people declare their opposition to it? The best answer I could generate is that discrimination does not go away because we, the discriminators, do not want it to go away. Why? Because we benefit from it. We may, however, be willing to let it be tamed and made far less costly to society, especially if we remember that the victims are still rebelling and will no longer accept their unfair treatment.

This study has gone through several revisions and many people have helped me in the process. The students in my two freshman seminars made many helpful comments. Linda Shaeffer was in on the conception of the project, but her other interests prevented her from continuing. My colleagues Andrzej Brzeski and Will Rochin raised several important points, which led to revision for which I am grateful. I am also grateful to Victor Stango for his help as research assistant, to Carl Eby for editorial assistance, and to the staff of the Economics Department, especially Donna Raymond and Marlene Baccala, for taking charge of the various versions of the manuscript. Last, but not least, my publisher and editor Henry and Romayne Ponleithner have my thanks and appreciation for their accommodation and help.

September 1994   ELIAS H. TUMA
Davis, California

Contents

List of Tables

THE PERSISTENCE OF ECONOMIC DISCRIMINATION

1

Discrimination in Its Many Faces

No doubt every one of us has come in contact with unequal treatment in one form or another, directly or indirectly. It may be by hearing a friend tell his or her story, watching a colleague fret about unequal treatment in the workplace, living it on the bus, or reading about it being dealt with in the law courts and in the legislative arena of one country or another. How often have we read about a black person who could not rent a room or buy a house in a certain neighborhood because of race, or how many times have we heard of a Jewish person being prohibited from joining a club, owning property, or taking a job because of his/her ethnic origin? How many times have skilled workers been denied jobs or promotions because they are women? These are examples of discrimination.

While we tend to focus on current conspicuous cases of discrimination, as in South Africa, or on situations where the victims have become active and vocal, as in the United States, the fact is that discrimination has been a common behavior throughout the known history of most present-day societies, although its form and the identity of those engaged in the act of discrimination have changed from time to time. If we go back in time, we find evidence of discrimination by race, ethnic origin, or by gender among the Greeks and Romans, the Asiatic societies, the Hebrews and the Arabs, and among European societies in their development from the feudal period to the present. It has been especially common in the societies that may be considered extensions of European society, east and west, as they encountered other races and ethnic groups less advanced and powerful than they were.

Discrimination may be reflected in the cultures and languages of various societies in ways that suggest that a differential treatment, positive or negative, is appropriate for certain groups or individuals simply because of their race, ethnicity, or gender. We see it reflected in the literature, prose or poetry, in the laws and customs, and certainly in the daily interactions between members of society. Probably the most convincing evidence of discrimination, however, is the existence of laws enacted to prohibit it or to eliminate its vestiges from days past.

Yet, even when people are aware of discrimination in their society, they do not always consider it improper, unjust, unfair, or inefficient. Until very recent times, slavery was considered acceptable as long as it was confined to certain groups specified by the enslaving society. Ethnic minorities have almost always been treated unequally by those in the majority, as if they had less right to what society can offer than the others and as if their mere toleration by the majority removed any suspicion of discrimination.

Probably the worst case of unacknowledged discrimination is that against women. Throughout history women have been told what to do; they have been excluded from decision-making; they have been treated unequally in matters of ownership, inheritance, choice of a mate, and freedom of mobility. They have been excluded from educational and economic opportunities, without regard for their wishes. Ironically, women have usually been told that they were excluded from various functions and occupations for their own protection. The discriminators have admitted that they do indeed discriminate, but insist that they do so in favor of women and not against them. Yet when women have sought freedom from discrimination, the discriminators have rarely listened to them.

One may ask whether it is any more just to discriminate in favor of than against one group or another, for there are two sides of the coin: when we accord preferential treatment to men, we must be discriminating against women, and when we give special rights to the majority we must be denying the minorities certain rights or privileges. When we give certain racial groups easier access to jobs, housing facilities, and education, we must be depriving other racial groups that must share these opportunities. It is difficult to deal with negative discrimination against certain groups without first recognizing that certain other groups or individuals may be benefiting from this discriminatory behavior.

After all, why doesn't discrimination go away in spite of the numerous attempts made to abolish it? Is it possible that those who discriminate have a vested interest in discrimination, that the policy-makers have no intention of abolishing it, or that their attempts are only half-hearted gestures intended to mislead and redirect activities against discrimination and maintain the vested interests of those who do discriminate?

We are asking these questions mainly from the economic standpoint, even though discrimination has roots and branches in culture, religion, literature, and technology—all of which may sustain and perpetuate discrimination. Our main focus will be in the area of political economy of racial, ethnic, and sex discrimination, that is, on discrimination that is primarily a result of prejudice, which leads to economic inefficiencies and high social costs to society.

DEFINITIONS AND CONCEPTS

Discrimination against, or in favor of, an individual, a group, or a nation means giving that party a different and unequal treatment compared with that given to others in similar situations simply because of specific features of that individual, group, or nation. For example, two individuals may be equally qualified for a job, but only one of them is given an interview, or both may be hired but one at a different rate of pay or under different terms of employment, solely because of race, ethnicity, or gender. Discrimination may be inflicted by an individual, a group, or a nation. The reasons for it may vary, but discrimination always changes the distribution of scarce opportunities against or in favor of one party unless measures are set in motion to offset such redistribution.[1]

Although we usually think of discrimination as being practiced against rather than in favor of someone, it is not unusual to find it practiced to favor certain groups or individuals. The net result in either case is a redistribution in favor of some, and against others. If certain groups are excluded from membership in a club for which they are qualified, they are discriminated against and deprived of certain benefits. The members in good standing may accrue benefits as a result because they have more space, privacy, and chance to associate with people like themselves. They may also have more opportunities to conclude deals and agreements with counterparts than they would if the club's door were open to all. If certain groups are excluded from employment in an enterprise or sector, other groups will have easier access to employment in that enterprise or sector. Yet those excluded may be critical to the survival of the enterprise and the continued existence of opportunities, so that excluding them reduces the total employment opportunities and thus deprives the discriminators of opportunities.

Discrimination may limit the opportunity to acquire endowments or investment in human capital, at capacity utilization, or the rewards received for services rendered. Discrimination against individuals may take the form of depriving them of equal access to investment in human capital—education, training, health, etc. Limiting their access to employment and business opportunities may result in underutilization of capacity. Or discrimination may consist of underrewarding a worker, with lower wages, limited promotions, or less favorable working conditions than those of others, solely because of that individual's race, ethnicity, or sex.

Discrimination may operate by exclusion or by inclusion. A person may be discriminated against by being excluded from certain occupations, investment opportunities, or rights such as ownership and inheritance.

Discrimination operates in the form of forced inclusion, for example, by reserving lowly occupations for certain racial, ethnic, or gender groups that have limited choice in what they do. For example, in the United States the garment industry is mainly reserved for women, low-paid farm work for Mexicans, and unskilled work for blacks, sometimes with little regard to the merits of the individuals.

The object of discrimination may be an individual, a group, or a nation with characteristics that are different from those of the discriminator. The differences may be racial features, ethnic characteristics, gender, religion, occupation, skill, education, residence, age, or seniority in a given place or job situation. In most cases the target of discrimination combines several of these differences, which reinforces prejudice and the practice of discrimination. Economic discrimination is not always practiced by a numerical majority against a minority, but by a more powerful group against a less powerful one when the power gap is substantial enough to sustain the discriminatory behavior and preserve its benefits to the discriminator.

Racial discrimination is usually based on genetic features such as color and physical characteristics. Some are favored because of the color of their skin, hair, or eyes, while others with the same skin or hair color are discriminated against because of other genetic or racial features. Fair-haired blue-eyed people have been favored in most Middle Eastern and Muslim societies since the early days of Islam and the Arab nation. Black people, on the other hand, have been discriminated against for centuries both in East and West largely because of their skin color and other physical features. When the Muslims were in power and enslaved both African blacks and European whites, they discriminated against the former and in favor of the latter.

Ethnic discrimination is somewhat similar, although the distinguishing ethnic features are in some cases cultural—linguistic, religious, behavioral—rather than physical. In most cases, however, cultural affiliation and physical differentiation are combined to create an identifiable ethnic target for others within the same racial group. Ethnic minorities in the Middle East are numerous, but most people there think they can easily identify a Kurd, an Armenian, a Jew, or a Druze Arab, even though all of these groups share the same racial origin. In the United States, most people think they can identify a Chicano, a Jew, or an Arab. Whether or not they actually can is not important; what is important is that they think they can and hence discriminate.

Discrimination by gender, the least complicated form of discrimination, is the most difficult to explain and rationalize on the level of society, which suffers when women are underpaid. It is not difficult to explain when practiced by individual employers, however, who discriminate by paying women less than men simply to realize economic gains.

In addressing economic discrimination, our focus will be on differential treatment based on race, ethnicity, or gender. We will not deal with economic inequality emanating from other features, such as differences in qualifications, natural endowment, or political and social loyalties. Our focus is not on economic class differentiation but on discrimination because of prejudice against or in favor of certain racial, ethnic, or gender groups. However, differential qualifications due to underendowment resulting from discrimination are relevant in this study.

We will observe and analyze economic discrimination as it is reflected in the patterns of distribution of six categories of rights and opportunities: rights of ownership, rights of inheritance, access to acquired endowment, freedom of economic and business decision-making, access to economic and business opportunities, and levels of compensation and rewards. The rights of ownership, inheritance, and access to acquired endowment may collectively be classified as rights to equal endowment; deprivation of any of these rights will result in underendowment. Freedom of decision-making and access to economic and business opportunities may be grouped as the right of equal capacity utilization; deprivation of either of these rights will result in underutilization. Finally, deprivation of equal compensation and rewards will result in underrewarding. These three forms of discrimination, on which we shall focus, overlap and sometimes reinforce each other so that their effects become cumulative and lasting.[2]

Discrimination may be considered rational behavior if its practitioner uses it consciously as a mechanism and the shortest path to achieve a certain objective. But "rational" private discrimination is not necessarily rational from the standpoint of society. On the contrary, the gains of the private discriminator may translate into costs to society.

Discrimination may be considered rational if it is based on the knowledge that it will lead to a given goal at the least cost. Though a person practicing discrimination may be receiving wrong information without knowing it, his/her behavior may be rational. If, on the other hand, that person discriminates without information, or assumes that the available information is correct without checking, or knowingly considers it correct when it is incorrect, or refuses to question its accuracy or correctness, such discrimination is nonrational and prejudicial. To say that such behavior is based on religion, custom, or tradition does not make it rational. Nor will it be rational if people discriminate just to "follow the leader" or as part of a mob rule devoid of any logical or physical grounds. That simply is discrimination because of prejudice, group prejudice that leads to collective discrimination. When a woman is not hired for a certain job because no woman has ever been hired to do that job, even though she may be as well qualified as any man holding that job, the decision is clearly based on prejudice and a form of collective discrimination.

Discrimination that is rational may have the same net results as discrimination that is prejudicial and nonrational, but treating it may require different approaches. For example, the rational discriminator may be shown that there are other ways to attain a goal, or that other goals may be pursued with equal or more gain than those achieved by discriminatory behavior. In contrast, prejudicial discrimination may be hard to combat; providing additional information, by counseling, or by example, sometimes generates equally prejudicial acts by those discriminated against. To understand discrimination, one must consider the behavior of the discriminating party as well as the behavior of the party being discriminated against. For example, when deciding whether or not to employ members of a minority group in competition with members of a majority group, it is not sufficient to analyze only the actions and reactions of the majority as if the minority will accept what is coming to them passively. The rational discriminator would anticipate the reactions of the minority group, immediate or delayed, before trying to justify the discriminatory behavior.[3]

Discrimination against racial, ethnic, and gender groups may have different bases. Racial discrimination, whether rational or nonrational, may be traced back to whether the discriminator believes that the members of a given race deserve equal rights, have equal qualifications, or are capable of equal productivity. Discrimination against ethnic groups, in contrast, has sometimes been described as a response to the behavior of those ethnic groups themselves. The argument is that a group's ethnic bonds and collective efforts to attain superiority or security for its members may make the group itself a discriminator and that it is discriminated against in response to those efforts. In this way an act of ethnic solidarity by a minority group may be used as a reason for discrimination against that group by the ethnic majority or by other minorities. Thus the victim is to blame.[4]

This theory of discrimination, which may apply to race as well, has been criticized by Edna Bonacich for at least three reasons: first, ethnic and racial groups tend to interbreed and redefine their affiliation in new situations; second, shared ancestry does not guarantee harmony or prevent conflict; and, third, conflicts based on primordial grounds, racial and ethnic, tend to vary in form and content. Accordingly, Bonacich concludes that "ethnic, national, and racial solidarity and antagonism are all socially created phenomena" and cannot explain discrimination.[5] Instead, Bonacich introduces another class theory of her own.

All class theories, however, lead to the same explanation, namely, that capitalists will exploit those below them in class status, and exploitation becomes racial and ethnic especially when the exploited are citizens of other nations or less-developed countries. Such exploitation by capitalists is aided by the cooperation of the leaders of the exploited countries; this is the theory of imperialism presented as a step "towards an integrated class approach."[6] Unfortunately, reducing all discrimination to class exploitation tends to defuse the issue of race and ethnic discrimination. Bonacich would have to explain discrimination against racial and ethnic minorities by others of the same class. For example, capitalists and executives often discriminate against other capitalists and executives who are of the same economic class, as is frequently the case in discrimination against Jews. Moreover, to accept the capitalist exploitation theory as an explanation for the source of discrimination, it would have to be shown that noncapitalist societies, including Socialists and Communists, would not discriminate on the basis of race or ethnic affiliation, in theory and in practice; this, however is not the case, as will be shown below.

The U.S. Commission on Civil Rights has identified three sources of discrimination: individuals, organizations, and structures. Individuals may discriminate as personnel officers, administrators, employers, teachers, real estate agents, etc. These individuals use their authority to express their own prejudices, often hiding behind tradition, law, and regulations. Organizational discrimination is usually built into the bylaws of an organization, such as limitations on credit to women and minorities because of specified qualifications. Exclusion of certain individuals and groups because of security precautions, or because of physical characteristics such as height and weight, though irrelevant for the purpose at hand, are examples of organizational discrimination. Structural discrimination is a self-sustaining form of discrimination. For example, "discrimination in education denies the credentials to get good jobs. Discrimination in employment denies the economic resources to buy good housing. Discrimination in housing confines minorities to school districts providing inferior education, closing the cycle in a classic form."[7] In most cases all three forms are interlocked.

COSTS AND BENEFITS OF DISCRIMINATION

Assuming there are both benefits and costs to discrimination, who are the beneficiaries and who are the losers? Are members of the majority always beneficiaries and members of the minority always losers? Are men always the beneficiaries and women always the losers? For example, would the nonblack plumber benefit if the black plumber were discriminated against?

Or would male lawyers benefit if female lawyers were discriminated against? I suggest that it is the employer who benefits, or the contractor (corporation) for whom the work is done. One might think that when a black man or a woman is paid below marginal product, or less than the wage of the nonblack or male worker, respectively, the nonblack or male worker would receive an additional wage ranging up to the difference between what the black man or the woman actually receive and what they would have received in the absence of discrimination.[8] I propose that no such overpayment occurs. The savings on the wages paid to the black man or the woman worker or any other party victimized by discrimination, if they do exist, are appropriated by the employer. There is no reason why the employer would want to give away those reductions in costs. As long as those who are not discriminated against are being paid a market rate, or a wage equal to their marginal product, they feel favored over others who receive less. The same applies to earnings from investment capital owned by the discriminated-against party. If the earnings are below market rates, or if the costs of the investment are above market rates, the difference accrues to the investment company or the lending institution, not to the other investors.[9]

The material benefits to the discriminator may be illustrated by the example of youth workers and students, who often are paid less than the minimum wage. Whether such workers' marginal product is truly below minimum wage is doubtful, as some might argue to justify their lower wages, and in no case is it evident that the savings on these wages are given as bonuses to other workers.

There is, however, a positive type of discrimination that benefits certain racial or ethnic numerical minorities, usually because of a stereotyped assessment of them as superior to others. Among these are Americans and Europeans working or residing in third world countries, the Copts in Egypt (though it may be difficult to identify them as a racial or ethnic minority), the Armenians and Jews in the Middle East, and North-European migrants in the New World, such as the Scandinavians, Germans, and English.[10]

Now a new group of "unhyphenated American" whites is being identified. These are whites originating in Northern and Western Europe who avoid the WASP (white, Anglo-Saxon, Protestant) identity because it is sometimes used in a derogatory manner.[11] It is interesting that the privileged groups feel discriminated against when their preferential treatment is eliminated in order to equate them with others, as in what is called "reverse discrimination."[12]

Positive discrimination or favoritism toward certain minorities may be regarded as the other side of negative discrimination, but this is not exactly so. The gains of one group are not necessarily the losses of the other group. In fact, it may be argued that positive discrimination does not always generate gains to the favored group in absolute terms, though it may do so in relative terms. For example, in Israel an Ashkenazi (European) Jew is favored over a Sephardi (Oriental) Jew, and a Sephardi Jew is favored over an Israeli Arab (who also is a citizen and a Semite), and the Israeli Arab is favored over an Arab worker commuting from the Occupied Territories who is not a citizen. I propose that the Ashkenazi Jew is remunerated at no more than the marginal product, and all the other groups are remunerated differentially at below that level. The savings in all these cases go to the discriminator.

The reward for a favored group may be in the form of higher wages, lower opportunity costs, or lower transaction costs, which are always translated into material benefits. For example, to have preference in getting employment because of preferred minority status means less time and money must be expended to find a job. To have a priority in promotions, credit, or housing accommodations could mean lower cost in making the transaction. The same differential applies to unemployment. The favored will suffer less than others, because they may be the last to be fired and the first to be rehired, regardless of seniority.

If all the wage savings from discrimination are appropriated by the employer, one might question the rationality of firing the lower-paid workers before the higher-paid on the grounds that the latter are a favored minority. The mystery, however, disappears when we remember that the jobs occupied by the two contrasting groups are not always perfectly substitutable and that members of the favored group have more power in the market to threaten the welfare of the nondiscriminating employer. These types of favoritism and discrimination will be illustrated in the next two chapters.

So far we have discussed benefits and costs of discrimination from the private standpoint. Costs and benefits may also accrue to society as a whole, in which case they are identified as social costs and benefits, and they may be accrued and distributed differently from private costs and benefits. As a rule, whenever realized output is less than potential output, there is a loss to society, and anytime the output is brought closer to the potential or the potential output is raised, we may consider it a benefit. If such results occur because of discrimination, then social costs and benefits are realized, regardless of what happens in the private sector. For example, when blacks, Jews, Arabs, or women, because of their race, ethnicity, or gender, are excluded from positions for which they are best qualified, total output is less than the potential, and society loses. Anytime members of disfavored groups are rewarded at less than the market wage or are delayed in promotions or deprived of investment opportunities, they suffer from disincentives, and society loses, even though the discriminator may realize a gain in the business. It is important to note that the private gainer cannot compensate society for the social loss because the gain is realized by redistribution of the smaller output realized, and regardless of how it is redistributed, it will not replace the lost output.

Are there social benefits from discrimination? As far as can be determined, there are no economic gains, for there are no economic activities that cannot be performed at least equally well without discrimination. Once it is agreed that the best qualified should get a given job, a perfect market will attract the best qualified. Similarly, "perfect" planners would recruit the best qualified. Discrimination in such an environment has no place and its occurrence will always incur costs to society, but no gains. Discrimination is possible only in an imperfect market or under an imperfect or imperfectly implemented plan, but in neither case are social economic benefits evident.

However, aggregate sociopolitical gains may accrue from discrimination. One might argue that discrimination is a source of political stability, for example, in the colonial environment, in which discrimination suppresses opposition. That, however, may be only an argument to rationalize colonialism, itself a form of discrimination against whole societies. Such an explanation is tautological. Others might argue that keeping women at home and out of the lucrative job market is a way of stabilizing the family and society. Yet such stability cannot be viable nor can total output be maximized as long as women are not free to make a choice. At the same time, society suffers a loss because of the exclusion or underutilization of women. It is not evident that sociopolitical stability can be enhanced by discrimination or achieved more easily, or at a lower cost, than it would be in the absence of discrimination. On the contrary, the histories of the United States, South Africa, and the Middle East are replete with incidents of instability resulting from economic and sociopolitical discrimination.

WHY DOESN'T DISCRIMINATION GO AWAY?

This question might seem rhetorical, but it is not, since many attempts have been made in recent history to abolish discrimination. If discrimination entails social costs but no social benefits, and if public policy tends toward the removal of discrimination, as has been publicized in recent decades, why doesn't it go away? We have looked briefly at some explanations of discrimination in an attempt to understand its existence and continuation. At this point one other explanation may be added: the private gains from discrimination and the economic power and dominance of the gainers, at the expense of both the private victims and society at large, have been sufficient to sustain discrimination. Private gain represents private power, and private power represents a major influence in society. The welfare of the private discriminators becomes identified with the welfare of the larger group or the majority in power terms. When the laws of society impose discrimination, enforcement appears to be a social service by authorities, who are supposed to be guardians of law and order. When no laws impose discrimination, social institutions are mobilized to accommodate discrimination as a service to the powerful group of potential gainers.

This is the same phenomenon we observe in the cases of imperialism, colonialism, exploitation of third world countries, and of the working classes by their employers. A small group of beneficiaries is able to convince the rest of society that their own welfare is the welfare of society and therefore should be protected. The same happens when discriminatory behaviors are legislated, as in South Africa, the United States, and Israel: discrimination is sustained in the name of law and order. Sometimes it is claimed that the evidence of discrimination is inadequate and therefore little can be done about it. At other times intervention by society on behalf of the victims is made so costly by the beneficiaries of discrimination that intervention has to be stopped. Thus, discrimination continues. Therefore, as long as economic gain from discrimination is possible, and as long as economic gain and accumulation lead to power, discrimination may be expected to stay.

The only way to eliminate economic discrimination is to make it too costly to discriminate and to realize economic benefits from it. Inasmuch as such measures may require a total transformation of the economy and society, which is unlikely within a foreseeable time horizon, taming discrimination, rather than eliminating it, so as to minimize its private and social costs, may be the most efficient alternative.

PLAN OF THE STUDY

The next two chapters will illustrate the ubiquity and variety of racial, ethnic, and gender discrimination. In Chapter 4 we will attempt to estimate the social costs and the social benefits of discrimination, if such can be observed. Chapter 5 will explore the economic theories and explanations of discrimination and present an interdisciplinary framework to explain it. This framework is based on the idea that material gain, accumulation, and power are at the root of discrimination. Chapter 6 evaluates the measures that have been applied historically to deal with discrimination, including affirmative action, and explores what remains to be done. Chapter 7 will deal with the issue of why discrimination does not go away. The conclusion is that discrimination cannot be eliminated. The only way to deal with it is to tame it.

Our approach is comparative and historical, drawing on examples from different periods and countries to show how ubiquitous discrimination has been. It is more qualitative than quantitative, though we shall utilize quantitative data as much as possible to illustrate the points under discussion. Our emphasis is on whether discrimination exists and whether its results are positive or negative, not on the exact measure of discrimination, which does not affect the conclusions, and also because data are not available for most periods and countries. We will emphasize the role of institutions, especially that of government, and highlight the social costs and benefits of discrimination, which have been largely neglected in the literature. In general, this study is best described as an essay in synthesis, with the hope that the results will influence policy and help to minimize the negative social and private effects of discrimination.

NOTES

1. For an economic standpoint, see Lester C. Thurow, *Poverty and Discrimination* (Washington, D.C.: Brookings Institution, 1969), 2.

2. For a different set of economic discrimination behaviors, see pp. 117-18.

3. On discrimination and prejudice, "Racism," *Encyclopaedia Britannica*, 1974, vol. 15, 360-61; Norman R. Yetman, ed., *Majority and Minority*, 4th ed. (Boston: Allyn and Bacon, 1982), 9-17.

4. Minority and majority are here used not as numerical measures but in the sense of who holds power and control over resources.

5. Edna Bonacich, "Class Approaches to Ethnicity and Race," in Yetman, *Majority and Minority*, 65.

6. Ibid., 65-77.

7. John Lescott-Leszczynski, *The History of U.S. Ethnic Policy and Its Impact on European Ethnics* (Boulder, Colo.: Westview Press, 1984), 202-5.

8. Marginal product means the additional output created as one more unit of input is added to the production process. It is relevant in this case, given the neoclassical theory that economic efficiency dictates equating wage with marginal product.

9. These points will be elaborated in Chapter 4.

10. I remember how in the 1960s in Saskatchewan, Canada, the North Europeans were considered to be at the top; the Ukrainians, who were a numerical majority, came next; and all others came third—probably with some differentiation among them. Opportunity seemed to be distributed for no evident reason other than ethnic origin. A recent immigrant to the province, I was often reminded of that kind of differentiation, as if to indoctrinate me into that "caste" system.

11. Stanley Lieberson and Mary C. Waters, "The Rise of a New Ethnic Group: The 'Unhyphenated American,'" *Items* 43, no. 1 (March 1989): 7-10.

12. Lescott-Leszczynski, *History of U.S. Ethnic Policy*, xi.

2

Economic Discrimination: Race and Ethnicity

Because economic discrimination has always overlapped other forms of discrimination, it has usually been difficult to isolate the causes and the effects of each type of discrimination. The differentiation between racial and ethnic groups has rarely been distinct. Furthermore, the meaning of discrimination has varied according to time, place, and the economic agents involved. The most complex form of discrimination is that against women. Does treating women differently from men mean discrimination against them? Is it possible that certain types of differentiation, such as sparing women heavy manual work, may simply protect women and discriminate in their favor? Is it legitimate to consider such differentiation as discrimination even if women willingly accept the role to which they have been socialized and do not perceive it as discrimination against them? Although we shall focus on racial and ethnic discrimination in this chapter and on gender discrimination in the next, it seems efficient to include gender in this definitional section.

Our approach is to consider the act of discrimination as an objective fact, whether the victim is aware of it and accepts such treatment or not. In either case, economic costs and benefits accrue and are differentially distributed according to the racial, ethnic, or gender affiliation of the individual. Some may argue that certain forms of discrimination (e.g., between sexes) are no more than forms of labor division. Men, for instance, are hunters, and women are homemakers. Such an argument would be convincing only if the division of labor were based on conscious decisions by the individuals. If a woman chooses to be a homemaker, it should be her privilege to be one, and no discrimination can be construed. However, if a woman is trained and expected to become a homemaker, and prevented or ostracized if she chose another occupation, that would be discrimination. Some might argue that such specialization is a cultural characteristic of a given society and not intended as discrimination against women. In that case we would consider the whole culture as discriminatory against women.

Others might argue that religious convictions and theology dictate that men and women assume specific occupational roles in society. The same rule, then, would apply: to the extent that women have less choice than men do, we would consider religion to be discriminatory against women. What if it could be shown that men are expected to adopt specific roles and have no more choice in the matter than women do? For example, if a man chose to be a homemaker, most societies would consider him a pervert and would penalize him socially; we would consider him discriminated against by society. However, because men have historically dominated religious and social organization, one can argue that men do have a choice. A man who deviated would thus be discriminated against more by his own group than by women.

Women have been discriminated against occupationally and economically in all societies and religions since the dawn of history. Even when a woman assumed the role of a ruler through a system of succession, from Cleopatra to Catherine the Great to the Tudor Queen Elizabeth, society has tended to look upon her as a fluke rather than as a woman fulfilling her role freely.   Exceptions, of course, exist, as in the case of Indira Gandhi, Margaret Thatcher, and Benazir Bhutto, all of whom were elected to office according to rules established mainly by men. In these cases there has been positive discrimination in favor of these specific women.

Social scientists and historians have often suggested that "racism"—discrimination on the basis of genetic or physical features—is associated primarily with the rise of capitalism in the West.[1] I propose, however, that racial discrimination has historically overlapped ethnic discrimination, which existed long before the advent of capitalism. I propose further that whenever two racial or ethnic groups have come in contact and economic gain as a result of discrimination has seemed possible, discrimination has been consciously practiced. To suggest that no racism or racial discrimination existed in precapitalistic society may be true only to the extent that in these societies different racial groups did not interact and hence such discrimination did not exist. However, ethnic discrimination has existed in all societies on which we have records. Ethnic discrimination has usually become most apparent after war, territorial occupation, human subjugation, or detention pending the payment of tribute or ransom to the conqueror, who usually was of a different ethnic origin than that of the victim. Such discrimination has persisted after war and conflict have ceased, as long as economic gain could be realized.

The argument that racial discrimination has been a creation of capitalism implies that discrimination is a domain of a given economic system. On the contrary, I suggest that discrimination against racial, ethnic, or gender groups is bound to prevail in any economic system in which it brings economic gain to the discriminator. If, however, discrimination cannot create economic gain, as in an ideal communal or collective economy, it will not exist.

The same argument would apply regarding discrimination against women, or gender. As observed by Bridenthal and Koonz, in early societies clan members shared what they had on a "remarkably egalitarian basis. With the development of private property and political institutions to safe-guard it, inequalities developed inside the clan, between families, and along sex lines." The development of capitalism widened the gap, "and women's role within the family declined commensurately."[2]

An interesting argument that might indirectly support the idea that racial discrimination is a creation of modern capitalism dates back to the early sixteenth century, suggesting that racism and slavery had not yet begun when the blacks were brought to America. This is a truism of American his-tory, but racism and slavery had prevailed in other societies and economic systems before they were practiced in the New World or under capitalism. The debate centers around the question of whether prejudice created slav-ery or slavery created prejudice, which eventually became institutionalized in the legislation of the colonies of Virginia and Maryland in the seven-teenth century.[3]

Much of the argument could be avoided if one considered the following points: first, laws usually are passed to institutionalize what already exists. Prejudice and the enslavement of blacks predated the legislation. Laws were passed simply to justify enslavement and protect the interests of the slaveholder. Second, slavery in the colonies was a continuation of a system of slavery that had existed for many centuries. Black slavery was only a variation on the pattern of enslaving the conquered and the less protected. Least protected, the blacks of Africa were easy prey for invaders and slave-traders, who considered them less than human. Prejudice had existed among the stock from which the American people descended long before the blacks arrived in America. The rest of this chapter will illustrate these points by referring to different historical periods, societies, and economic systems.

The presentations in this and the next chapter are not exhaustive histori-cal records of discrimination, but comparative essays to illustrate its exis-tence in different periods, places, and economic systems. The discussion will emphasize forms of economic discrimination and its potential costs and benefits as reflected in the six categories specified in Chapter 1, whether by underendowment, underutilization, or underrewarding. For example, equality of opportunity in this case relates to equality of opportunity to acquire endowments in the form of human and material capital, the utilization of these endowments, and the attainment of equal rewards when they are utilized. Furthermore, equality of opportunity should be understood to begin at birth, not at the time one enters the job or housing market.

DISCRIMINATION IN THE ANCIENT AND MEDIEVAL PERIODS

Race and ethnicity were not clearly differentiated in ancient times. Racial and ethnic minorities were primarily aliens to the community, outsiders, and therefore relatively weak. This diffusion between ethnic and racial origins, however, declined gradually during the medieval and modern periods (the latter beginning roughly around the eighteenth century). Accordingly, discrimination against both racial and ethnic groups will be addressed as a single topic until they become distinct in historical records and in the economic behavior toward them in the late Middle Ages.

It has been suggested that racial conflict was foreign to ancient civilizations, such as those in India, the Middle East, or Africa, and that racial exploitation and race prejudice are products of modern nationalism and capitalism, especially in the Western world. The Hellenic Greeks divided people according to cultural and ethnic affiliation, but not race: people were Greeks or barbarians who did not adopt the Greek language or culture. The Greeks intermarried with these other groups, though they considered themselves superior to them. Alexander the Great married a Persian and encouraged others to intermarry with non-Greeks.[4] Yet even in this case, ethnic differentiation continued, along with estate differentiation, which Cox considers class differentiation rather than racial or ethnic differentiation. However, it could not have been simply class differentiation, since lower-estate people were usually from a different ethnic origin than those of the upper estate.

The Babylonians and the Greeks, for example, enslaved only foreigners or those of another ethnic and cultural origin. Conquered slaves were usually differentiated from credit-slaves (people who had defaulted on a loan), and from children sold by their parents into slavery to save them and themselves from starvation and death. Conquered slaves could be sold but could not be manumitted except by their masters. In contrast, credit-slaves were freed automatically upon payment of their debts.[5] Among the Hebrews, Jewish slaves had to be freed after six years of enslavement, but not aliens taken into slavery, who remained slaves until manumitted by their masters.[6]

Slaves in the Greek world were of two types: those coming from indigenous groups and those who were conquered aliens. Those in the first group were used in the economy and had limited rights (like serfs), as if they were under "house arrest." In contrast, conquered aliens were chattel slaves who were sold in the market and had no rights; these were "bought Barbarians."[7] These two types may be classified as voluntary and involuntary slaves. Those in the first group might have allowed themselves to be enslaved because of debt or to get protection; they could not be sold, and they could redeem themselves upon repayment of the debt. In contrast, involuntary slaves, who were conquered during war or kidnapped in piracy during peacetime, could be sold as chattels, killed, or disposed of as the slaveowner wished.[8]

A similar form of differentiation may be observed in the Roman Empire. Slavery and discrimination were based on ethnic and cultural differentiation and on the fact that the slaves, mostly prisoners of war, were taken from among occupied peoples, who, by definition, were not Romans. The more the empire expanded, the greater the supply of slaves and the more slavetraders were attracted to Rome. Trade and breeding were also important sources that sustained supply.[9] Slave dealers usually followed the army to take advantage of the fortune they could realize by buying slaves directly after battle for very low prices. The supply of slaves was ample for a long time. During the days of the Gracchi brothers slaves were so cheap that they displaced most of the poor class of free workers.[10] Freed slaves, however, were allowed to assimilate, sometimes granted citizenship and allowed to rise in the ranks of the empire, which may have misled Cox to conclude that no racism was practiced amongst the Greeks or Romans.[11]

Slaves may not have been of a different racial origin than their masters, but they were aliens or of a different ethnic origin. This, however, does not demonstrate that there was contact between different races and racism did not appear. To reach such a conclusion would be a fallacy. For example, because a black person may reach a high position in America does not mean that racism no longer exists in U.S. society. All of Cox's illustrations apply to inter-Caucasian contacts. They hardly show that race differentiation would not have occurred had there been interaction between races. Ethnic discrimination has been evident whenever and wherever ethnic interaction has occurred.

An illuminating picture of slavery in the Roman Empire may be seen in North Africa in the days of St. Augustine. Slaves for the North African trade were captured in raids on native tribes. Slaves sometimes included Roman provincials who might have been free (but not Roman) citizens in the countryside. Or they were children stolen or sold by their parents for a given number of years to avoid death by starvation.[12] It may be noted that Augustine did not consider slavery abnormal. Presumably Christ "did not come to change slaves into free men, but to make bad slaves good ones." This discriminatory ethic toward slaves had a parallel in the discrimination men practiced against women in the Augustinian era: adultery by men was considered morally wrong, but not sexual relations between a man and his slave, since the slave was the master's property to do with as he pleased. Strangely enough, a free woman who had sexual relations with her slave would be brought to court for adultery. St. Augustine, however, considered both actions morally wrong.[13]

In North Africa or the Barbary States in later years, various conquerors enslaved, traded, and left behind vivid reminders of their actions. The Muslims who swept over North Africa and parts of Europe started what has become known as Christian slavery.[14] Aliens from a different ethnic origin enslaved by the Arabs and North Africans were held for ransom, put to work on development projects, or sold, depending on the expected profitability of the transaction. At times, in the sixteenth century, "so many slaves were taken, and such was their enfeebled condition, that numbers were sold by the captors for an onion each."[15]

Racism was also evident among the occupiers in their treatment of those under them who were not enslaved. The Janizaries, or soldiers of the Turkish sultan, rebelled against their Turkish masters in the seventeenth century and set up their own government in Algiers under the titular leadership of a dey (uncle). Under the Janizaries no local people could hold office or work in government. The Janizaries had the right of way and their posterity were automatically privileged, but only if the mother was a Turk, not a Moor or North African. However, the son of a Janizary father and a Christian mother would have his father's status and privileges. Ironically, Christian slaves who converted to Islam were freed and given privileges as Janizaries, though such privileges were beyond the reach of the native Muslim Moors and Moriscoes. In another way ethnic and racial discrimination was evident in the treatment of Moors and Jews by the Janizaries. Moors and Jews caught in the act of theft would lose their right arm, but neither was allowed even to accuse a Janizary of theft. On the other hand, slaves who had to depend on theft to survive could openly steal from Moors and Jews but not from other slaves, without fear of punishment.

The Europeans of medieval and early modern Europe were equally discriminatory against other ethnic groups, including other Europeans. In 1682 the Algerians released 600 prisoners to the threatening French; when 64 of those released were found to be English, the French returned them to the dey, rather than send them into freedom.[16]

The Europeans, from the days of the barbarian invasions of the Roman Empire, considered slavery an integral part of the war society they formed. War was the major source of the slaves who were found everywhere in that society. Sometimes prisoners of Roman blood were enslaved and sold, but usually they had the right to buy their freedom by paying back the sum the master had paid for them or by serving him for five years.

While slavery was considered a humane alternative to killing a war prisoner or bearing the cost of feeding him, it was also an important source of material benefit, whether by sale or by using the slave in production. This rationalization of slave trading persisted until after the abolition of the slave trade. It was also argued, however, that if not killed or traded, the slaves could breed until they were strong enough to overpower their owners.[17] If the slave could not be used efficiently in production, or if there was a danger of losing him for one reason or another, the owner would maximize his benefits by selling his "perishable" capital in the market for as much, and as soon, as possible. The Europeans, however, did differentiate between penal slavery, slavery for indebtedness, and the slave trade of people who had been conquered and captured in battle or kidnapped by bandits for sale. The former two groups were not free for a given period of time or until a debt was paid. The latter were slaves indefinitely or until manumitted by their master. European slavery extended to Italy, Ireland, Scandinavia, and to the Slavic countries: "Tenth century Prague, according to Arab travelers, was one of the great markets of the slave trade."[18]

Cox looks at the Asians of the medieval period and concludes that race was not a problem because the Huns, Saracens, Moors, Seljuk Turks, Ottoman Turks, and Tartars who penetrated into Europe and sometimes enslaved white people felt no racial antagonism.[19] However, all of these invaders and the invaded Europeans were Caucasian, so no occasion for racism occurred. The same argument would apply to absence of racial discrimination in medieval Europe. All interaction was between different ethnic groups of the same racial origin. Therefore one cannot conclude from the European society that the medieval Europeans were immune to racism. All one can say is that racism probably did not exist because there was no occasion for it to exist. The first sustained racial contact with black Africans, Native Americans, Chinese, and Japanese, who had different racial features, came in the late Middle Ages and was a precursor to the development of the capitalist system, after which racism did develop, as the history of the New World indicates.

There is a tendency to believe that Asiatic and Middle Eastern people did not develop a racist attitude toward people of other racial origins. The evidence, however, is rather weak, and it seems to contradict that belief. For example, among the Hindus and the Arabs, the Jews and the Christians, there has always been a tendency to favor white over black and light over dark as marks of beauty, especially in women. The Japanese and Chinese apparently were aware of racial differences but presumably did not develop an attitude of prejudice and discrimination. Yet, both seem to have had a bias against people with features different from their own. In the sixteenth century a Chinese mandarin "likened the hairiness of the Portuguese sailors to that of monkeys."[20]

Also, contrary to some observers' conclusions, the Arabs did have a racist attitude toward people of other colors; the color black is associated with slavery. In Arabic it is said "black as a slave." The color white, on the other hand, is associated with beauty, purity, and innocence. Even though the Arabs enslaved both blacks and whites during and after their expansion period, they have usually accorded better treatment to white than to black slaves. Whites were held as slaves mostly for pleasure or for ransom, while blacks were to do the menial work, castrated to serve in the *harem* (women's quarters), or to be traded on the market. After the advent of Islam, the Arabs, like the Greeks before them, considered other people ignorant and looked down upon them, occupied their lands when they could, and made them pay a *Jizyah* or special tax, usually imposed on non-Muslims who also happened to be non-Arabs.

In conclusion, it appears that race and ethnicity were not clearly demarcated in ancient and medieval times. As outsiders, those of a different racial or ethnic origin were treated differently from and less equally than the native people. When distinct, however, race did play a role as a source of discrimination, even among slaves. White slaves were treated better than were black slaves, and slaves of other races and ethnic groups were less protected than local slaves. In all the cases above, the slaves had no rights of endowment, utilization, or reward. They survived at the mercy of their owners.

In the ancient and early medieval worlds, people did discriminate on the basis of ethnic differences. In public service, in obtaining titles, in the ownership of real estate, and in the practice of certain professions, ethnic minorities have always found themselves treated differentially from the majority. Different ethnic minorities were discriminated against differently. In some cases a certain minority group might be discriminated in favor of, rather than against, though such situations were rare. In this section I shall look at the treatment of ethnic minorities who were presumably free citizens or residents of their countries, but who received less than equal treatment before the law and in the market place, primarily because of their ethnic origin.[21]

Ethnic differentiation has usually overlapped class (estate) differentiation in the sense that ethnic minorities have often been from lower economic classes. A problem of definition therefore complicates our analysis. Recently the concept of *underrepresented groups* has come into use. (A variation of the concept is the underrepresented nations in which ethnicity and nationality overlap, as in Belgium, Switzerland, Yugoslavia, and the former USSR.)[22] An underrepresented group may be united by religion, ethnic origin, nationality, or other characteristics, with the only common denominators, the fact of underrepresentation, itself a form of discrimination, and a vulnerability to other forms of discrimination. Our present concern, however, is only with ethnic groups and economic discrimination. Whether economic discrimination is in favor of or against a group has to be determined, contrary to the implication that ethnic minorities have always been "economic peripheries" or at the bottom of the scale, as suggested by Riccardo Petrella.[23] An ethnic group may be peripheral on the political scale but high up on the economic scale, as has been the case with Jews, Armenians, and others, especially Caucasian whites in third world countries.

As noted above, ethnic differences were generally associated with being foreign or alien in early and late medieval Europe, presumably because mobility was mainly related to war and its effects, or to trade and commerce, which rarely led to permanent settlement by foreign merchants. Foreigners, therefore, were probably the main differentiated ethnic groups within a country, and they continued to be treated as aliens until they left the country or were fairly well assimilated in the community. The motives for discrimination varied according to place and time, but two factors seem to be most important. On one hand, the discriminating local people tended to look down upon foreigners, especially if they were traders and peddlers. On the other hand, they discriminated against them because they appeared to be a threat to the local people's economic and business security. For example, though the Roman Empire was dependent on Africa for grain and oil provisions, Africans were looked down upon as barbarians and certainly less equal than Romans.[24]

The treatment of ethnically different people by Europeans varied also according to whether those people were needed by the local economy and whether they had powerful patrons in the community. The Italians who traveled throughout Europe and the East were sometimes privileged and occupied prestigious positions; they might be admirals in the navy of another city or country, or they were put in charge of the mint. Other times, however, they had to be satisfied with lowly jobs as mercenaries in foreign armies or as pawnbrokers for the lower classes in other countries. Their treatment as aliens often varied according to the strength of the position of the Pope at the time. Nevertheless, as outsiders they were easily sacrificed to satisfy local interests, as illustrated by the brothers Mouche and Biche Franzesi of Florence, who rose in France to be the king's revenue and financial agents. However, when an inflation crisis occurred, the king did not hesitate to use them as scapegoats to appease the people. Similarly, the French and English authorities usually extended protection to Italian merchants and Jews, but neither group was safe from erratic waves of hostility and confiscation. They simply had less than equal rights in these countries.[25]

The treatment of ethnic minorities who had not assimilated also varied in accordance with the demand for their services in the market. Medieval towns formed independent economies and often monopolized certain aspects of trade to protect local welfare. Whenever local interests seemed threatened by foreigners, the latter were put under restriction. In the expansion years of the twelfth and thirteenth centuries foreign merchants could join merchant guilds, trade in cities other than their own, and come and go freely as long as they paid certain dues and "submitted to being in scot and lot in all things concerning the gild."[26] However, when the towns were no longer in need of provisions from the outside, restrictions were imposed on them and their freedoms were reduced[27]

The place of ethnic minorities in the economies of the medieval and early modern periods was best reflected in trade and commerce, which usually were shunned by the native majority. This occupational division of labor was illustrated in medieval Poland: in the thirteenth century large-scale trade was dominated first by Germans, and then by Italians and by Armenians, who were especially dominant in the southeastern territories. The Scots dominated peddling from the fifteenth century on, and some of them became wealthy merchants. Dutch and English merchants also played important roles in the Polish economy at that time. After the *potop* (invasion) in the middle of the seventeenth century, assimilation of those minorities became significant, so few appeared as non-Polish, except for the Jews, who would not assimilate. Yet from then on, Jews were able to dominate Polish commerce.[28]

The Jews, in general, preferred to face economic discrimination in the market place rather than assimilate. (Only economic discrimination against Jews is treated here.) The fact of discrimination in selling to or buying from Jews is evidenced by the need to issue royal decrees making discrimination against Jews illegal. Such decrees were issued in various places between the twelfth and seventeenth centuries. Jews had to have special permission to travel, and special protection to trade on equal footing with others, and this discriminatory behavior was often approved by the central authorities. In 1559 Sigmund August allowed the town of Sandomierz to exclude Jews from selling any goods in the town "on pain of confiscation." During the sixteenth century many other localities excluded Jews from their economies or expelled them altogether with royal approval.[29]

One of the arguments for excluding Jews from commerce was that their participation would make goods cheaper and thus undermine the interests of local merchants. Another argument was that Jews forestalled the purchase of goods by meeting the sellers before they reached the market place, thus undercutting other merchants. Guild charters usually excluded Jews from membership and from participation in trade within the jurisdiction of the guild. Some towns, especially in the seventeenth century, permitted the Jews to come to markets and fairs, but only when special protective measures had been taken, to make sure that they would not "get ahead of the Christians."[30] In a revealing study of the interaction of economics and discrimination, Hillel Levine tries to explain anti-Semitism in Poland as economic in origin. The Jews were blamed for being efficient in managing the estates of the gentry and thus causing the return of serfdom. They were also blamed for being efficient in conducting trade and finance, for producing alcoholic beverages, which drained capital from the people, and for Poland's failure to industrialize concurrently with Western countries. The Jews were used as scapegoats whenever the powerful majority found it to its benefit to do so. Although Levine reaches conclusions beyond the power of his evidence to support, the fact of discrimination against Jews and other minorities, for economic reasons, can hardly be contested.[31]

Complaints against minorities in Poland were not confined to Jews. They were addressed against Armenians, Lithuanians, Scots, and others who competed with locksmiths, watchmakers, pewterers, and shoemakers. To avoid discrimination on charges of misbehavior in the market place, Jews created their own system of self-discipline. As Armenians, Italians, Scots, and Germans became "Polanized" and assumed new economic roles, Jews were able to expand their own roles in spite of discrimination against them.[32]

The most common form of minority status in the Europe of the sixteenth to eighteenth centuries was that created by religious differentiation, as between Muslims and Christians in the Ottoman Empire, or between different denominations of Christianity in the rest of Europe. Ethnic minorities also existed, but usually the problem was treated by allowing as much national/ethnic autonomy as possible within the larger political entity, as in the Holy Roman and Ottoman empires. There were Czechs, Slovaks, and Serbs within the kingdom of Bohemia, and Germans in the kingdom of Poland and in Hungary. A weak central authority and an emphasis on autonomy made it possible to avoid ethnic minority-majority conflicts, though not so with regard to religion; religious minorities, however, are not treated in this study.

A more problematic type of minority-majority relationship was created in the sixteenth and seventeenth centuries by the colonizing English in Ireland and abroad. In the typical colonialist situation, a small minority set itself up as the master ethnic group over a large majority of another ethnicity. Domination by the English in Ireland and their behavior toward the native Irish have been compared to their behavior towards the Indians of Virginia, although the Irish were not annihilated as were the Indians when the colonists sought to take their land and dominate the economy.[33]

Another form of minority relationship prevailed among groups of Christians (native or foreign) within the Ottoman Empire. From the sixteenth through the early part of the twentieth century, Christians tried to secure privileges of extraterritoriality within the Ottoman Empire. The native Christians, Orthodox, Catholic, and Protestant, turned for protection to foreign Christian governments, especially those of Russia, France, and England, respectively, who encouraged them to do so. In addition, the Christian governments sought extraterritoriality for their own citizens who traveled to or resided within the Ottoman Empire for trade and business purposes, on the assumption that the Ottoman authorities discriminated against both native and visiting Christians. The "solution" offered was in the form of capitulations or concessions by the Ottoman sultan to these groups in agreement with their protective governments.

These capitulations guaranteed that the personal status of Christians native to the empire would be governed by their own religious principles. On the other hand, foreigners residing in the empire would be governed by the civil laws of their own countries. The impact of these capitulations varied according to the terms and power of the negotiating country in comparison with that of the Ottoman government. Until the late seventeenth century the capitulations were offered to the natives of Britain, France, and Russia who resided in or traded within the Ottoman Empire, as privileges or favors by the sultan, who was at the peak of his power in relation to those countries. By the eighteenth century, when the distribution of power had been relatively equalized, the capitulations became objects of negotiation between equals. However, from the beginning of the nineteenth century, when Ottoman power was in relative decline and industrializing Europe was on the move, the capitulations became obligatory, with terms virtually imposed on the Ottoman authorities. From then on, the benefits enjoyed by the Christian Europeans represented major economic concessions such as access to the Ottoman market, highly favorable customs duties, and full autonomy in civic and religious governance. It should be noted, however, that privileges accorded citizens of these powerful countries did not transfer well to the Christian natives of the Ottoman Empire, who were still discriminated against and sometimes harshly mistreated.[34]

To conclude, the ancient and early medieval periods witnessed a diffusion between race and ethnicity. Ethnicity, however, became more distinct in later periods. The common denominator between the victims of discrimination in these periods was their alien and weak status. Whether as slaves or as unequal ethnic minorities, they suffered from underutilization and underrewarding. They were a source of economic benefit to their owners or employers, though sometimes they were accused of displacing local people and members of the majority because of their competitively low remuneration. Data are too sparse for any details regarding employment, wages, and incomes.

DISCRIMINATION IN THE MODERN PERIOD: CONTINUITY AND CHANGE

Diffusion between race and ethnicity did not end in the medieval period. A new form of diffusion has evolved in the modern period, most distinctly and formally in the United States. Five overlapping racial/ethnic groups in the United States have been defined, as follows:

"White, not of Hispanic Origin," including people from Europe, North Africa and The Middle East.

"Black, not of Hispanic Origin," including blacks of African origin.

"Hispanic" - Persons of Mexican, Puerto Rican, Cuban, Central or South American, or other Spanish culture or origin, regardless of race.

"American Indian or Alaskan Native."

"Asian or Pacific Islander," including East Indians, Japanese, Chinese, Polynesians, etc., which is a mix of various races and ethnic groups.[35]

The last U.S. census divided Asians into nine subgroups. The ethnic composition of the U.S. population and its distribution by education and managerial occupations among male members 25-54 years old for 1980 are shown in Table 2.1. Also shown is the distribution of poverty, affluence, and per capita income. Interestingly enough, all ethnic groups include segments of affluent and below-poverty income recipients. The table also shows that

TABLE 2.1
SIZE AND CHARACTERISTICS OF 50 MUTUALLY
EXCLUSIVE RACIAL/ETHNIC GROUPS IN 1980

	Percent			Men 25-54	
	Below Poverty Line	Affluent[a]	Per Capita Income[b]	Mean Years College	Percent Prof./ Mgr.[c]
U.S. Total	11	12	$11.2	1.7	28
Hispanic Groups					
Cuban	12	9	10.6	1.7	25
Mexican	22	3	6.8	.7	11
Puerto Rican	34	2	6.1	.6	13
Other Spanish	16	7	8.9	1.5	21
Racial Minorities					
Amer. Natives	25	5	6.9	1.0	19
Asian Indians	8	12	13.2	5.3	60
Black	27	4	7.1	1.0	14
Chinese	13	16	11.9	3.6	42
Filipino	6	9	10.9	2.8	27
Japanese	5	23	14.6	2.9	42
Korean	8	11	10.2	3.4	36
Vietnamese	34	3	5.8	1.4	17
Other Races	21	7	8.8	2.2	26
White Ethnic Groups					
American	10	9	10.0	1.0	18
Amer. Indian	13	6	9.0	.8	15
Armenian	9	19	13.6	2.6	38
Austrian	5	25	15.5	3.3	49
Belgian	7	14	12.3	2.0	36
Canadian	6	7	13.4	2.2	40
Croatian	4	16	13.2	2.1	38
Czech	6	16	13.3	2.2	35
Danish	5	16	13.2	2.3	34
Dutch	8	12	11.7	1.7	29
English	8	15	12.5	2.0	32
Finnish	7	13	11.5	2.1	31
French	8	10	11.6	1.5	27
French-Canadian	6	11	11.7	1.5	25
German	6	14	12.3	1.8	30
Greek	7	16	12.2	2.0	35
Hungarian	6	18	13.5	2.3	36
Irish	8	13	11.8	1.8	29
Italian	6	14	12.1	1.8	31
Lebanese	7	17	13.1	2.8	40
Lithuanian	5	20	14.6	2.6	42
Norwegian	6	15	12.7	2.2	33
Polish	5	11	12.8	2.0	32

TABLE 2.1 (continued)
SIZE AND CHARACTERISTICS OF 50 MUTUALLY
EXCLUSIVE RACIAL/ETHNIC GROUPS IN 1980

	Percent			Men 25-54	
	Below Poverty Line	Affluent[a]	Per Capita Income[b]	Mean Years College	Percent Prof./ Mgr.[c]
Portuguese	7	10	10.9	1.1	19
Rumanian	6	27	15.3	3.3	49
Russian	6	32	17.9	4.0	59
Scandinavian	5	16	12.3	2.7	41
Scots-Irish	5	18	14.1	2.4	37
Scottish	5	20	14.4	2.7	40
Slovak	4	13	13.4	1.8	27
Swedish	5	17	13.7	2.4	37
Swiss	6	18	13.6	2.5	36
Ukrainian	5	17	13.6	2.5	36
Welsh	5	18	13.0	2.6	39
Yugoslavian	7	18	13.7	2.1	33
Not elsewhere classified	6	14	12.4	2.4	36
Not Rpt.	5	11	11.7	2.3	23

Source: U.S. Bureau of the Census, Census of Population: 1980, Public Use Microdata Sample. Reprinted from Reynolds Farley, fn. 36
[a]This reports the percent of individuals in households whose pre-tax cash income equaled at least six times the poverty line.
[b]Shown in thousands: 1987$.
[c]This shows the percent of employed men holding professional or managerial jobs in April 1980.

not all whites nor all Asians nor all those of European descent have the same distribution. There are wide ranges within each of these groups.[36] Table 2.2 shows the distribution of annual earnings for men 25-54 and their deviation from the national average. Here, too, it is evident that within each larger ethnic group (e.g., Asians) there are variations in earnings.[37]

The Hispanic minority, as conspicuous as the black, has been less outspoken in defense of its rights to equality. The data on Hispanics are somewhat lacking, especially for the period preceding 1970. For a comparative viewpoint, Table 2.3 shows income ratios of blacks and Hispanics to whites. Three observations may be made regarding these data: (1) Blacks and other races have held a relatively constant income ratio to that of whites, ranging from 60% to 65% between 1972 and 1983. (2) Blacks have a lower income ratio to that of whites, ranging from 55% to 62% over the same period. (3) Hispanics have experienced a declining ratio, ranging from 71% to 65% of whites.

TABLE 2.2
ANNUAL EARNINGS OF MEN 25-54 AND DIFFERENCES FROM THE NATIONAL
AVERAGE FOR 40 MUTUALLY EXCLUSIVE RACIAL/ETHNIC GROUPS IN 1980

	1979 Annual Earnings[a]	As Percent of Total
U.S. Total	$23.4	100
Hispanic Groups		
Mexican	19.3	83
Puerto Rican	19.6	84
Other Spanish	21.3	91
Racial Minorities		
Amer. Natives	19.1	82
Black	18.6	80
Chinese	26.8	115
Japanese	26.4	113
Other Races	20.3	87
White Ethnic Groups		
American	21.3	91
Amer. Indian	20.8	89
Austrian	29.4	126
Belgian	27.2	116
Canadian	23.7	101
Czech	25.5	109
Danish	25.4	109
Dutch	23.5	101
English	24.1	103
Finnish	27.3	117
French	23.2	99
French-Canadian	23.8	102
German	24.4	104
Greek	25.7	110
Hungarian	27.8	119
Irish	24.5	105
Italian	25.5	109
Lithuanian	27.3	117
Norwegian	24.7	106
Polish	25.6	110
Portuguese	25.4	109
Russian	32.4	139
Scandinavian	25.7	110
Scots-Irish	25.4	109
Scottish	25.7	110
Slovak	26.5	114
Swedish	25.6	110
Swiss	24.2	104
Ukrainian	25.5	109

TABLE 2.2 (continued)
ANNUAL EARNINGS OF MEN 25-54 AND DIFFERENCES FROM THE NATIONAL
AVERAGE FOR 40 MUTUALLY EXCLUSIVE RACIAL/ETHNIC GROUPS IN 1980

	1979 Annual Earnings[a]	As Percent of Total
Welsh	25.7	110
Yugoslavian	28.0	120
Not elsewhere classified	24.6	105
Not Rpt.	22.1	95

Source: U.S. Bureau of the Census, Census of Population: 1980, Public Use Microdata Sample. Reprinted from Reynolds Farley, fn. 36
[a]Shown in thousands: 1987 dollars. Estimates of earnings assume a person worked 2000 hours. Analysis is restricted to all persons reporting positive earnings in 1979.

TABLE 2.3
MEDIAN FAMILY INCOME 1972 TO 1983 (IN CURRENT DOLLARS)

	Median Income					Median Income Ratio		
Year	All Races	White	Black and Other Races	Black	Hispanic	Black & Other Races (to White)	Black (to White)	Hispanic (to White)
1972	11,116	11,549	7,106	6,864	8,183	0.62	0.59	0.71
1973	12,051	12,595	7,596	7,269	8,715	0.60	0.58	0.69
1974	12,902	13,408	8,578	8,006	9,540	0.64	0.60	0.71
1975	13,719	14,268	9,321	8,779	9,551	0.65	0.62	0.67
1976	14,958	15,537	9,821	9,242	10,259	0.63	0.59	0.66
1977	16,009	16,740	10,142	9,563	11,421	0.61	0.57	0.68
1978	17,640	18,368	11,754	10,879	12,566	0.64	0.59	0.68
1979	19,661	20,502	12,380	11,644	14,569	0.60	0.57	0.71
1980	21,028	21,904	13,843	12,674	14,716	0.63	0.58	0.69
1981	22,388	23,517	14,598	13,266	16,401	0.62	0.56	0.70
1982	23,433	24,603	15,211	13,598	16,230	0.62	0.55	0.66
1983	24,580	25,757	15,887	14,506	16,956	0.61	0.56	0.65

Sources: U.S. Bureau of the Census, *Current Population Reports*, Series P-60, 1948-1984; and U.S. Bureau of the Census, *The Social and Economic Status of the Black Population in the United States: An Historical Overview, 1790-1978*, 1979, p. 31.

The sources of discrimination vary between one racial or ethnic group and another. However, since blacks have faced the most extreme and varied discrimination, we shall concentrate on that minority to illustrate its effects.

Racial discrimination in the New World, against the blacks, Chinese, Japanese, and the indigenous people, is well documented. Although the slave trade was suspended early in the nineteenth century, slavery was not legally abolished until the second half of that century. Even then, racial discrimination did not end, in the United States, Latin America, Europe, or

Africa. The worst case of sustained racial discrimination in the twentieth century has been in South Africa, where the policy of apartheid has replaced classical slavery in law and practice.

The form of racial economic discrimination in the modern period has varied from place to place. Often it has combined underendowment with underutilization and underrewarding. Exclusion of certain racial groups from specific opportunities, such as the ownership of property, entry into certain occupations, and the right to equal wages for equal work, or from equal opportunities in education, vocational training, or in acquiring other basic prerequisites for economic improvement and economic equality has been common. In the case of slavery, discrimination included underendowment, underutilization, and underrewarding of blacks and Indian slaves forced to work for no reward other than subsistence. At other times, discrimination has taken the form of expropriation, as in the case of the American Indians who, having lost their land and earning opportunities, have been reduced to dependence on the federal government for survival. The beneficiaries in both of these cases were the discriminating whites, although the benefits were differentially distributed among them.

Racial discrimination against blacks assumed an economic role early in the mercantilist period (sixteenth and seventeenth centuries), when European powers competed for larger pieces of the expanding trade and frontier territories, East and West. The profitable slave trade formed a part of the triangular trade, which joined Africa with Europe and the New World.[38] According to documents dating back to the second half of the seventeenth century, the British Royal African Company shipped about 5,000 blacks a year to the West Indies in the thirty ships at its disposal. These numbers increased substantially by the next century because merchants, managers, lenders, and the British Parliament supported the slave trade. Parliament allocated annual grants to secure forts and factories in Africa, thus assuring the planters better opportunities to acquire slaves and make money by shipping surplus slaves to Spanish and French colonies. The purpose was both aggrandizement of the state and enrichment of the agents active in the trade. The welfare of the black was of no concern at any time. Blacks and other Africans and Asians were considered a subclass without any rights, or with lesser rights and no claim to equality with whites.[39] This attitude still prevails in Britain toward immigrants from those continents. The British approach to blacks (and women) is basically reflected in the common law, which regards both blacks and women as "the property of their masters," not entitled to have "an independent legal identity."[40] The same attitude prevails in other European countries almost with no exception.

The British attitude toward non-English and non-white people carried over to the United States, where immigrants were pressured to assimilate to the Anglo-Saxon way of life in the new land. In 1699 Virginia imposed a tax on servants coming from anywhere except England and Wales; this tax, however, was gradually lifted from other Europeans.[41]

The blacks transported from Africa were a mixed group: some came from the Bantu tribes; some were Sudanese; others were Nilotic Negroes and black and brown Hamites; others came from the tribes of the East African great lakes; some were pygmies and Hottentots; some had traces of Berber and Arab blood. A conservative estimate suggests that about ten million blacks were transported to the Americas between the fifteenth and nineteenth centuries.[42] In the United States, they were kept in bondage until emancipation in the Confederate states in 1863, and then in the United States in 1865, with few questions of rights for them being raised, except by a tiny minority. The philosophy of the period was clearly expressed by the Virginia *Examiner* in 1854:

Let us not bother our brains about what *Providence* intends to do with our Negroes in the distant future, but glory in and profit to the utmost by what He has done for them in transplanting them here, and setting them to work on our plantations. . . . True philanthropy to the Negro begins, like charity, at home; and if Southern men would act as if the canopy of heaven were inscribed with a covenant, in letter of fire, that *the Negro is here, and here forever; is our property, and ours forever; . . .* they would accomplish more good for the race in five years than they boast the institution itself to have accomplished in two centuries . . . .[43]

And so it was until emancipation.

Enslavement and deprivation of all legal rights, loss of control over self and family, and separation from the family through individual sale were the fate of the blacks. They could not bear arms, which was a right of every American; even in the "liberal" north, Massachusetts, Connecticut, Rhode Island, and New Hampshire, slaves could not strike a white person or be on the street after 9:00 P.M. They could not buy liquor, and they could be bought and sold at the owner's command. However, in contrast to slaves in the South, Northern slaves could own property, testify against whites, and learn to read and write.[44] It is not clear, though, how Northern slaves could own property if they could be traded at the owner's will or be readily evacuated from the property. It is ironic also that some observers considered the conditions of the black slaves to have been more favorable than those of white and free workers: in contrast to free white workers, the slaves presumably had security of old age pension, guaranteed employment, and health care, if only because they were a form of capital investment the slave owner wanted to protect.[45]

The conditions of the blacks were influenced by the demand for labor in opening up new territories and economic expansion: in periods of severe scarcity, whatever civil or human rights they had were eroded.[46]

Probably the best demonstration of the relationship between racism, slavery, and economic benefits for whites is the decision by the U.S. government to send freed slaves back to Africa. The state of Liberia was created to accommodate them, and while the returnees might have agreed to go back, it is evident that few other options were open to them. Furthermore, they clearly were no longer wanted in the United States once they became free labor, harder to exploit, and an apparent threat to white workers. Thus, beginning in January 1820, tens of thousands of blacks were shipped aboard the U.S. *Elizabeth* to settle in the new country of Liberia. They were helped to resettle by the American Colonization Society, a nongovernmental agency that enjoyed the backing of the U.S. government. The question, of course, is why did the United States send back to Africa free blacks who were already in the country while it encouraged white immigration from Europe?[47]

Abolition of slavery by Britain and emancipation of the slaves in the United States brought an end to legal slavery but not to discrimination against blacks, nor did white attitudes toward blacks change substantially. The blacks were freed but not given citizenship. The Thirteenth Amendment (Civil Rights Bill) of 1865 did not give them citizenship either. That came only with the Naturalization Act of 1879.[48] Blacks were freed but given no source of income to depend on, no compensation for lost opportunities, and few facilities to help them adjust to their new conditions. Economic discrimination against them continued to be a source of material profit for discriminators. Since that time, blacks have earned less than whites for similar jobs, had less access to jobs they are qualified for than whites, suffered more unemployment than whites, and enjoyed fewer opportunities for education and training than whites. The laws have been changed, but the economic incentives to discriminate have not been removed, and the disincentives to discriminate have not been made strong enough to end discrimination.

After emancipation, blacks were gradually segregated legally from whites in most aspects of public life: schools, transportation, recreation, and other services. There was segregation before emancipation, though probably not as much as after emancipation.[49] The overall policy toward blacks, like that toward the American Indians, catered to the racist attitudes of the whites. Even though the Indians were considered, at least by some whites, a superior people with their own culture, they were often lumped with the blacks as inferior people who existed primarily to serve the white majority. For example, during Reconstruction, blacks were encouraged to settle in the territories designated for Indian resettlement, both to implement segregation and to avoid ceding any white-owned territory to blacks.[50] This policy was probably also intended to weaken both blacks and Indians by pitting them against one another.

Segregation may have been based on the theory of "separate but equal," but such an intent was not even approximated by the segregation laws passed by the states. On the contrary, those laws were passed because white policy-makers believed strongly in the inequality of the races. Furthermore, those who believed in the doctrine of "separate but equal" were no doubt idealistic or misled, because such a doctrine could not have worked anywhere, and no evidence existed to show otherwise.

Under the new system of segregation inequality was inherent because blacks were starting their life of freedom at a much lower level of endowment in the form of education, material endowment, and skill than whites were. As a result, they were unable to compete with the whites on equal terms. Fewer opportunities and doors were open to them because of segregation. With freedom came new forms of discrimination, sanctioned by law and exploited by the potential beneficiaries. Discrimination and exploitation were possible in spite of laws protecting individual and civil rights, because of the high costs of litigation (both in time and money), the vagueness of the laws against discrimination, and the fact that the blacks were not powerful enough politically or materially to lobby for more equalizing legislation. These factors may explain in large part why blacks in the United States still suffer from economic discrimination, 130 years after emancipation, despite frequent resort to the courts, civil disobedience, and lobbying for better legislation.

Some economic benefits were realized by blacks in the First World War and during the 1920s. The increased demand for labor during the war helped to open new opportunities, and blacks took advantage of them. Postwar restrictions on immigration meant more opportunities for blacks. These benefits, however, were quickly lost as the Depression set in, even though Franklin Roosevelt tried to give the blacks new opportunities in government employment and services.

The advent of the Second World War and pressure by the National Association for the Advancement of Colored People (NAACP) made some breakthroughs possible, especially in military service. Blacks had been used little in the military and thus had been excluded from any benefits the military offered whether in education, chances for mobility and advancement, or benefits to veterans. Under the threat of a march on Washington, on June 25, 1941, a week before the scheduled march, President Roosevelt issued Executive Order 8802, which prohibited discrimination in defense contract work "'against any worker because of race, creed, color, or national origin.'"[51] By the end of the war, the number of blacks in the military had increased significantly, though it was nowhere near proportional to their size in the population, nor were their assignments similarly distributed in specialization as were those of whites. Because they had had fewer endowment opportunities, they remained concentrated in the lower ranks. It was claimed that discrimination could not be eliminated by the stroke of a pen and, therefore, a slow pace was fully justifiable.

The civil rights movement grew during the 1950s and 1960s. Rebellion against segregation and the Vietnam War, the advent of relatively liberal administrations, and the rise of passive resistance against discrimination under Martin Luther King and the NAACP combined to bring about new legislation and a better mechanism for law enforcement against discrimination. Eventually segregation in public schools and discrimination in employment were declared illegal.[52] All-white educational institutions were opened to blacks. Bus segregation was ended; restaurants were integrated; housing segregation became illegal; and more job opportunities became available to blacks, especially at the professional and vocational level. Furthermore, the wage gap that had always existed between white and black labor was gradually narrowed so that in a few professions it has almost disappeared, though the overall ratio of black/white family incomes has not improved. According to official figures, the ratio was 60% in 1907-9 Immigration Commission records. Census reports for later years show a ratio of 51% in 1947, 54% in 1964, and 58% in 1985.[53]

Racial discrimination exists in other countries as well, for example, in Britain (the only European country with a sizable community of non-Caucasians), and in South Africa and Namibia. It also exists in Malaysia, Indonesia, and in various Latin American countries. Blacks in Britain suffer the same types of economic discrimination as do blacks in the United States, with one difference: the blacks of Britain are mostly voluntary immigrants who therefore do not suffer the same psychological and sociological forms of deprivation that blacks do in the United States. However, the rules governing economic discrimination, written or not, in the two countries are similar. They depend on the level of technology and the demand for unskilled and easy-to-exploit labor, the structure of the market and its compatibility with discrimination, and the distribution of power.

There are suggestions that discrimination against blacks in Britain will continue to be a problem as long as they are not fully assimilated, which does not seem possible unless they lose their identity as blacks and all physical differences are neutralized. However, the degree and form of discrimination they face depend on whether a given job is in demand by whites or not; the more in demand it is, the more threatening blacks are considered to be, and the more discrimination they are bound to face. Undesirable jobs are available to blacks more easily. Finally, the distribution of power in the market makes a difference. For instance, union membership gives workers a bargaining power that seems to help reduce discrimination against them; it is not clear, however, whether discrimination within union ranks continues to exist, as it did in the United States for a long time.[54]

Discrimination has been evident in the differential wages and take-home incomes of different racial and ethnic groups in Britain. For example, "while two thirds of British men took home over £12 a week, only half of the West Indian men did so," presumably because British men worked overtime. In 1962 the average "male manual workers wages in Britain were £15 17s. 3d. and for women £8 0ss 10d. The Jamaican immigrants...averaged £10 15s. 0d. a week (30 percent less than average) in the case of men and £6 13s. 0d. (20 percent less than average) in the case of women."[55] Differences in earnings, however, are widest among other occupational groups. According to recent surveys, Asians and West Indians in Britain earned uniformly lower incomes than whites, as shown in Table 2.4.

TABLE 2.4
EARNINGS OF DIFFERENT BRITISH RACIAL GROUPS COMPARED

Male Full-time Employees by job level	Average Gross Weekly Earnings	
	White £	Asian and West Indian £
Professional managerial	184.70	151.80
Other nonmanual	135.80	130.40
Skilled manual/foreman	121.70	112.20
Semiskilled manual	111.20	101.00
Unskilled manual	99.90	97.80
All male employees	129.00	110.20

Source: Jeanne Gregory, Sex, Race and the Law (London: Sage Publications, 1987), 21.

Treatment of blacks in South Africa and Namibia is a classic case of racial discrimination based on the conviction that one race is superior to another, and that discrimination is an acceptable way of realizing economic gain. While a movement toward less discrimination was under way in the Americas, the opposite was happening in South Africa. The problem started early in the nineteenth century, when white colonists began to take the land held by the African tribes, usually on a communal basis as it was held by the Native Americans in the Western Hemisphere. Land appropriation and expansion of settlement were accomplished by force and by legal actions based on laws enacted by the whites to serve their own purposes. As early as 1809 legal limitations were imposed on the mobility of Khoikhoi tribes to make room for white expansion. Land expropriation left many native blacks landless and thus a source of cheap black labor. After the abolition of slavery by the British in 1834, the white Boers began their Great Trek—the fan-shaped northward exodus—beginning in 1836. At the same time black Zulus were expanding westward at the expense of black Bantus, who were crushed as communities and forced to migrate. The white Voortrekkers took advantage of this instability, claimed the best land by seeing to it that large areas of land were emptied, by force if necessary. When the Zulus resisted, they, in turn, were crushed by the superior military force of the whites.

The Africans who stayed behind were subjected to severe discrimination. For example, in the Natal Republic, Africans could not stay in settled areas except as servants, they could not own land, and they had to carry passes. Resident Zulu men were rationed out to work for white farmers whether they liked it or not.[56] The problems for blacks became more serious when diamonds and gold were discovered in 1867 and 1886, respectively, and the demand for labor increased rapidly. The prospectors were anxious to get as much labor as cheaply as possible, which led to more alienation of native land to create landless people and new sources of labor.[57]

Between 1870 and 1900 all South African chiefdoms became subject to white rule. Even the black peasantry, which had started to emerge between 1830 and 1870, was squeezed and manipulated both to appropriate their land and increase the supply of labor. To crush the peasantry "legally," the Boer republics resorted to discriminatory legislation. In the mid-1890s they introduced the "Squatters' Law," according to which only five African families could be employed on a single white farm. Surplus families had to move on. In the Transvaal, the 1908 Natives Tax Act levied a higher tax on squatters than on labor tenants, thus forcing the squatters to become tenants dependent on white landowners. In Natal, access to land was made difficult for Africans, and in 1904 they were prohibited from buying crown land at all. Location Acts (1892, 1899, 1909) in the Cape were used to tighten the pressure on squatters. The 1913 Natives Land Act made it necessary for an African to get special permission from the governor-general to purchase or rent land outside the "scheduled" areas.[58] By the time the Union of South Africa was formed in 1910, about seven percent of the South African territory was covered by reserves; the scheduling just about doubled that amount. Thus the Africans were contained within a small percentage of their hereditary land areas by force and legislation.[59]

The demand for labor affected white workers as well. The poor whites sometimes suffered badly, but they were able to organize into trade unions.

Blacks were not permitted to organize. As a result, skilled and semiskilled jobs were usually reserved for whites, while blacks were confined to unskilled work. By the early 1920s segregation at work between whites and blacks was in force. The Mines and Works Amendment Act reinforced the 1911 act, which legalized the color bar in mining. The Industrial Conciliation Act established collective bargaining, mediation, and arbitration between employers and white workers. However, the 1925 Wage Act established a wage board to recommend minimum wages and working conditions for unorganized labor (the black majority), to be approved by the Minister of Labour. Other measures included the 1922 Apprenticeship Act, which mandated minimum qualifications for technical education and skilled jobs such that only whites could qualify.[60]

The white-black conflict reached its most traumatic stage with the institutionalization of *apartheid* following World War II. The apartheid plan aimed to reduce the number of blacks in areas designated for whites, developing reserves for separate African habitation, and establishing white industries close enough to black settlements to assure employment opportunities for labor and labor supply for the industrialists.[61] To implement apartheid, mobility of the blacks was restricted. No one could move from one area to another without having a job, which could not be secured in advance. Deportation of "illegal" migrants back to their native homelands (Bantustans) has been resorted to frequently since the early 1950s.

The movement against apartheid has been transformed into a national liberation movement, with the blacks seeking majority rule in South Africa, an arrangement resembling the resolution of the conflict in Rhodesia. Apartheid has now been legally ended and a newly constituted multiracial government, including coloreds, has come to power, with the black majority forming the government.

In economic terms, however, the blacks have continued to suffer from underendowment, underutilization, and underrewarding. They have been deprived of equal opportunities in educational facilities, job opportunities, housing, wage rates, and political participation. The loss to blacks has no doubt been a gain for whites—at least for certain members of the white community, since there may be losers among the whites as well. According to Barbara Rogers, the Bantustan policy was meant to keep African workers dependent on white employers, rather than to obstruct their technical and educational progress.[62] Yet the blacks remained undereducated, underskilled, and far below the technological levels achieved by workers in the white economy. Social and political segregation and economic exploitation seem to have been the objectives of apartheid. Such segregation has in the process made it unnecessary to create a formal color divider between the two races. An economic divide has been dictated by the differential qualifications of the two groups and the institutionalized deprivations imposed on the less qualified blacks.

While racism has peaked and is beginning to decline in South Africa and Namibia, ethnic discrimination has continued to be a source of economic deprivation for ethnic minorities in other parts of the world. As in earlier periods, there has been a diffusion between ethnicity and other features of minorities, such as language, culture, religion, national sentiment, own perceptions of self-esteem, as well as racial origin. Our focus continues to be on distinctions based on ethnicity, national identity, and attributes that are considered unique to a community, especially by its own members. The Basques in Spain, the gypsies in Yugoslavia, the Armenians in Russia and Turkey, the Hispanics in the United States, and the Jews outside Israel are perceived as ethnic minorities in the countries in which they live, both by themselves and by the majorities in those countries.

In recent decades the definition of ethnic minority has become entangled with national origin, which in turn is associated with a given territorial entity. The Armenians are associated with Armenia and the Turks with Turkey, in the sense that the Armenians form a nation with origins rooted in Armenia. Thus, wherever they are found outside Armenia and Turkey, Armenians and Turks form ethnic minorities. This is the definition of ethnic minority that will be adopted in relation to the modern period.

As we have seen, the ethnic minority problem is not new in Europe or the Western world at large. Minorities have always existed, and their status has always been in jeopardy because of discrimination. What has changed, however, are the increasing tendencies toward individualism and competition, and the decline of the philosophy of "live and let live" that prevailed in earlier times, and this may have accentuated minority-majority conflict. Increasing economic and social mobility through competition involved the stronger groups using the weaker groups as stepping stones toward their higher goals. I suggest that it has continued to be possible in the modern period for members of the "power" majority, not only the state, to exploit or discriminate against the weaker members of the "power" minorities and realize economic benefits at their expense, either by excluding them from certain opportunities, or by underrewarding them for equal performance.

In Switzerland and Belgium, Italy and Spain, we find ethnic minorities that are often at odds with the majority. Even when there is no absolute majority, as in Switzerland or Yugoslavia, each minority group at times finds itself in conflict with others. The reason is that both the majority and minority groups consider themselves native to the country in which they reside and try to preserve some of their ethnic or unique characteristics, even when such interests clash. The French-speaking Swiss minority leans toward French culture, but it considers Switzerland its home. The Basques of Spain regard Spain as their home and expect—as do the Turks in Cyprus and the Algerians in France—to be able to preserve their own unique characteristics in their homeland. Economic discrimination, however, seems to prevail whenever a given ethnic minority appears weak and alien to the ethnic majority in the respective country.

The Algerians and other North Africans in France represent an ethnic minority that has much in common with many minorities in other parts of the modern world. Though French Algerians seek acceptance and assimilation rather than separatism, they are regarded as aliens in France and as less than equal by the European French. Algeria was under French rule between 1832 and 1962. As former political dependents of France, Algerians could travel to, work, and reside in France. After Algerian independence, cooperation between the two countries was resumed, but on a much more restricted basis. Labor migration to France continued, and a serious ethnic minority problem has evolved. Algerians, even those who have acquired French citizenship, are treated by other French citizens as less equal, in pay, housing, promotions, and other opportunities. The problem becomes more serious in periods of crisis and unemployment. No real solution has been proposed. It should be noted, however, that minority children in France are given equal public opportunities to acquire minimum endowments of education and health benefits, which may eventually remove the grounds for economic discrimination.

World War II created many minorities in Europe, East and West, with problems similar to those of the North Africans in France. Prosperity in Western Europe may have kept the lid on economic ethnic differences throughout the 1950s and 1960s. Once economic crises began to appear in the 1970s and 1980s, minority workers began to feel the impact. Migrant and alien workers have been subjected to pressure, by persuasion, the promise of financial compensation, and by force, to go back to their homelands.

Another distinct ethnic minority group that has faced open discrimination is the East Indians in the British Commonwealth countries that formerly composed the British Empire. After the abolition of slavery in the British Empire in 1834, East Indians were encouraged to migrate to fill jobs previously occupied by slaves in various parts of the Empire. To encourage such mobility, a system of indenture was utilized according to which workers contracted as tenants for a given period of time in payment for their transportation to the designated destinations. Large minorities of Indians grew up as a result in Canada, South Africa, Kenya, and Britain to satisfy the labor demand of a few powerful employers. Because they were hard-working, innovative, and willing to work for lower wages, they were in great demand on farms and ranches and in lumber camps.[63]

When the conflict with minorities became serious, Canada and other parts of the Commonwealth took measures to limit Indian immigration. Following extended debates regarding the presumed equality of all British subjects and the open rejection of such equality by South African whites, the British government agreed that each country should be free to decide its own population policy, declaring that it would be difficult to transplant white European culture and society to other parts of the world and at the same time keep an open immigration policy in those countries to all races and ethnicities.[64] However, limiting migration did not improve treatment of the existing minorities.

Probably the best illustration of the attempt to exploit ethnic minorities and at the same time to transplant and keep white European culture "pure" is the treatment of the Chinese, East Indians, and Japanese in British Columbia. When they were needed, these minorities were imported and given work, but once they were no longer needed, they were pressured and sometimes forced to leave the province. They were degraded, called John Chinaman, boys, and Japs. They were also subjected to school and housing segregation, and were always employed for lower average wages than those of the whites. This movement to keep Canada white reached its climax between 1850 and 1940.[65]

Treatment of the Chinese in British Columbia was no worse than their treatment in the United States. The Naturalization Act of 1879 excluded them from U.S. citizenship, and restrictions were imposed on Chinese immigration long before they were on any other foreign group so as to keep out the "yellow peril." They were discriminated against by the 1882 Chinese Exclusion Act, which kept them as aliens. The 1885 Alien Contract Labor Act made it illegal for a Chinese who had returned to China to come back to the United States, a restriction not imposed on other groups.[66] Since then the use of immigration policy has become a standard approach to regulate the racial-ethnic composition of the U.S. population, especially through the Quota Acts of 1921 and 1924, which based quotas on the proportional composition of the population by national origin in 1920.[67] Those of European background were, by definition, given the lion's share of the immigration quota.

Discrimination, however, has also characterized ethnic groups among whites in Canada. For example, Anglos in Quebec have a marked income advantage of almost 40% over the average income, while the Francophones' disadvantage is almost 80% of the average because of their ethnicity.[68]

East Indians today exist as minorities in Britain, Canada, Kenya, and South Africa. They are worst off in South Africa, where only recently they won some representation in Parliament as Coloreds. In all these countries they are considered minorities, often receiving lower wages, underrepresented in public administration, and treated less than equally in everyday life, though they may be equal before the law. Because their economic efficiency or "productive superiority" would be a threat to the white community were they to have equal rights and privileges, there is a continuing tendency to keep them "domiciled" to contain that threat.[69]

In the past, Indians in Africa were the "middleman" minority, filling a vacuum between the white colonists and the blacks. In parts of Asia they were one middleman minority among others, including the Chinese. In Malaysia the stratification put the Europeans at the top, followed by the Chinese and then the Indians, after whom came the native Malays at the bottom. The Indians were brought in to do manual labor in mines, rubber plantations, and transportation, and to fill lower managerial and craft jobs, as well as lower civil service positions. The Indians were and are discriminated against by both the Europeans and the Chinese.

The Indians in Malaysia worked mostly for wages, while the Chinese worked on contract. The wage workers had housing and health benefits, but even with these benefits, "the total real wage of a Chinese [rubber] trapper has been usually at least a third higher than that of an Indian counterpart." The wages of Indians went down when rubber prices went down, but they did not go up when the prices went up. Their living conditions were poor, their educational facilities underfunded, and they had little land to settle on in comparison with the Chinese and the Europeans. At school they were instructed in the native languages, though learning English was the way to move up the economic ladder, and children 10-12 years old were encouraged by estate owners to go to work, rather than attend school. Even after labor organization started following World War II, the wages of Indians were far below those of the Chinese and Europeans.[70]

The problem of Indians in Africa and Asia raises a new issue because it mixes ethnic with racial elements. As Caucasians the Indians share a common racial origin with the British but a different ethnic origin, but like the Hispanics in the United States, they are ethnically different from the "Anglos" and racially and ethnically different from the blacks and the Chinese. Like Hispanics in the United States, they are treated better than the blacks, but certainly not as well as the whites and the Chinese.

The same phenomenon of racial-ethnic diffusion is evident in the case of the Chinese in Southeast Asia, particularly in Indonesia. The Dutch ruled Indonesia for many years before its independence in 1945. Chinese immigrants were imported into the Islands to fill occupational gaps between what the Dutch would do and what the native Polynesians would do. The Polynesians engaged mostly in farming, while the Chinese worked in trade, commerce, and finance. The Dutch were landowners and government officers. The treatment of the Chinese was in many ways similar to that of the Indians in Africa, though the Chinese were not allowed to own property, while the Indians were. Neither group could assimilate, because of racial and cultural differences, even though assimilation was encouraged.

The Chinese, who were concentrated in Java and Sumatra, occupied an intermediate position in "a colonial caste structure" that was racially stratified: the Europeans were on top, then the Chinese, and then the Indonesian natives. In the early period the Chinese acted as tax farmers, operators of pawnshops, and in trade, including the salt trade and the opium trade on behalf of the Dutch government. Gradually they branched out into money lending, wholesale trade, purchasing and processing raw material for export, especially rubber, and banking. These specializations were enhanced by the Agrarian Law of 1870, which restricted landownership to natives although enforcement of the law was lax especially with respect to rubber plantations controlled by Europeans. Both Indonesians and Chinese were subjected to a pass system imposed by the Dutch. Living standards were also differentiated according to this racial stratification system at all levels of income.[71]

In 1946, the Indonesian republic offered citizenship to all Chinese born in Indonesia who had resided there continuously for five years, unless they had opted for a Chinese nationality. The issue of citizenship was complicated, however, by the fact that China had allowed dual citizenship to all Chinese wherever they resided. Once the Dutch were out of power, the Indonesian majority tried to circumscribe the role of the Chinese in the national economy, though the Chinese still managed to expand their role and increase their wealth, mostly at the expense of both the Dutch and the Indonesians. The Dutch were active in the economy until the major nationalization campaign in 1957-58, but since Indonesian projects were still inadequate to replace Dutch projects, the Chinese were always ready to step in to fill any emerging vacuum. The Indonesians were restricted by lack of expertise and capital, but they had the licensing authorities on their side, which led to what has become known as the "'Ali Baba firms' (Ali the Indonesian front man obtained the licenses, Baba the Chinese with the trading connections and capital)."[72]

Attempts by the Indonesians to nativize the economy and their apparent inability to compete with the Chinese led first to covert hostility and then open violence against them between 1959 and 1968. Since then, violence has been contained, but anti-Chinese sentiment and detestation are still rampant. The Indonesians feel that the Chinese minority is robbing them of their native wealth and depressing their living standards. Such feelings are translated into violence, especially in periods of crisis. According to some observers, violence against the Chinese, who are held responsible for high prices, is correlated with periods of inflation and unemployment.[73] Discrimination against them, therefore, is supposed to be a way of retrieving economic benefits that would otherwise have accrued to the Indonesians. A case in point is the rubber industry in Sumatra. The Indonesians, mostly small farmers, produce the rubber, and the Chinese process it into slabs or sheets for export or export it raw for processing. The Chinese have capital to extend to the farmers and command of the market and know-how, so that the Indonesian farmers have become dependent on them, to their disadvantage as they see it.[74]

The ethnic minorities of the Middle East are another example of people who face chronic conflict with the majorities and with each other. Wars, the breakup of the Ottoman Empire, changes of national boundaries and transfers of population, plus multiplicity of religious faiths have resulted in fragmented communities in most countries of the region. Minorities in the Middle East are more often distinguished by religious differences than by ethnic or racial differences. Christians, Muslims, and Jews are separated by religion, though religious minority groups are also often identified by their cultural, ethnic, and perception affiliations. Yet they are all Caucasian and Semitic, and they often identify with their native countries. The Copts in Egypt are the best example of a minority's national identification, with Egypt as *their* country; this same form of minority national identification is illustrated by the Maronites, the Greek Catholics, and the Greek Orthodox communities in Lebanon, Syria, and other Middle Eastern countries, all of whom consider their country of residence as their national home as well. Though religious conflict in the Middle East—at least as serious as their ethnic conflict—is outside the scope of our discussion, the idea that the Jews are a nation and the Arabs are a nation, that the Kurds are a nation, as are the Armenians, has transformed minority-majority conflict into an ethnic-national conflict.

The problem of ethnic minorities in the Middle East has a little different character from minority problems elsewhere. It usually reflects favoritism or positive economic discrimination in favor of a minority that is already better off than the majority in terms of economic, educational, or other opportunities. The Christians, the Jews, the Bahais, the Armenians, and the Greeks in the largely Muslim countries of the Middle East have usually had higher levels of education and living standards than the Muslim majority.

This favored position dates back almost to the days of the Crusaders, but more formally to the fifteenth century, when Western Christian countries sought privileges in Muslim countries, including the protection of native Christian communities, as discussed above in the context of the Ottoman capitulations.

By the end of foreign rule, the traditions and institutions of such favoritism had become established. The Muslim ruling majority has tried to abolish these privileges by applying countermeasures that are themselves discriminatory. These countermeasures are well illustrated by the treatment of the Copts in Egypt and the various Christian communities in Lebanon, where the conflict has led to socio-economic and political disasters, the most recent of which has plagued Lebanon for the last eighteen years.[75]

Ethnic discrimination in the Middle East extends to the nationals of other Middle Eastern countries regardless of religion: for example, Egyptians in Jordan, Iraq, and Saudi Arabia are treated less equally than are natives regarding the rights to own property, operate a business, hold permanent government employment, or acquire citizenship and assimilate. Such Arab nationals (though from sister Arab countries) are often discriminated against and treated less well than would be a foreigner from the West, such as an American, a French, or an English professional doing the same work as the Arab national of another country.

A somewhat similar form of ethnic discrimination in the Middle East is experienced in internal Jewish relations and in Jewish/Arab relations in Israel. The Sephardic (Oriental) Jews are discriminated against by the Ashkenazi (Western) Jews, and the Arabs in Israel are discriminated against by both Jewish groups. The Ashkenazi Jews, who have dominated Israel in terms of political power and their seniority to the Sephardic Jews in populating and developing country, have brought with them the superiority complex of the Western world toward Oriental people, including other Jews. As a result, a three-tier stratification has arisen in Israel: Ashkenazi Jew, Sephardic Jew, and Arab in that order. Within each of these strata there may be other forms of stratification, by country of origin, religion, length of residence in the country, etc. This form of ethnic discrimination has been costly and destabilizing, reducing work opportunities, causing housing segregation, and leading to misallocations of resources for development and the improvement of services. Though discrimination is legally prohibited, administrative power is distributed in such a way as to perpetuate the three-tier stratification.

The problem of discrimination in Israel, when discussed openly by Israelis, is said to exist because there has been insufficient time for the ethnic integration of Jewish communities gathered from around the world, and because of the state of war between Israel and its Palestinian and other Arab neighbors. Discrimination against Arabs is considered a result of the need for security measures to protect the state. Neither the Sephardic Jews nor the Arabs, however, are convinced by these explanations. No doubt economic benefits accrue to someone when a Sephardic Jew is paid less than an Ashkenazi Jew doing the same work, or when a Sephardic Jew is denied a job in favor of an Ashkenazi Jew. Similarly, the employer who pays a lower wage to an Arab but receives the same amount of output, or more, than he receives from a Jew, benefits from such discrimination; therefore discrimination persists.

One other form of discrimination in the Middle East should be mentioned, namely, the presumed discrimination against the Kurds, who are spread out over parts of Turkey, Iran, Iraq, Syria, and the Soviet Union. The Kurds consider themselves a nation, originally from Kurdistan, and have tried unsuccessfully to consolidate their communities and create an independent state of their own. None of the countries involved has allowed it. The Kurds charge that by being denied such independence they are discriminated against. This form of discrimination, however, is not a result of their unequal treatment as citizens, but of their desire to separate from the nation and create a new citizenship and a new national state. While charges of economic discrimination have been voiced, the thrust of the Kurdish movement has been political; therefore it falls outside the scope of our study.

In conclusion, the Middle East shares with the rest of the world the practice of discrimination in favor of or against certain ethnic minorities. Discrimination there, as elsewhere, seems to be aimed either to redress inequalities or to exploit potential benefits, and the existing power structures allow it to continue.[76]

Finally we need to explore the place of ethnic discrimination in Socialist economies, the former USSR and Eastern Europe. According to Marxist theory, discrimination is not a matter of race, ethnicity, or sex. It is a result of the conflict between classes. Since classes would be abolished in Socialist society, there could be no discrimination in such a society. And since people are expected to contribute according to their ability and be rewarded according to their contribution in socialism or to their need in communism, there could be no exploitation. Therefore, once capitalism has been abolished and replaced by socialism, economic discrimination will no longer be possible. What do the facts tell us?

First, ethnic minorities have existed in Russia and Eastern Europe for centuries as a result of war, Russian expansion, shifting of boundaries, and population transfers. For example, in the most recent census

Czechoslovakia had Czechs (65%), Slovaks (29%), Hungarians (4%), and some Germans, Poles, Ukrainians, Jews, and others. Poland had 98% Poles, but also had Ukrainians, Jews, Belorussians, Germans, and others. This composition has changed greatly since the interwar period because massive forced population transfers took place after World War II. The census of 1979 enumerated 92 national groups in the Soviet Union. The Russians formed 52.4% of the population, 16.2% were Ukrainians, the Uzbeks were 4.7%, etc. Fifteen nations qualified as union republics. Hence, ethnic minorities continue to exist within the Socialist world.[77] Now that the Soviet Union has been dissolved and a form of capitalism is under way, all the minorities have begun seeking independence on ethnic national grounds, both peacefully and by force.

Second, it is agreed that neither the USSR nor the countries of Eastern Europe fully achieved the state of communism, and few achieved the full state of socialism, in which all means of production are nationalized and all workers are compensated according to their contribution. Employment and wages in the Socialist economies were part of the economic plan, which was influenced more by partisan-political considerations than by the productivity of a sector or team of workers. However, there is no evidence that ethnic discrimination was practiced with regard to wages or rewards within agriculture or industry. Discrimination among individuals within both sectors was more evident on the basis of one's rank in the party, association with the power structure, and sex, which will be discussed later. In housing, in entering a university, or in landing the right job, one's position in the party made a difference, regardless of ethnic origin. The scale of compensation was established by the planning mechanism or the party structure, but once it was established, it applied to all workers in a given category or industry.

Ethnic political conflict in the former USSR, however, is evident as a national concern, not as a minority-majority conflict. The various ethnic groups that inhabit the former USSR and Eastern Europe regard themselves as nations and expect to be treated as equals. However, there is apparently a feeling that certain nationalities are treated more equally than others in economic terms, with Russians at the top, and other nationalities below them, such as the Latvians, the Uzbeks, etc. Like the case of the Kurds, this problem is outside the scope of our analysis.

There are arguments that the allocation of resources and investment capital is influenced by the ethnic composition of the population in a region or a republic, and that is why certain ethnic groups remain traditional, underdeveloped, less educated, and in lower occupations and positions than others, as in Azerbaijan and Kazakhstan. Whether such allocation is intended as discrimination is not evident, but the objective facts remain: certain republics have developed faster than others. It is true that sometimes the absorption capacity and the promise of achievement are lower in one region than in another and therefore that investment in that region would be lower than in the other. The fact that such a region is inhabited by an ethnic group that forms a minority in the federal structure, but a majority in the individual republic may not be coincidental, because absorptive capacity of investment is cumulative. Once a republic falls behind (or might have been behind at the start), it may be difficult for it to catch up unless extra efforts are made to speed up its development. Whether the majority in the federal system would be willing to devote extra resources to enable the minority to catch up is uncertain. It has not happened in the Western capitalistic countries, nor are there indications that it should be expected to happen in the Socialist countries, the Marxist analysis notwithstanding.[78]

Nevertheless, there is little evidence that discrimination exists in Socialist economies against individuals because of their ethnic background, on the job, in occupational rewards, or in housing. Discrimination in these areas, or one should say favoritism, is tied mostly to one's position in the party, closeness to the power machinery, and to education and occupational status. It should be noted, however, that economic discrimination against individuals because of ethnicity or race has rarely been discussed in the Soviet Union as an existing problem.[79]

CONCLUSIONS

Six common features of racial and ethnic discrimination have been illustrated in this chapter. First, whenever racial and ethnic groups have interacted, economic differentiation has become evident. Second, in most cases discrimination has been directed against minorities rather than in their favor. Third, economic discrimination in favor of racial minorities has prevailed whenever that minority has been backed up by a powerful racial, political, or economic power, such as Europeans and Americans in third world countries, the Chinese in Southeast Asia, and Christians in Muslim countries. Fourth, economic discrimination has always been associated with differential power distribution, the existence of an "alien" minority, and the prospect of private economic gain for the discriminators. Fifth, the form and intensity of discrimination have varied according to the demands of the market as perceived by the "power" majority, ranging from slavery, through apartheid, to subtle differentiation in the market place. Finally, economic discrimination between ethnic and racial groups seems to have been common to various periods, countries, and economic systems, and to become more evident in periods of economic crisis than in periods of prosperity and growth.

NOTES

1. "Racism," *Encyclopaedia Britannica*, 1974, 15, 361-63; Oliver C. Cox, "The Rise of Modern Race Relations," in William Barclay, Krishna Kuman, and Ruth P. Simms, *Racial Conflict, Discrimination and Power* (New York: AMS Press, 1976).

2. Renate Bridenthal and Claudia Koonz, eds., *Becoming Visible: Women in European History* (Boston: Houghton Mifflin, 1977), 5, 7.

3. See the first three articles by John B. Duff and Larry A. Green, eds., *Slavery: Its Origin and Legacy* (New York: Thomas Y. Crowell, 1975).

4. Cox, "Rise of Modern Race Relations," 84-85.

5. Muhammad A. Dandamaev, *Slavery in Babylonia: From Nabopolassar to Alexander the Great* (626-331 B.C.), trans. Victoria A. Powell (De Kalb, Ill.: Northern Illinois University Press, 1984), 648.

6. W. O. Blake, *The History of Slavery and the Slave Trade: Ancient and Modern* (Columbus, Ohio: J. and H. Miller, 1859), 2.

7. Yvon Garlan, "War, Piracy and Slavery in the Greek World," in M. I. Finley, ed., *Classical Slavery* (London: Frank Cass, 1987), 10-11.

8. Blake, History of Slavery, 18-20.

9. By K. R. Bradley, "On the Roman Slave Supply and Slavebreeding," in Finley, Classical Slavery, 43.

10. Blake, *History of Slavery*, 146-49.

11. Cox, *Rise of Modern Race Relations*, 85-86.

12. Gervase Corcoran, O.S.A., *Saint Augustine on Slavery* (Roma: Institutum Patristicum, 1985), 24-25.

13. Ibid., 27, 29-30.

14. Ibid., 69-71.

15. Ibid., 76.

16. Ibid., 79-90.

17. Ado Boahen, "Politics in Ghana, 1800-1874," in J. F. A. Ajayi and Michael Crowder, eds., *History of West Africa*, Vol. II (New York: Columbia University Press, 1972), 174.

18. Marc Bloch, *Slavery and Serfdom in the Middle Ages*, trans. William R. Beer (Berkeley: University of California Press, 1975), 27.

19. Cox, *Rise of Modern Race Relations*, 86.

20. "Racism," *Encyclopaedia Britannica*., 1974, 15, 361.

21. Isolated data may be gleaned from the pages of the *Cambridge Economic History of Europe*, Vol. I, 2nd ed., ed. M. M. Postan (Cambridge: Cambridge University Press, 1966).

22. Charles R. Foster, "The Underrepresented Nations," in Charles R. Foster, ed., *Nations Without a State: Ethnic Minorities in Western Europe* (New York: Praeger, 1980), 1-6.

23. Riccardo Petrulla, "Nationalist and Regionalist Movements in Western Europe," in Foster, *Nations Without a State*, 17.

24. Frank W. Wallbank, "Trade and Industry Under the Later Roman Empire in the West," *Cambridge Economic History of Europe*, Vol. II, eds. M. M. Postan and H. J. Habakkuk (Cambridge: Cambridge University Press, 1952), 81-82.

25. Robert S. Lopez, "The Trade of Medieval Europe: The South," in *Cambridge Economic History of Europe*, Vol. II, 318-19.

26. A. B. Hibbert, "The Economic Policies of Towns," *Cambridge Economic History of Europe*, Vol. III, eds. M. M. Postan, E. E. Rich, and Edward Miller (Cambridge, Cambridge University Press, 1963), 181-82, 193-94.

27.   Ibid., 197-98.

28.   Gershon David Hundert, "The Role of the Jews in Commerce in Early Modern Poland and Lithuania," *Journal of European Economic History* 16, no. 2 (Fall 1987): 249.

29.   Ibid., 253-54.

30.   Ibid., 255-59.

31.   Hillel Levine, *Economic Origins of Anti-Semitism: Poland and Its Jews in the Early Modern Period,* (New Haven: Yale University Press, 1991), especially Chs. 2 and 3.

32.   Hundert, "Role of the Jews," 268.

33.   A. C. Hepburn, ed., *Minorities in History* (New York: Edward Arnold, 1978), especially Chs. 3 and 4.

34.   E. H. Tuma, "The Economic Impact of the Capitulations: The Middle East and Europe: A Reinterpretation," *Journal of European Economic History* 18, no. 3 (Winter 1989): 663-82.

35.   John Lescott-Leszczynski, *The History of U.S. Ethnic Policy and Its Impact on European Ethnics* (Boulder, Colo.: Westview Press, 1984), 50-51.

36.   Farley Reynolds, "Blacks, Hispanics, and White Ethnic Groups: Are Blacks Uniquely Disadvantaged?" *American Economic Review, Papers and Proceedings,* 80, no. 2 (May 1990): 238-39.

37.   Ibid.

38.   Barclay, Kumar, and Simms, *Racial Conflict,* 137.

39.   Robert Norris, "Document: Memoirs of the Reign of Bossa Ahadee...and a Short Account of the African Slave Trade, 1789," in Barclay, Kumar, and Simms, *Racial Conflict,* 128-39.

40.   Jeanne Gregory, *Sex, Race and the Law: Legislating for Equality* (London: Sage Publications, 1987), 13.

41.   Leonard Dinnerstein and Frederic Cople Jaher, eds., *The Aliens* (New York: Appleton-Century-Crofts Educational Division, Meredith Corporation 1970), 4.

42.   W. E. B. Dubois, "The Black Worker," in Dinnerstein and Jaher, *Aliens,* 97.

43.   Ibid., 99.

44.   Dinnerstein and Jaher, *Aliens,* 5.

45.   Dubois, "Black Worker," 102.

46.   Dinnerstein and Jaher, *Aliens,* 6.

47.   Abeodu Bowen Jones, "The Republic of Liberia," in J. F. A. Ajayi and Michael Crowder, eds., *History of West Africa,* Vol. II (New York: Columbia University Press, 1972), 308ff.

48.   Lescott-Leszczynski, *History of U.S. Ethnic Policy,* 13-14; Gregory, *Sex, Race,* 13-15.

49.   For these and other opinions and findings, see Joel Williamson, ed., *The Origins of Segregation* (Boston: D.C. Heath, 1968), especially 6-20.

50.   Christine Bolt, "Red, Black and White in Nineteenth-Century America," in Hepburn, *Minorities in History,* 120-21.

51.   Donald R. McCoy and Richard T. Ruetten, "Towards Equality: Blacks in the United States During the Second World War," in Hepburn, *Minorities in History,* 145.

52.   For details of these measures, more below in Ch. 6 and in Lescott-Leszczynski, *History of U.S. Ethnic Policy.*

53.   Richard Vedder, Lowell Gallaway, and David Klingman, "Black Exploitation and White Benefits: The Civil War Income Revolution," in Richard F. America, ed., *The Wealth of Races: The Present Value of Benefits from Past Injuries* (New York: Greenwood Press, 1990), 133.

54.   Bob Hepple, "The British Industrial System and Racial Discrimination," in Barclay, Kumar, and Simms, *Racial Conflict,* 146-154.

55.   Bob Hepple, *Race, Jobs and the Law in Britain* (London: Penguin Press, 1968), 59.

56.   Mats Lundhal and Eskil Wadensjo, *Unequal Treatment: A Study in the Neo-Classical Theory of Discrimination* (New York: New York University Press, 1984), 212.

57.   Ibid., 213.

58.   Ibid., 214-15.

59.   This drama of land appropriation and cheap labor drama has been enacted by Israel in the Occupied Territories of Palestine and to an extent against the Arab citizens of Israel.

60.   Ibid., 218.

61.   Ibid., 220.

62.   Quoted in Lundhal and Wadensjo, *Unequal Treatment,* 236.

63.   T. G. Fraser, "Imperial Policy and Indian Minorities Overseas, 1905-23," in Hepburn, *Minorities in History,* 155.

64.   Ibid., 156-57.

65.   W. Peter Ward, *White Canada Forever* (Montreal: McGill-Queen's University Press, 1978), especially Chs. 1 and 9.

66.   Lescott-Leszczynski, *History of United States Ethnic Policy,* 14-20.

67.   Ibid., 24, 26.

68.   Morton Weinfeld, "Affirmative Action in Quebec's Middle and Upper Management in the Private Sector," in William C. McCready, ed., *Culture, Ethnicity, and Identity: Current Issues in Research* (New York: Academic Press, 1983), 364.

69.   Fraser, "Imperial Policy," 160.

70.   Kernial Singh Sandhu, *Indians in Malaya: Some Aspects of Immigration and Settlement, 1867-1957* (Cambridge: Cambridge University Press, 1969), 259.

71.   J. A. C. Mackie and Charles A. Coppel, "A Preliminary Survey," in J. A. C. Mackie, ed., *The Chinese in Indonesia: Five Essays* (Melbourne: Nelson in Association with the Australian Institute of International Affairs, 1976), 4-5.

72.   Mackie and Coppel, "Preliminary Survey," 13-14.

73.   Mary F. Somers Heidhues, *Southeast Asia's Chinese Minorities* (Hawthorn, Victoria: Longman, 1974), 100-101.

74.   K. D. Thomas and J. Panglaykim, "The Chinese in South Sumatran Rubber Industry: A Case Study in Economic Nationalism," Ch. 4 in Mackie, *Chinese in Indonesia.*

75.   The ethnic minorities of the Middle East include Armenians, 5% of the Lebanese population; Arabs about 17% of the Israeli population; Kurds, about 19% of the Turkish, 23% of the Iraqi, 10% of the Iranian, and 8% of the Syrian populations. The Berbers (though they do not identify with a separate nationality) compose 40% of the population in Morocco, and 15-20% in Algeria. Minority Rights Group, *World Directory of Minorities* (Chicago: Longmans, 1990), 176-214.

76.   On minorities in the Middle East see also A. H. Hourani, *Minorities in the Arab World* (London: Oxford University Press, 1947); Joane Nagel, "The Conditions of Ethnic Separatism: The Kurds in Turkey, Iran, and Iraq," *Ethnicity* 7 (1980): 279-97; Milton Esman and Itamar Rabinovitch, *Ethnicity, Pluralism, and the State in the Middle East* (Ithaca, N.Y.: Cornell University Press, 1988); R. D. McLaurin, *The Political Role of Minority Groups in the Middle East* (New York: Praeger, 1979); Ruth Klinov, "Ethnic Discrimination in the Israeli Labor Movement," Hebrew University, November 1991 (mimeo).

77.   Robert R. King, "Eastern Europe," in Robert G. Wirsing (ed.),. *Protection of Minorities* (New York: Pergamon Press, 1981), 86, and Teresa Ratowska-Harmstone, "The Soviet Union," in Wirsing, *Protection,* 120.

78. For a more recent look at ethnicity in the USSR see Teodor Shanin, "Ethnicity in the Soviet Union: Analytical Perceptions and Political Strategies," *Comparative Studies in Society and History* 31, no. 3 (1989): 409-24.

79. In addition to the sources above, see David K. Willis, *Klass: How Russians Really Live* (New York: St. Martin's Press, 1985), Ch. 12.

3

Economic Discrimination: Gender

Sex discrimination against women, and occasionally against men, has been a major issue of contention in the post-World War II period, though more intensively in developed than less developed countries. Like discrimination against minorities, gender discrimination is practiced by a stronger party against a weaker party in expectation of gaining economic benefits. It may take the form of exclusion by limiting the acquired endowment, which depends on education and training, by underutilization, which limits the kind and duration of employment, and by underrewarding or underpayment relative to payment made to the other sex, and probably relative to the marginal product. Discrimination against women, the commonest form of gender discrimination, entails social costs that cannot be compensated for by the private benefits that may accrue. Accordingly, economic gender discrimination entails a net social cost and a loss to society.

Whether there are social benefits to discrimination against women is not evident. If they did exist, they would be sociological and cultural, not economic. Some observers contend that keeping women at home helps to stabilize the family, raise better educated and mannered children, and promote morality and ethics, which contribute to the stability of society. These uncertain potential benefits must be weighed against the impact on the family and society of depriving women (or men) of the freedom of choice, which is certainly diminished by discrimination.

Discrimination against women has been common throughout history in all economic systems, in varying degrees of intensity and hurt. In this chapter we shall illustrate the ubiquity of discrimination against women by looking at the place of women in the economy in various periods and places, beginning with ancient and medieval society.

GENDER DISCRIMINATION IN ANCIENT AND MEDIEVAL SOCIETY

Women were treated differentially in all ancient and medieval societies, although one might debate whether the differential treatment was intended to be discriminatory or not. However, by our definition, to the extent that the unequal treatment was imposed on women by men, it was a form of discrimination.

History has usually been written with most of the focus on men, on the elite, and from the viewpoint of writers who have been men. Even so, these writers have admitted that the status of women seems to have deteriorated over time. The fact that most historians have been men may also explain, at least in part, the scarcity of information regarding the place of women in ancient and medieval societies and to a certain extent in present-day society. Brave attempts have been made recently to "restore women to history." The results have been collected in volumes on which this chapter depends heavily.[1] Most of the literature, however, is outside the economic sphere; therefore, our presentation gleans information from these interdisciplinary sources to answer the questions raised in this study.

In ancient society Babylonian women seem to have enjoyed a higher status than did women in later periods. They could own property and dispose of it as they saw fit. They had a right to inherit a part of the husband's estate, and they could conclude contracts, but they could not appear as witnesses to a contract. According to the Code of Hammurabi they could enter into partnerships and trade, and they could conduct lawsuits independently of their husbands. However, there are suggestions that Hammurabi accorded a more restricted role to priestesses than to priests, though it is not explained why.[2] The ancient Egyptians also accorded women a status that was equal or superior to that of men. Women could own property, work in various professions, and participate in public affairs side by side with men. Upon marriage men had to promise not only to respect but also to obey their wives.

In contrast, the Greeks and Romans reduced women to total dependence upon men. In ancient Athens, for example, women had no opportunities to be educated, were confined to household activities, and had no voice in public affairs. In Sparta, however, almost the opposite prevailed: women enjoyed a large measure of equality with men in politics, economic affairs, sports, and in social interaction. It is not clear why women fared so much better in Sparta than in Athens during the same period. In ancient Crete women had a superior position to men. Theirs was a matrilineal society in which women had larger living quarters than men. Kinship and residence followed the mother, not the father.[3] On the other hand, Roman women were treated as subservient to men, with little indication of citizenship or rights as independent individuals. They could not inherit property, they had no access to education, and they had no social life of their own. Women of the higher classes enjoyed comfort and wealth and had the help of servants, but only by virtue of the status of their husband or some other male relative on whom they depended. Women of lower classes, including slaves, worked with men but received fewer benefits than men and were subservient to their own male relatives as well.

Feudal Europe saw few changes in the status of women: among feudal families, women were ladies of leisure, except in the absence of the lord, when they could exercise full authority in his name. Women of the lower classes and serfs, who did all kinds of work outside the house, were always paid less than men and with no means of redress or protection often were treated worse than men by feudal lords or their agents. Women were definitely subservient to men and dependent on them except when men or lords delegated power to them, as they would to an agent or foreman.[4]

The decline of feudalism and the rise of towns in Europe brought a little improvement in women's position. They won a little more freedom of choice. Women of the lower classes could migrate and work in towns, live on their own, and make some decisions regarding their own personal lives. However, they were limited to certain trades, were invariably paid less than men, and rarely acquired positions of management or master artisanship. Few could become guild members, except in separate women's guilds, or succeed their dead husbands. Women did not usually run shops but leased them to craftsmen and thus became rentiers.

Upon the death of her husband, a woman could inherit all or part of a farm and operate it. However, even in late medieval and early modern Europe, women's earnings were considered only a supplement to men's earnings or a reward for less significant responsibilities and therefore could be depressed. In the cottage industry, where the family worked as a team, the man directed, managed, and controlled the shop and all the family resources. By the same token, underpayment of women was justified as being only a supplement to the family income. In general, however, underrewarding resulted from the perception that women were weaker than men in bargaining and in the eyes of society.

To summarize, in contrast to their status in Babylonia, Minoan Crete, and ancient Egypt, women in Europe up to the Industrial Revolution lived a life of inequality, monotonous employment, and subservience to men before the law and in society. They had little choice in what they did, where they lived, and how they lived. They did what was expected of them. It is often argued that women's lower status was due to their devotion to caring for their children, or to their need for protection while their children were young. Yet, their status hardly improved when they no longer had dependent children. The less-than-equal treatment of women was often justified as being consistent with the Judeo-Christian ethic, which predominated in medieval and early modern Europe.[5]

Throughout most of the history of large parts of Africa, women (wives) were exchanged for cows. (Men, as husbands, were never exchanged that way.) The cows were used to enrich the male members of the wives' family, while the wives exchanged for the cows had to work the land of their husband and thus increase his wealth. There are suggestions that in the earlier forms of African society, especially the pastoral, a certain degree of egalitarianism between the sexes existed. The work was done by the family as a team, and the men and women performed various duties interchangeably.[6] There is, however, some doubt regarding the interpretation of the roles: women were responsible for food supply but that did not mean they controlled it or that they acquired power, authority, or independence by that means. Women probably participated in activities often performed by men, in addition to their own duties, but that would not prove they enjoyed equality, unless it can be shown that they participated in deciding who did what, which is not evident.

The presumed egalitarianism between men and women apparently suffered as a result of the advent of Islam in Africa and the increasing value attached to the ivory and horn trade. Islam restricted the sphere of women to the home, and trade enhanced the role of men as hunters and increased their ability to invest in more wives.[7] Both interpretations depend on whether women actually had occupied an equal position earlier, which certainly is not established. It is true that according to Muslim law, *Shari'a,* a woman could inherit only half the share of a man, but women and men did not inherit equally before Islam either.

The place of women in Africa apparently deteriorated again in the nineteenth century, though it may be argued that this had happened earlier because of the threat of drought, the slave trade, and capitalism. The scarcity problem and introduction of the plow apparently encouraged male domination by inducing men to take control of the land and cultivation, while slavery and capitalism did so by "distorting and commodifying the value of women's labor," thus forcing them to seek male protection.[8]

Division of labor varied in different parts of Africa before the twentieth century. In early Sudanese states, such as Ghana, Mali, Songhay, and the Hausa city-states, there was more division of labor by gender than in other parts of Africa, though women's activities seem to have been shared with men. For example, women worked around the house and cared for children, while men prepared the land for farming. Here, too, the advent of Islam seems to have altered these relationships, presumably reducing the status of women in political and economic terms.[9] During the medieval and early modern periods (1400-1800), new crops were introduced in Western Africa and the hinterland. Trade also expanded, including the slave trade. These developments did affect the status of women, but they rarely engaged in large-scale lucrative trade or held positions of power. Interestingly, slave owners preferred women slaves because they could be more remunerative, and more easily exploited by male owners and controlled by female owners.[10]

Gender discrimination in Western Africa and the hinterland seems most evident in the institution of woman-woman marriage, according to which one woman played the role of husband and married another female to control her labor, children, and wealth or simply to assume the more powerful role of a husband. Apparently such an arrangement did not interfere with other roles or the traditional division of labor by sex. Similarly, daughters in this type of family had authority over female in-laws who were not of the same kinship, presumably only in the absence of male heirs.[11] Even when the society was organized along matrilineal lines, it was understood that authority resided in men, and women were subservient to the male relative.[12]

Contact with Europeans brought many changes to West Central Africa, but attitudes toward women changed little. Women continued to be items of trade, sources of labor, subservient to and dependent on men. As the male-dominated slave trade expanded, women lost both power and business. Slave wives brought from far away were preferred by men because. without male relatives around to look after their interests, they were less demanding.[13] The preference given to slave wives no doubt increased the vulnerability and undermined the place of free women. Whether free or enslaved, women were dominated by men.[14]

Looking into the history of Asia, we find women treated as inferior by men from the earliest days of recorded history. The caste system, presumably adapted by the Aryans occupying India around 1500 B.C., was one way to isolate and exclude "indigenous people and those of mixed descent as outsiders." These became the *sudra* or servants, fourth class. The Aryans had a patriarchal family system in which "women were considered a part of the male's property in the same way as a field belonged to the men of the family." Women could participate in business, in agriculture and manufacturing, as well as in public administration. What became of their earnings, though, is not clear. One tenet of the caste system in India held that ritual purity would be realized by vegetarianism, teetotalism, and "increased control over women." Such control included "women's disinheritance from

immovable property . . . and their exclusion from the productive economy," by seclusion or *purdah*. In addition, men's control over women's sexuality was an important factor.[15]

In Buddhist India women participated in religious ceremonies and traditions, but Buddhist nuns were subordinate to Buddhist monks.[16] Women's
status declined gradually in relation to that of men, so that by 500 B.C.
women were treated as *sudras*. They were not allowed to wear the "sacred
thread" or perform the sacrifice even as partners with their husbands.[17] In
the Mauryan Empire (322-183 B.C.), which was the first centralized state in
India, a woman had property rights to her dowry, *sirdham,* which was given
to her by her parents and later augmented by her husband. Though most
dowries were in the form of jewelry, over time the dowry concept became
broad enough to include immovable property.[18]

During the Gupta era (320-540 A.D.), women in India were brought up
according to the rules of the patriarchal family, which were similar to those
of Confucian China. According to the Laws of Manu, which represented the
ideals of the *Brahmans,* or highest *varna,* or class, "in childhood a female
must be subject to her father, in youth to her husband, and when her lord is
dead, to her sons; a woman must never be independent." Women, like sons
and slaves, had no property rights; what they earned belonged to the men
who owned them.[19]

However, though men's proprietary rights in women were legally recognized in early India, there are indications that the implementation of those
rights would have met with social disapproval if it hurt women.[20]

Legal rights to property in India varied according to tradition. The
Dyabhaga tradition, unique to Bengal, allowed a widow to inherit her husband's property only if he had no male heir; the Mitskara tradition, which
prevailed in the rest of India, did not give any property rights to a widow.
With the advent of Islam, Indian women began to practice *purdah* or veil-
ing. The Turkish Muslim occupation of India apparently intensified the
seclusion of Hindu women. The *harim* or seclusion of women, *zenana* in
India, has been described both as an institution of oppression and as a
source of protection and opportunity to achieve power and influence.[21]

Prior to 1500 A.D. women seem to have enjoyed a higher status in
Southeast Asia—Burma, Malaysia, Singapore, Thailand, Cambodia, Laos,
Vietnam, Indonesia, and the Philippines—than in most other places.
Though little is known of the early history of women, it appears that in the
late medieval period, women still occupied a higher status in Southeast Asia
than in other regions, and the "value of daughters was . . . never questioned...as it was in China, India, and the Middle East."[22] Marriages were
monogamous, and women had a right to divorce and had virtual autonomy.

Women were active in the economic sphere as traders and skilled managers, though little is said about rights of ownership, conditions of work, or equality with men. There is no reason to believe that equality existed in this region since it was exposed to Buddhism, Confucianism, Christianity, and Islam, all of which make women less than equal with men. Nevertheless, women enjoyed more independence in Southeast Asia than in any of the other regions of Asia.

The colonial period, 1500-1800, did not bring improvement to the status of women. On one hand was a stereotype of Javanese women as "docile dolls or sensual and fecund sexual partners." On the other hand, women were known as money managers and efficient business operators, though with limited property rights.[23] Evidently the colonial powers, Spain, Portugal, and Holland, exercised much control over the institutions that affected the place of women in the economy. Women were not equal to men in those Western societies, so one could not expect a great improvement in their status under colonial rule.

Women had a different status in China, Japan, and Korea. In all three societies women were associated with such taboos and undesirables as menstrual blood, postpartum discharge, and dominance over men through sexual activity.[24] In Confucian teaching women were to be "unselfish, loyal, self-sacrificing, and chaste in the service of father, husband, and ruler." In ancient Japan and Korea there were *amas,* or communities of women divers who were significant contributors to the economy. In these communities the mother's economic, ideological, and emotional roles often conflicted with Confucian ethical codes, which gave supremacy to men. The Confucian code does not give property rights to women. Therefore women were considered the cause of conflict among male kin when they requested that the property inheritance be divided. In Buddhism, "women alone come to symbolize all that must be transcended in order to achieve enlightenment." In Taoism the female deity was the "patron deity of all women . . . but was the special guardian of singing girls, dead women, novices, nuns, adepts, and priestesses," all of whom were "outside the traditional Chinese family."[25]

Confucianism and Buddhism discriminated against women by attributing to them limited rationality and inability to cope with affairs of state or public life; hence their dependency on men. Neo-Confucian teachings were even harsher on women, imposing on them rules of chastity, controlled sexuality, and complete obedience and loyalty to men. Footbinding, begun probably in the seventeenth century, might have been instituted to limit the mobility of women and force them to devote their attention to chastity and loyalty to the man in their life. Humiliating and painful, it crippled women and forced them to devote their attention to beauty and sexuality to please men.

Neo-Confucianism did not have the same impact on women in Korea. Until to 1600 A.D. men in Korea were not considered superior to women; inheritance was divided equally between sons and daughters; both sexes participated in the ancestor ceremonies; female lines were as important as male lines; and remarriage by women was not unusual. After 1500 A.D. change began to take place, presumably because of changes in landholding systems that favored men over women. When women lost the right to hold land, they lost their ancestral ceremonial rights and with them their relatively equal status.[26]

Change in Japan was slow but steady. By the fourteenth century inheritance rights for women had been abolished, presumably because of the rise of a warrior class that opposed property division; and if a woman did have an inheritance it was only for life. With loss of landed property Japanese women, like Korean women, lost their ancestral ceremonial rights and with them their relatively equal status. Women's role in trade and manufacturing was still important. Their status, however, began to decline again by the end of the sixteenth century. By the nineteenth century, in spite of claims of reform by men in favor of women, famine and poverty increased infanticide, which was practiced primarily on females. It became a matter of choice between the mother and the infant: to allow the mother to work and feed herself or let both of them perish (apparently the contest did not threaten the male members of the family). Similar declines in the status of women were evident in Korea and Japan after contact with the West, presumably because of poverty, Western intrusion, war, and unrest. The official response to these crises in Japan was to reject Western influence for reform and reimpose strict rules that segregated schoolchildren, established separate curricula, and brought back the ethics of the "good wife" and "wise mother" into the family and society.[27]

Latin America and the Caribbean offer still another view of women's place in society in relation to that of men. In pre-Columbian societies, "women everywhere were subordinated and excluded from public life."[28] There was a fairly well-defined division of labor, though it is not clear who defined it. Among the Aztecs, only men enjoyed the religious, economic, and prestige benefits society offered. Women were socialized to be "good women" who did spinning and weaving and embroidery and cared for home and family. Their "lower" status followed them after death. Their spinning wheels and weaving instruments were buried with them, while men had their slaves buried with them. In some communities marriage was monogamous and women were able to practice any of fifteen crafts and professions, though thirty-five were open to men.[29]

Among the Incas women participated in religious rites, but priesthood was reserved for men. Spinning, weaving, and embroidery were considered the right tasks for women. Men could have "secondary" wives. When certain communities were conquered, the conquerors took a portion of the occupied land and left the rest to the conquered people, who were expected to provide *mit'a* or labor service. Women, however, were exempted from the labor service, though they were expected to do their share of weaving labor. The Incas generally saw the role of women to be in the home.[30]

Conquest by the Europeans brought about basic changes in the role of women. Establishment of the *encomienda*, feudal estate, carried obligations to care for the Indians, convert them to Christianity, and assimilate them into Hispanic culture. As it turned out, the *encomienda* was a brutal form of exploitation. Amerindian slavery extended to men and women, but women were exchanged among the conquerors as gifts to be held as concubines or as the men decided. Indian noblemen often gave their daughters or sisters to the *conquistadors* to maintain alliances and noble privileges. Indian noblewomen were able by this means to secure privileges for themselves and others. What is not evident is whether women, noble or not, had a choice in the matter of being exchanged as gifts. Common Indian women, however, were given away by their fathers or were taken by force to prepare food and provide sexual satisfaction for the conquerors.[31]

The colonial society was marked by gender, class, and race distinctions:

When gender is taken into account, the following picture emerges, admittedly modified by exceptions. Although the conquistadors and their male descendants lost to the Crown some of the prerogatives they had sought to retain, and although the administration of the colonies remained in the hands of Spanish royal officials, because of their sex and race, Spanish men (i.e. white men, either born in America or in Spain) were nevertheless given superior status, economic benefits, and a subservient labor force composed of men and women who were Indian, African, or belonged to a *casta*. But Spanish women, either *criollas* or *peninsulares*, [born in America or in Spain respectively] were equal to Spanish men only in terms of race. In fact, they were legally subordinated to white men because they were viewed as the weaker sex, needing protection from the father, if they were unmarried, or the husband, after marriage. They could not hold public office or become lawyers, were banned from positions of authority, and were therefore subject to restrictions that applied to slaves or Indians. Their status was defined by their father or their husband, but, because of their race, they were superior to Amerindians of both sexes or anyone of mixed race and, of course, slaves. *Mestizos* and *castas* were racially mixed groups that lived on the margins of the Spanish community, engaged in petty trades or manual skills. They were separated from the whites of both sexes because of their mixed racial ancestry and also because they worked. Physical work was a degrading activity for a Spaniard and had to be avoided whenever possible. *Mestizos* were excluded from certain public offices and could not be ordained unless they were of proper background and legitimate; free blacks suffered the same restrictions that were applied to the *mestizos* and, additionally, were forbidden to carry arms, buy liquor, or assemble. *Mestizas* were subordinated to *mestizos* because of their sex, but all in turn were superior to Amerindians. In this group, women continued to be subordinated to men, as they had been since before the Conquest, and, although both men and women were legally subjects of the Crown and free vassals, they were also considered legally minors. Furthermore, because they had to pay tribute to the king or to the *encomenderos* and perform forced labor, they were in fact subordinated to the Spaniards of both sexes and were regarded as fit only for servile tasks. On the other hand, Amerindians were also divided by class, although the Indian nobility stood substantially below the Spanish nobility. African slaves were at the bottom of the social scale because they were legally debased, and women slaves fared worse than male slaves, once again because of the sexual dimension of their master's power.[32]

Women of the slave-owning class could themselves be slaveowners. They could own property and manage it. The dowry was the property of the woman but was managed by the husband, who usually added ten percent of his assets to it. If a marriage was dissolved or annulled, the woman received back the dowry and its income, and she could manage both if she remarried. Married women had no legal position and became minors upon marriage, but they could be given the authority to act on their own by their husbands. Slave women, in contrast, had no rights of any sort, although they were freed more frequently than men, presumably because their labor was less valued than that of men. The status of colonial women was undermined by the religious world, just as it was by the lay world of class, status, and race. Spanish women, like Catholic women everywhere, could not be priests. Amerindian women could not take vows as nuns, and when they were finally permitted to, in 1724, candidates had to meet conditions not imposed on whites.[33]

The treatment of women by men, in the secular as in the religious world, was influenced by color and racial difference.

In practice, the colonists' attitudes toward women depended on their social position and color. They did not look on a white woman with those same eyes with which they looked on black or Amerindian women. However, rather than a double standard of values, there was a double standard of expectations and of enforcement. Expectation of deviation from behavioral ideals demanded of the white woman varied inversely with the decreasing degree of whiteness and the financial means of the woman.[34]

The eighteenth century saw the beginning of reform and attempts to help educate women and elevate their status, but significant change did not come until after the independence of Latin America from the colonial European countries a century later. Women were active participants in the struggles for independence in most fields of endeavor, short only of physical combat. Nevertheless, following independence they were again reduced to their original legal and social status, as has been true of independence movements in India, Algeria, and other countries. Apparently independence promoted equality for men in legal and rhetorical terms, and sometimes in real terms, but not for women. Women could not hold public office, vote, advocate, or be a witness in court. On the contrary, they continued to be treated as minors, the same as slaves, invalids, criminals, and the retarded.[35] In the Caribbean, abolition of slavery brought some changes. Women had to gradually retreat from agriculture, although they often were sole breadwinners, who owned the farms, marketed the product, or worked as agricultural laborers.[36]

Women in the Middle East and North Africa share some of the histories of women in both sub-Saharan Africa and Asia, but they have distinctive histories of their own as well, especially those associated with seclusion, the veil, and subordination to men. Often attributed to Islam, these phenomena predated Islam by centuries. Their status began to decline with the advent of the agrarian-urban culture around 3500-3000 B.C. Urban life generated economic change and the development of crafts, trade, and new wealth. It appears that gender-based divisions of labor were evident at this time. Given the patriarchal family system, the father wanted to keep wealth in the family and thus resorted to controlling his wives' and daughters' sexuality and social activities as a way of maintaining purity of descent; hence the restriction of women to the household.[37] But how did men acquire the authority or power to control women's sexuality or restrict them to the household in the first place?

Withdrawal of women from outside activities and confinement to the house seem to have increased over time, which made women more and more dependent on men for their living. This became evident in the period extending to A.D. 600, the threshold of Islam, after which a reversal in women's status seems to have occurred. Until that time, women, especially of the elite class, were visible in the economy. They traded and managed wealth, which they could acquire from family, trade, or sometimes inheritance. Nevertheless, even when women worked outside the home, they rarely earned as much as men; therefore men exercised more control over resources of the family. Prior to Islam polygamy was permitted in order for a man to have more children. To facilitate marriage, a part of the father's estate was designated to provide a dowry for the daughter and bride-price for the son. According to Sumerian law a divorced wife had a right to half her dead husband's assets for the upkeep of their children and for a dowry to remarry after the children had reached maturity. The restriction of women's status, however, was more evident in the legal and political spheres. The veil was introduced in this period also as a symbol of chastity which was required by men; prostitutes were forbidden to wear the veil and were punished for doing so.

Some pre-Islamic traditions continued in the early period of Islam. Women remained visible and active in public life, but gradually they went into seclusion. Islamic society legitimized the change, though it is not explained why the change occurred. A woman in the early period could choose a husband; later she could not. The argument that the increase in wealth associated with the expansion of Islam encouraged patriarchy and reduced women to dependency does not have much evidence to support it. Islam allowed polygamy, endorsed patriarchy, and set the inheritance of a female at half of that of a male. A woman could inherit one-eighth of her husband's estate, while he would inherit one-fourth of hers if they had no children. Islam, however, did forbid female infanticide, which was common in the early period. The teaching of Islam defines a good wife as "one who obeys her husband and guards his secrets." In return for supporting his wife financially, the husband is empowered to punish her by "admonishing her, sleeping in a separate bed from her, or beating her."[38]

Though the *Shari'a* did not bar women from court proceedings or public life, the endorsement of seclusion and the veil by tradition and the example of Prophet Mohammed's wives made it seem improper for women to deal with strangers. As a result, they usually had to relinquish the management of their wealth to a male relative, which depressed their status and possibly their wealth.

The advent of Turkish rule (thirteenth to eighteenth centuries), did little to change the status of women in the Middle East. After adopting Islam and the *Shari'a*, the Turks gradually modified their treatment of women, depressing their status below what it had been in their own Turko-Mongolian society. In that society elite women had played important roles in court and public life. After the adoption of Islam, seclusion, the veil, obedience to the husband, and a reduced right to inherit became the fate of women. There was some variation in the status of women, however, because there were, and still are, different ethnic and religious communities in the Middle East that did not follow the *Shari'a*, such as Christians and Jews. These, however, were too small a minority to make a difference in society at large, at least not before the twentieth century and the penetration of Western powers into the region. Moreover, women were not treated more fairly in these communities than they were under *Shari'a*.

GENDER DISCRIMINATION IN THE MODERN PERIOD: CONTINUITY AND CHANGE

The modern period began at different times in different countries. For the expanding, industrializing countries of the West, the modern period meant industrialization, urbanization, and eventual transformation of the economy and the polity into a relatively free enterprise economy and a Western-type democracy, all of which have evolved over the last two centuries. In that context, women faced new situations and had new roles to play. In Socialist countries the modern period began in the twentieth century. In third world countries, the modern period began in the second half of the twentieth century. Here we shall be concerned mainly with the process of transformation and its impact on the place of women regardless of chronology.

If we look at Europe during the Renaissance and Reformation, we find women's status to be deteriorating from its low level during the feudal and medieval eras. The revival of Roman customs and the adoption of the basics of Roman law had a negative impact on the place of women in society. This revivalism was accompanied by fundamentalist Christian movements during the Reformation. Calvinism and other theologies resorted to new and more conservative interpretations of the Bible that put women back in positions of almost total dependency and low status.[39]

The French Revolution was a first step toward reversing that trend. However, though the French Revolution introduced ideas of equality, fraternity, and liberty, its impact on women, like that of the Enlightenment, was more rhetorical than substantive. The Code of Napoleon emphasized the role of women first and foremost as mothers and teachers of their own children, rather than as equals with men who make their own choices. The picture we see in Europe was common to an extent in the United States as an extension of the former. The Constitution of the United States did little to increase the freedom of choice for women or to equalize them with men.[40]

The Industrial Revolution was the decisive force that broke those traditions and ushered in a new era, or at least set the stage for change.[41] Economic expansion and factory work meant that work outside the home became necessary. Movement to the cities meant a break in the unity of the family and in the pattern of control over the migrating members. By the same token it reduced the dependence of the migrating women on their fathers and husbands. Now they could earn income on their own and acquire some economic independence as well. During the industrial expansion era women of the upper classes continued to be ladies of leisure, who enjoyed the benefits of wealth and the luxury of choosing to do or not to do social service. However, they acquired such privileges by virtue of the position of their male relatives. Women of the lower classes, the workers, worked in the factory as well as in the home, took the lowest-paid jobs or jobs not wanted by men, and suffered abuse and humiliation far more than did men. In addition they continued to be controlled by the men in their homes. Women of the middle class had more options: some were ladies of leisure and did charitable work; others stayed home to take care of their children, cater to their husband's needs and demands, or supplement family income with earnings from traditional activities such as spinning, weaving, food preservation, sewing, etc. Still others went to work in the factories and other jobs in the market place. These factory workers of the middle class were the group that basically tried to break tradition and bring to women a sense of equality and worth they had not had before.

As the twentieth century began, women gained a new venue for employment in the field of communications: telephone, telegraph, and typing. Gradually women replaced men and the clerical profession became the domain of female workers. Finally, there were rural women, who continued to work with their husbands on the farm, in addition to their housework. These wives and mothers may have controlled the money in the till as family bankers, but decisions were still made by the husbands or by the men in the family.

Work in the factory was soon routinized, and women, even though they had little education, were in more demand than men for factory jobs. It was fully accepted that women were better workers, easier to control, and cheaper to pay; hence they were a better profit-maker for the employer than male workers. Even when women worked together with their husbands, they usually were paid less. This was true in England, France, Germany, Italy, and to an extent in the United States.

The industrial economy demonstrated the need for education, which in this case was extended to women as well. Although the professions were still closed to women in Europe and the United States, especially law, medicine, engineering, and theology, women began to dominate in midwifery and teaching, especially at the lower levels. The lower the grade, the more preferred women were as teachers: they did a better job and accepted lower salaries. On the other hand, the higher the grade and the more leadership responsibilities a job entailed, the lower the proportion of women who held it. Women were relegated to the positions least wanted by men, regardless of qualifications.[42]

Neither attitudes toward women nor their legal position changed much as industrialization advanced. According to findings of the U.S. Commission on Civil Rights, "throughout much of the 19th century the position of women . . . was in many respects, comparable to that of blacks under the pre-Civil War slave code. Neither slaves nor women could hold office, serve on juries, or bring suit in their own names, and married women traditionally were denied the legal capacity to hold or convey property or to serve as legal guardians of their own children."[43]

This attitude has not vanished even within the most developed countries. As late as 1955, Adlai Stevenson advised women to "'influence man and boy' through the 'humble role of housewife.'"[44] If a woman chose to go beyond the traditional role, say into a career, "she ran the risk of losing forever 'as a woman, her chance for the kind of love she wants.'"[45]

Women of the twentieth century have continued to work outside the home, even more so than before. However, as recently as the 1920s and 1930s, they usually worked in "sex-segregated" occupations, pursuing mostly "women's work," especially in textiles or in the service industries. Women continued to receive lower pay than men, presumably because they "neither needed nor deserved" to be paid similar wages. Even where men and women worked together and did the same work, women were paid much less. A woman social worker in the United States received 80% of a male social worker's pay. A female finisher in a paper-box factory received half as much as a male finisher.[46] This same attitude prevailed in the United States, England, and France, and in most other countries.

Both the First and Second World Wars enhanced women's roles in the economy. Many new occupations were opened to them, and their rate of participation in the economy increased significantly, especially in the Soviet Union and other Socialist countries. Change came also in the form of increased education, delayed marriages, and more freedom in making personal decisions.[47]

Tables 3.1 and 3.2 illustrate changes in Britain and the United States. On the positive side, a higher percentage of women were in the professions in 1981 than in earlier years. There were more women in business among the proprietors, administrators, managers, and skilled people. On the negative side, there were more unskilled workers among women than in earlier years; there was a sustained concentration of women as schoolteachers and nurses, and in the service industries; women were concentrated in the lower-paying jobs, in other than productive industry, and very few of them were able to reach the top in their careers. This picture was true even in the USSR in the 1960s, when "men outnumbered women in highly skilled occupations by four to one . . . . Even today . . . women's work is of less consequence than men's."[48]

The ideal situation to achieve equality between women and men was expected to prevail in the Israeli kibbutz (collective settlement), built upon such utopian principles as collective ownership, equality of the sexes, and shared responsibilities in all aspects of life in the community. Women were to be freed of family responsibilities by transferring those responsibilities to the community and establishing dormitories for children with expert care on behalf of the kibbutz. However, even in the kibbutz those ideals have not been sustained. Women have been gradually shifted to the "nonproductive" occupations or to the services, just as they have been in Israel as a whole; Table 3.3 illustrates.[49]

The fact of inequality between men and women in the market place seems hard to dispute. As late as 1983, women's earnings in Britain were 50-55% of men's earnings in similar occupational and age statuses, just as it had been between 1950 and 1970. Similarly, women's earnings in the United States were 60-66% of men's earnings in the early 1980s in most occupational classes, an improvement over earlier years. This pattern of

TABLE 3.1

OCCUPATIONAL CLASS OF GAINFULLY OCCUPIED BRITISH FEMALE
POPULATION AS PERCENTAGE OF TOTAL (SELECTED YEARS)

Occupational Class	1911	1931	1951	1971	1981
Professional					
Higher	6.0	7.5	8.3	6.1	11.1
Lower	62.9	58.8	53.5	51.4	56.4
Employers and proprietors	18.8	19.8	19.9	23.8	21.5
Managers and administrators	19.9	13.0	15.2	15.6	18.7
Clerical workers	20.2	44.2	58.8	70.9	71.0
Foremen, inspectors, and supervisors	4.2	8.7	13.4	17.4	20.4
Skilled manual	24.0	21.3	15.8	14.4	14.5
Semiskilled manual	40.0	42.1	40.7	47.6	44.8
Unskilled manual	15.5	15.0	20.3	36.8	42.0
All occupations	29.6	29.8	30.8	36.5	39.9

Source: A. T. Mallier and M. J. Rosser, Women and the Economy (Houndmills, Basinstoke, Hampshire: Macmillan, 1987), 2.

TABLE 3.2

OCCUPATIONAL CLASS OF GAINFULLY OCCUPIED U.S. FEMALE POPULATION
AS PERCENTAGE OF TOTAL (SELECTED YEARS)

Occupational Class	1910	1930	1950	1970	1980
Professional, excluding nurses and noncollege teachers	17.5	23.0	19.7	22.7	30.7
Nurses and noncollege teachers	81.4	80.3	81.5	76.7	78.3
Proprietors, managers and administrators, including farm	6.7	7.6	8.6	14.6	24.2
Clerical and kindred	34.3	49.4	62.2	73.8	80.1
Sales workers	14.5	18.3	34.0	40.1	45.3
Craft and kindred	11.5	3.6	3.1	4.9	6.0
Operatives	22.5	23.2	24.0	31.8	32.0
Laborers	17.9	11.5	10.1	10.2	14.2
Services					
Household	83.3	81.8	94.9	96.9	97.5
Nonhousehold	46.8	50.8	44.9	55.8	58.9
All occupations	21.2	22.0	27.8	37.2	41.9

Source: A. T. Mallier and M. J. Rosser, Women and the Economy, 1987, 54.

TABLE 3.3
PERCENTAGES OF MEN AND WOMEN IN PRODUCTION AND SERVICES
IN THE KIBBUTZIM AND IN ISRAEL (JEWS ONLY) IN 1973

	Production	Services
Kibbutzim		
Men	77.2	22.8
Women	27.3	72.7
Israel		
Men	46.7	53.3
Women	24.3	75.4

Source: William M. Boskoff, "Women and Work in Israel and the Islamic Middle East,"
Quarterly Review of Business and Economics 22, no. 4 (Winter 1982): 101.

underpayment is common to most developed countries, as Table 3.4 shows, although a few improvements may have occurred since these data were collected.[50] Apparently discrimination persists in payment at both the preentry and postentry levels, and in the process of promotions. This is true even in teaching, in which women predominate in numbers, but not in seniority or rank, in the United States and in Britain. In both countries the percentage of women declines as the scale of pay rises and as a shift is made from teaching to the administration of schools.[51]

TABLE 3.4
COMPARISON OF FEMALE AND MALE EARNINGS (ANNUAL) (SELECTED YEARS)

Under 60% of Male Earnings	60-65% of Male Earnings	65-70% of Male Earnings	70% of Male Earnings
Japan (1975)	Australia (1971)	Czechoslovakia (1970)	Hungary (1972)
	Austria (1953)	France (1970)	Israel (1970)
USA (1974)	Belgium (1964)	Poland (1972)	
	Canada (1960-61)		
	Finland (1960)		
	UK (1975)		

Source: A. T. Mallier and M. J. Rosser, *Women and the Economy,* 1987.

In her study of the gender gap in a historical perspective, Claudia Goldin reinforces the findings above and notes contradictions to the hypothesis that "economic progress" narrows the differences between the sexes. Female to male earnings ratios have remained around 60% over the last three decades, though they have varied across occupations and over time. The ratio of female to male earnings rose from 46% in 1890 to 56% in 1930 and remained stable between 1950 and 1980. These differences, however, can be attributed only partly to discrimination. After allowance is made for differences in education and experience, the residual is regarded as a measure of discrimination resulting from the differences in earnings at the starting point and inequality in advancement. Such wage discrimination rose from about 20% of the difference in earnings in U.S. manufacturing in 1900 to about 55% of the difference in clerical occupations in 1940. These findings are similar to those of studies surveyed by the author relating to more recent periods.[52]

The picture was a little different in the former Soviet Union, where the female participation rate was almost equal to that of men, access to education and occupations was equal to that of men, and equal pay for equal work was the rule. However, because the structure of employment of women was biased in favor of services and less "productive" occupations, women ended up with less pay as a group than did men. It is also significant that in the USSR women's participation in the labor force did not relieve them of duties at home; men shared little in home care, and women ended up doing both the housework and the outside work. Nevertheless, as far as free choice was concerned, Soviet women were closer to equality with men than women were in the United States and Western and Northern Europe.[53]

It should be emphasized that a big gap continued between legislation and implementation in the Soviet Union, as in the West. The Soviet Constitution of 1936 reiterated the equality of women with men: "Women in the USSR have equal rights with men in all branches of economic, cultural, social, and political life. The implementation of these rights is assured by granting women the same rights as men to work, to pay, to social insurance and education and by government protection of mothers and children, by paid maternity leave, and by a wide network of maternity homes . . . ."[54] The economic plan, however, designed mainly by men, specified certain occupations for women and usually served society more than it promoted choice for women. As Rosenthal has observed, "The crucial factor in determining state policy remained constant: the needs of society as perceived and defined by the Communist Party."[55] And all the high-ranking leaders of the party were men.

Another significant aspect of the market place is discrimination against women within a profession or industry. A look at the economics teaching profession in the United States will illustrate. Women economists in general earn less than men economists at all levels. In 1973 female assistant professors earned between 90.8% and 86.2% of the earnings of male assistant professors. The ratio declined as the rank increased; female associate professors earned between 87.4% and 74.2% of what their male counterparts earned, while female full professors earned between 83.9% and 65.7% of what male full professors earned. However, female white economists earned substantially more (almost double) than black male economists did, though the gap tended to narrow as the rank increased.[56]

Through my own field observations, I have noted similar patterns in medicine and in the media. Promotions, management positions, and employment security are scarcer for females than for males, and the bias against women increases as the rank increases. The position of women attorneys is not much better, especially when a partnership is under consideration. Women have fewer opportunities of being promoted to an associate or a partner than do men. However, there has been an improvement in the opportunities for women lawyers, but apparently this has resulted in part from the need for women lawyers in cases related to the overall increased demand for lawyers and more frequent litigation in sex discrimination cases against business firms.[57] As far as the professions are concerned, women have made their greatest achievements in the Socialist countries. Table 3.5 compares these achievements internationally for lawyers, physicians, and dentists. Women of the Soviet Union, East Germany, and Poland exceeded all other countries by a large measure in all three professions. In the Soviet Union 36% of the lawyers in 1971 were women, compared with 3.5% in the United States and 6.1% in Sweden. In the Soviet Union, 75% of the physicians and 83% of the dentists were women, compared with 6.5% and 2.1% in the United States and 15.4% and 24% in Sweden, respectively.

In contrast to both the Soviet and American treatments of women, Nazi Germany represented a counterrevolution, rendering women totally dependent, protected, and used as its decision-makers saw fit. From somewhat equal roles during the political rise of Nazism to their return to traditional roles as mothers and homemakers in the late 1930s, and then to active participation in the war economy, women were always expected to respond to the designs of the authorities and their perceptions of the National Socialist economy and society. Few women participated in the leadership or in planning the new roles designated for women. They had their own organizations, but these were mainly for "feminine" activities. Women were directed to increase their reproduction of "pure" Germans and were given incentives to do so. They were also directed, as major consumers on behalf of their families, to promote certain products and businesses and boycott others, such as those owned by non-Aryans or Jews. Women usually complied, because of their own nationalism, their belief in their traditional roles as wives, mothers, and homemakers, or because they had no choice in the matter.[58]

In third world countries independence from imperial domination, higher standards of living, and industrialization have been the major preoccupa-

TABLE 3.5
PROPORTION OF WOMEN IN SELECTED PROFESSIONS, BY COUNTRY

Country	Occupation (percentage)		
	Lawyers	Physicians	Dentists
United States	3.5	6.5	2.1
USSR	36.0	75.0	83.0
United Kingdom	3.8[a]	16.0	6.9
Japan	3.0	9.3	3.0
Sweden	6.1	15.4	24.4
Germany (Fed. Rep.)	5.5	20.0	14.0
Germany (Dem. Rep.)	30.0	36.0	24.7
Italy	2.8	4.9	-
India	0.7	9.5	3.9
Denmark	-	16.4	70.3
Poland	18.8	36.4	77.0

Source: Marilyn Rueschemeyer, "The Demands of Work on Human Quality of Marriage: An Exploratory Study of Professionals in Two Socialist Societies," in George Kurian and Rafun Ghosh, *Women in the Family and the Economy* (Westport, Conn.: Greenwood Press, 1981).

[a] Barristers.

tions of policy-makers. The struggle for equality between men and women has not enjoyed a high priority in India and Pakistan, or in countries that established some form of socialism, such as Algeria, Iraq, and Syria. The Middle East countries probably display a good picture of the place of women in the economy in most Islamic countries. Though some countries, such as Syria and Iraq, are a little more liberal in their treatment of women than Saudi Arabia and Iran, most of them have been guided largely by the *Shari'a*, which assigns women to a dependent status. This tendency has been gaining strength in recent years with the growth of religious fundamentalism.

Children remain in high demand in third world countries, and women are encouraged to marry early and produce many children. Education of women, though expanded significantly, remains less extensive than men's, and it is also directed more toward the arts and humanities and away from the professions and sciences. The family continues to be a patriarchal institution in which women are dependent on and subservient to men. Women's earnings and employment remain complementary to, rather than competitive with, the earnings and employment of men. The influence of developed countries has no doubt brought about some changes, but these changes have remained limited. Women still predominate in domestic work, agriculture, and in lower-skilled and unskilled work. Few women enter business and the professions, and when they do, they find it hard to practice their professions or to reach high positions. A woman engineer in Saudi Arabia may be qualified but she will not be able to practice engineering. It would be a rarity to find a woman banker or a woman president of a corporation in the Middle East.

Participation rates of females in the labor force in the Middle East are still very low, relative to those in the developed countries, ranging from 3.8% in Iraq to 13.6% in Iran in 1975. These figures, however, are quite low even by comparison with those in other underdeveloped countries, such as Togo, Cameroon, the Ivory Coast, and Jamaica.[59] Women, however, have continued to demand some degree of equality, even though they tend to deny that they promote secularism. Given that they want equality within the *Shari'a* laws, it is unlikely that they will achieve a high measure of equality, as women have in Cuba, Russia, and France.[60]

Transformation in Africa during the colonial period brought about negative effects on the status of women. In most countries the change meant a transfer of control over land to men, and the strengthening of patriarchy at the expense of women and matriarchy. Rural women began to suffer when cash crops were introduced and made farming more attractive to men. Men also took up farming as technology changed and a light plow came into use, and it was assumed that women could not operate it. As a result, men began to assume control of the land and farming operations. These changes were enhanced by government policies (British in most cases) intended to replace collective land titles and holdings with private individual titles, which in most cases were awarded to men. Probably the best example of such transformation was in Kenya. In urban areas women continued to fill jobs not wanted by men such as domestic service and petty trade, and prostitution. A few women worked in factories, as in Southern Africa, but most of them were white Afrikaners or Indians (Colored). The majority of black women had no access to education and were not considered qualified to work in factories. It appears that this transformation was generally guided by Western influence and patterns, and by Islam and Christianity, which emphasized the domesticity and dependence of women.[61]

After World War II, most African countries acquired political independence through liberation movements in which women played important roles. Nevertheless, little effort has been expended since then by policymakers to meet the demands of women for equality and freedom. Thus, women today have little access to land ownership, and they face legal and political barriers that limit their access to credit and other opportunities available to men. Women, however, have more educational opportunities than they did before independence, but training and jobs they secure are stereotypically for women, as in Western countries.[62]

Arrival of the British in India in the seventeenth century ushered in a new period there, characterized by reform movements that gradually improved the status of women through education, delayed marriages, a prohibition on *sati* (widow burning) and female infanticide, as well as by relaxation of *purdah* and restrictions on the physical mobility of women. The British occupiers tried to justify their occupation of India as a means of improving Indian society through the elevation of the status of women. Some Indian observers, however, regarded the British reform attempts as attacks on the status of Indian males and the Indian family structure, in which women were totally dependent on men. Change did come gradually through legislation, education, Christian missionaries, and women's movements. By the beginning of the twentieth century some elite women owned property and acted as landholders and managers of their estates. When in the professions, women catered mostly to women, or they worked in factories and agriculture and as prostitutes.[63]

There is little information on the conditions of women's employment in India relative to those of men's employment. Despite the equal status conferred by law as of 1950, equality has not been realized. Recent reports show that the ratio of women to men in the population has declined drastically, suggesting that women suffer from malnutrition and higher mortality rates. Since the application of amniocentesis, or diagnosis of the sex of the fetus, has become common, 99 percent of fetus abortions have been female fetuses. Another negative change for women is a decline in their participation rate in the paid labor force, especially in agriculture and unskilled factory employment. In contrast, the number of professional women has increased. Nevertheless, women still occupy a subservient role to men in most aspects of life in India.[64]

Change in Japan went in the opposite direction from that in India. Except for compulsory education for both girls and boys introduced by new legislation after 1868, little improvement in the status of women took place in the late nineteenth and early twentieth centuries. On the contrary, the new civil code of 1898 transformed all of society into a legal model of the *Samurai* family--for women, perhaps the most oppressive formula in their history. Primogeniture was reinstated, patrilocality was assured, and the patriarchy was shored up by regulations that denied women their existence as juridical persons. In courts of law after 1898, all Japanese women were lumped together with mental incompetents and minors--unable to bring legal action without a male guarantor.[65]

Education became gender oriented and sex segregated to produce a "good wife, wise mother" culture. Women continued to work mostly in cotton and silk factories and on family farms. Women, however, did not accept this status silently. They continued to demand rights, organize movements, seek suffrage, and publish their own literature and critique of society. Nevertheless, little change in their status took place before the end of World War II.[66]

The end of World War II transferred power in Japan to the United States occupation authorities, who made sure that women had the right to vote, run for office, and enter the labor force freely. Although Japanese women were hired at the same entry level as men, they were encouraged to take leave to marry and have children and then return, and thus lose seniority and fall behind the men they had been equal to in rank and earning. Today in Japan women still stay home to take care of children and men continue to be the "declared" breadwinner.[67]

The trend in China was similar to that in Japan until the Communist party became powerful enough to bring about change in the regions liberated by the revolution. The most substantial change came after the revolution was complete. The marriage law of 1950 was considered the most radical step toward establishing the equality of women with men, at least in legal terms, since it freed women completely from all vestiges of the past. Implementation, however, has not been as fast, and the Chinese family, especially in the rural areas, still rests on patriarchal, patrilocal, and patrilineal foundations. Most probably the slow implementation is due to underdevelopment in education, mobility, and the economy, even though the grounds for full equality have been established.[68]

Discrimination against women in Latin America and the Caribbean has continued throughout the twentieth century, although movements for liberation have been initiated in most countries. Women sought better civil codes, expanded education, and self-sufficiency in decision-making. They wanted equality before the law. Yet working conditions for women remained poor: long hours, low pay, and no provisions for child care, health, or sanitation. These conditions deteriorated with job mechanization, which rendered women a relative surplus in the labor force.

The newly independent countries adopted laws based on Hispanic laws, which upheld male authority throughout society. However, the economic emancipation of women must have started. Single women and widows could then control property and act on their own behalf in legal matters, though married women were still subject to their husband's authority. Women composed an important part of the agrarian labor force, together with male Indians, blacks, mestizos, and mulattos. But change came slowly, so that even by the early years of the twentieth century a married woman in Argentina needed her husband's permission to engage in any profession; she still could not sign a contract, let alone expect equal treatment in business or the economy.[69]

Economic change in Latin America had a limited impact on women. Their rate of formal participation in the economy fluctuated, depending on the need for their labor and the availability of jobs not wanted by men. However, as illustrated by Brazil, women continued to earn lower wages than men, occupy more of the lower-paying jobs, and acquire less training than men. Their participation rate stabilized around the middle of the twentieth century at a rate of about 25%.[70]

Women's position in the rural economy was also depressed. Their claims on agrarian reform benefits were somewhat circumscribed because prequalifications tended to favor male farmers, both as recognized heads of households and as former tenants on redistributed plantations. The exception was in Cuba, where women were mobilized in rural work teams just as were men, both because of the need for their labor and in compliance with Communist doctrine.[71]

Among the most important improvements in women's rights in Latin America were the changes in the Civil Code of Argentina in 1926 which gave women some control over their earnings, allowed them to inherit property, and to engage in contractual agreements. They won the right to vote in 1932 in Puerto Rico, 1934 in Cuba, 1947 in Argentina, and 1958 in Mexico. In most cases improvement seems to have come after a revolution or the achievement of independence. The most extensive measures of equalization have been in Cuba under Fidel Castro and more recently in Nicaragua. Cuba has integrated women as equals almost completely in both theory and practice. The most recent measure came in 1976 when the Family Code mandated "the division of household labor and child care between men and women." Implementation, however, is still less than perfect, and women continue to carry out a disproportionate share of what used to be considered women's work.[72]

CONCLUSIONS

1. Women have always been treated differently than men, and almost always unequally. In Africa and Asia, in medieval Europe and in the Americas, women have made contributions to their respective economies, either through production or through redistribution by means of the dowry and bride wealth upon marriage. They have worked in agriculture and in trade as well as in domestic industry and at home. In virtually all cases, however, women have had little choice in what they have done or in the disposition of their wealth—even their own dowries and bride wealth. Society, managed by men, dictated the norms of economic behavior for women and made men the guardians of these norms.

2. Because women's performance in the economy has usually been in addition to their work in the home, it has been difficult for them to build careers, and this has made them seem dependent on men, whom society has considered to be the breadwinners. Though data are not available on the system of remuneration in the early periods, it is quite apparent that women

were restricted to lower-paid duties, considered less capable than men, and had weaker bargaining power than men.

3. Though women have made significant contributions to their respective economies, they have always been at a disadvantage even when major institutional and technological changes were taking place.

4. Individual women have gained prominence in various places throughout history, but in most cases women's high status and recognition have been a means to perpetuate a patrilineal heritage in the absence of a male heir.

5. Arguments that women's status has declined over time, especially following the Industrial Revolution, are subject to debate since it is not clear how much equality they enjoyed in earlier periods. In all periods, ancient and modern, women have had more restricted rights of ownership, inheritance, choice of occupation, and mobility than men. Sometimes women have been excluded from certain opportunities on the assumption that it is for their protection, but they have had no choice in the matter. The Enlightenment and the American and French revolutions failed to pay adequate attention to women's rights or to improve their status. While democracy, equality, and freedom for men were on the rise, women continued to suffer relative underendowment in education and training, underutilization and underrewarding in the market, as well as neglect in demographic policies and institutions, and discrimination in religious and social practices.

6. Sometimes women have avoided discrimination by manipulating the institutions governing society, as they did by adopting woman-to-woman marriages so that a woman would acquire all the rights of a male (husband), or patriarch of the family.

7. Finally, the modern period and industrialization have brought important changes to the economic life of women. Their rates of participation in the economy have increased, and so has their mobility. However, their levels of endowment, utilization, and rewarding have continued to fall far short of equality with men. Evidently much of the improvement has been formalistic and rhetorical, expressed in equalizing legislation, though the institutional and enforcement frameworks have remained unfriendly to women, and discrimination continues, virtually undiminished in quality and possibly in quantity.

NOTES

1. Organization of American Historians, *Restoring Women to History* (Bloomington, Ind: Organization of American Historians,1988); Renate Bridenthal and Claudia Koonz, *Becoming Visible: Women in European History* (Boston: Houghton Mifflin, 1977); Margaret

Jean Hay and Marcia Wright, eds., *African Women and the Law: Historical Perspectives* (Boston: Boston University African Studies Center, 1982); Asunción Lavrin, ed., *Latin American Women: Historical Perspectives* (Westport, Conn: Greenwood Press, 1978).

2. Ruby Rohrlich Leavitt, "Women in Transition: Crete and Sumer," in Bridenthal and Koonz, *Becoming Visible*, 56.

3. Ibid., 40.

4. See Joann McNamara and Suzanne F. Wemple, "Sanctity and Power: The Dual Pursuit of Medieval Women," 107-8, and Joan Kelly-Gadol, "Did Women Have a Renaissance?" in Bridenthal and Koonz, *Becoming Visible*, 145-6.

5. Muhammad A. Dandamaev, *Slavery in Babylonia: From Nabopolassar to Alexander the Great* (626-331 B.C.), trans. Victoria A. Powell (Dekalb, Ill.: Northern Illinois University Press, 1984); "Status of Women," *Encyclopaedia Britannica*, 19, 1974, 908-16; Theresa Schmid McMahon, *Women and Economic Evolution or the Effects of Industrial Changes upon the Status of Women* (diss., University of Wisconsin, 1912), Chs. 1-2.

6. Iris Berger, "Women of Eastern and Southern Africa," in American Historians, *Restoring Women*, 3-12.

7. Ibid., 15ff; Murray Last, "Reform in West Africa: The Jihad Movements of the Nineteenth Century," in J. F. A. Ajayi and Michael Crowder, eds., *History of West Africa*, Vol. II (New York: Columbia University Press, 1972), 24-26.

8. Berger, "Women of Eastern Africa, 19.

9. E. Francis White, "Women of Western and Western Central Africa," in American Historians, *Restoring Women*, 58-59.

10. Ibid., 61-63.

11. Ibid., 73. On female-female marriages, see also Margaret Jean Hay, "Women as Owners, Occupants, and Managers of Property," in Hay and Wright, *African Women*, 122.

12. J. Vansina, "Equatorial Africa and Angola: Migrations and the Emergence of the First States," in D. T. Viane, ed., *General History of Africa*, IV, UNESCO (London: Heineman, 1981), 557.

13. White, "Women of Western Africa," 83.

14. These attitudes toward women were institutionalized and bolstered by the law, written and common. See Hay and Wright, *African Women*, for more details.

15. Joanna Liddle and Rama Joshi, *Daughters of Independence: Gender, Class, and Caste in India* (London: Zed Books, 1986), 59, 61-62.

16. Barbara N. Ramusack, "Women in South and Southeast Asia," American Historians, *Restoring Women*, 4.

17. The *sudras* are the fourth *varna* or class, who were servants of the upper three classes. Only the untouchables are below them; they are "probably the indigenous people conquered by the Aryans;" Ramusack, "Women in South Asia," 3, 5-6.

18. A. S. Altehar, *The Position of Women in Hindu Civilization* (Delhi: Motilal Banarsidaes, 1956), 254-55.

19. Manu VIII, 416; Manu V, 148, in Ramusack, "Women in South Asia," 8-9.

20. Altehar, *Position of Women*, 275.

21. Ramusack, "Women in South Asia," 13. The acquired power was evidently used against other women, depending on seniority, favoritism, etc., so that women were discriminated against not only by men but by other women as well.

22. Anthony Reid, as reported in Ramusack, "Women in South Asia," 35.

23. Ibid., 36-39.

24. Sharon L. Sievers, "Women in China, Japan, and Korea," in American Historians, *Restoring Women*, 65.

25. Ibid., 65, 71, 73-74.

26. Ibid., 81-82. Why the change in landholding took place is not clear; perhaps it was because the neo-Confucian and Buddhist ethics, which favored men, triumphed.

27. Sievers, "Women in China," 83-93.

28. Marysa Navarro, "Women in Pre-Columbian and Colonial Latin America," in American Historians, *Restoring Women*, 3.

29. Ibid., 6-8.

30. Ibid., 11-12.

31. Ibid., 15-21.

32. Ibid., 25-26.

33. Ibid., 27-34.

34. A. J. R. Russell-Wood, "Female and Family in the Economy and Society of Colonial Brazil," in Lavrin, *Latin American Women*, 68.

35. Virginia Sánchez Korrol, "Women in Nineteenth and Twentieth-Century Latin America and the Caribbean," in American Historians, *Restoring Women*, 47.

36. Ibid., 57.

37. Guity Nashat, "Women in the Middle East 8,000 B.C.-A.D. 1800," in American Historians, *Restoring Women*, 3-12.

38. Ibid., 15-21, 30.

39. Sherrin Marshall Wyntjes, "Women in the Reformation Era," in Bridenthal and Koonz, *Becoming Visible*, 165-91.

40. Richard T. Vann, "Toward a New Lifestyle: Women in Pre-Industrial Capitalism," in Bridenthal and Koonz, *Becoming Visible*, 192-235; see also Ruth Graham, "Loaves and Liberty: Women in the French Revolution," in Bridenthal and Koonz, *Becoming Visible*.

41. Mary Lynn McDougall, "Working-Class Women During the Industrial Revolution," 262-79, and Therese M. McBride, "The Long Road Home and Industrialization," 280-95, in Bridenthal and Koonz, *Becoming Visible*.

42. *Encyclopaedia Britannica*, 19, 1974, 910-11; McMahon, "Women and Economic Evolution," Chs. 2-3; Susan Cahn, *Industry of Devotion: The Transformation of Women's Work in England, 1500-1660* (New York: Columbia University Press, 1987), 30-65.

43. John Lescott-Leszczynski, *The History of U. S. Ethnic Policy and Its Impact on European Ethnics* (Boulder, Colo.: Westview Press, 1984), Appendix, 201.

44. Juanita M. Kreps, ed., *Women and the American Economy: A Look to the 1980s* (Englewood Cliffs, N.J.: Prentice-Hall, 1976), 7.

45. Attributed to Margaret Mead, in William H. Chafe, "Looking Backward in Order to Look Forward: Women, Work, and Social Values in America," in Kreps, *Women and the American Economy*, 6.

46. Chafe, "Looking Backward," 13.

47. Bernice Glatzer Rosenthal, "Love on the Tractor: Women in the Russian Revolution and After," in Bridenthal and Koonz, *Becoming Visible*, 370-99.

48. Nelya V. Motroshilova, "Soviet Women in the Life of Society: Achievements and Problems," *International Social Science Journal* 35, no. 4 (1983): 737-38.

49. William Moskoff, "Women and Work in Israel and the Islamic Middle East," *Quarterly Review of Economics and Business* 22, no. 4 (Winter 1982): 89-103.

50. A. T. Mallier and M. J. Rosser, *Women and the Economy: A Comparative Study of Britain and the USA* (Houndmills, Basinstoke, Hampshire: Macmillan, 1987), 117-18, 180.

51. Ibid., 119-20.

52. For more details, see Claudia Goldin, *Understanding the Gender Gap: An Economic History of American Women* (New York: Oxford University Press, 1990), 59, 84, 117.

53. Mallier and Rosser, *Women and the Economy*, 180-89.

54. Quoted in Rosenthal, "Love on the Tractor," 389-90.

55. Ibid., 372.

56. Carol L. Jusenius and Richard M. Scheffler, "Earnings Differential Among Academic Economists: Empirical Evidence on Race and Sex," *Journal of Economics and Business* 33, no. 2 (Winter 1981): 95.

57. Jill Abramson, "For Women Lawyers, An Uphill Struggle," *New York Times Magazine*, 6 March 1988.

58. Claudia Koonz, "Mothers in the Fatherland: Women in Nazi Germany," in Bridenthal and Koonz, *Becoming Visible*, 445-73.

59. One should be careful in using these statistics because they seem to ignore the informal economy, which is quite important in the Middle East and in which women probably predominate. For continuation of the cultural impact of Islam, see Moskoff, "Women and Work in Israel," 89-95.

60. On the ambiguity of women's position in the Middle East, see Judith E. Tucker, "Women in the Middle East," in *Restoring Women to History*, especially 75-92.

61. Berger, "Women of Eastern Africa," 25-30; Eleanor R. Fabohunda, "Female and Male in West Africa," in Christian Oppong, ed., *Female and Male in West Africa* (London: George Allen and Unwin, 1983), 34-35.

62. Berger, "Women of Eastern Africa," 35-37; White, "Women of Western Africa," 94-97. For comparative statistics on women in West Africa, see Fabohunda, "Female and Male," especially Tables 2.1 (p. 37) and 2.4 (p. 50).

63. Ramusack, "Women in South Asia," 17-22.

64. Ibid., 26-29.

65. Sievers, "Women in China," 92.

66. Ibid., 92, 96-97.

67. Ibid., 108-10.

68. Ibid., 98-104, 110-11.

69. Korrol, "Women in Latin America," 38-53.

70. Marianne Shmink, "Women and Urban Industrial Development in Brazil," in June Nash, Helen Safa, et al., *Women and Change in Latin America* (South Hadley, Mass.: Bergin and Garvey Publishers, 1985), 134-64.

71. Carmen Diana Deere, "Rural Women and Agrarian Reform in Peru, Chile, and Cuba," in Nash, Safa, et al., *Women and Change*, 189-207.

72. Korrol, "Women in Latin America," 57-70.

Social Costs and Benefits of Discrimination

The effects of discrimination may be evaluated as material or nonmaterial, as private or social. Our concern is mainly with the material or economic effects, and the social or aggregate, rather than the private or partial. Private effects, such as those resulting from wage discrimination, have been the usual subject of study and analysis. Similarly, studies of discrimination in housing, education, and occupations tend to deal only with the costs to those discriminated against or the benefits to those who practice discrimination. These studies show differences in wages between those discriminated against and others. They also show that the victims are usually deprived of certain job opportunities, educational facilities, and housing facilities that are enjoyed by those who do not face discrimination.[1]

The private effects of discrimination relate to the distribution of benefits among individuals and the extent to which the gain of one may be the loss of another. The aggregate economy could remain unaffected, unless the redistribution of benefits also redistributes resources, opportunities, and incentives enough to increase or decrease aggregate output. Few studies, however, have dealt with the macro economic effects of discrimination as they are reflected in economic growth and efficiency of resource use or with the balance between the costs and benefits of discrimination. These are issues on which we shall focus in this chapter.

MACRO EFFECTS: CONCEPTUAL FRAMEWORK

If there were no discrimination and economic behavior were guided either by the market or by a plan, economic performance of the aggregate economy would be optimal. For optimal performance the following conditions would have to be met:

1. All resources are developed to the full within the overall constraints faced by the economy. For example, all people have access to education and

training to develop their capacities to the full, regardless of race, ethnicity, or gender. No one is deprived of the opportunity to improve, and no piece of land can be excluded from improvement and cultivation by arbitrary decisions that are inconsistent with market rationality or an economic plan free of discrimination. Each factor is allowed to develop according to its qualifications and comparative advantage in the production process.

2. All resources and available inputs, human and nonhuman, are fully employed.

3. Resources are utilized to satisfy demand as well as to maximize productivity of all factors of production. This can be achieved by allowing perfect mobility of the factors of production, either by means of the market, or by iteration on the planning board. Perfect mobility means that each factor will be specialized according to its comparative advantage and incentives. While the market is considered a perfect mechanism for such mobility, a perfect plan can achieve similar results by iteration. However, a perfect market and a perfect plan can achieve such results only if the economic system itself is perfect in the sense that all relevant facts are known, including the objective function or the objectives specified in advance, qualifications of the factors, flow of information, and constraints.

4. Production of commodities and services is organized in such a way that no more economies or diseconomies of scale can be realized, either by the market or by planning. A segmented market that does not permit an optimal scale of production would reduce efficiency and productivity.

If the conditions above are satisfied, we may consider an economy to be functioning at its optimum level. Any deviation from these conditions would create a gap between the realized and the optimal results. The size of the gap would indicate the size of the cost to the economy resulting from deviation from optimal behavior. If discrimination caused such deviation, the resulting gap would be the social cost of discrimination.

It is our hypothesis that economic discrimination against race, ethnic origin, and gender has inflicted considerable social economic costs wherever it has occurred. We propose also that these social costs have usually been overlooked because of the institutionalization of discrimination, change in expectations, or redefinition of the constraints facing the economy. Accordingly, once discrimination is deemed acceptable and expected, its effects may no longer be considered as costs.

Probably the simplest and most useful way of conceptualizing social benefits and costs is by reference to the production possibility frontier.[2] If all resources were used in the production process, with free mobility of inputs and outputs, and all inputs were endowed with material and nonmaterial capital to function at capacity, output would be on the production possibility frontier. Any interference in the economy that prevents production at the frontier, or moves it closer to the origin will reduce optimality and incur a social cost to the economy. Racial, ethnic, or gender discrimination that reduces full endowment and utilization of labor or reduces incentives by underrewarding so that total output falls short of the production possibility frontier will incur a social cost equal to the difference between realized output and output on the frontier.

In the next section we shall explore the proposition that discrimination against racial, ethnic, or gender groups may be rational behavior that is capable of realizing social benefits. We shall also explore the forms discrimination takes, as well as its magnitude, after which we shall analyze the process by which discrimination incurs social costs, the forms these costs take, and ways by which they can be estimated.

SOCIAL BENEFITS AND COSTS ILLUSTRATED

Social Benefits

It has been suggested that economic discrimination can bring about social economic benefits, benefits that are rarely acknowledged. For example, discrimination may be a source of efficiency and optimality within given economic and sociopolitical constraints in society in at least three ways.

1. Higher savings and lower consumption may be realized because lower wages are paid to those discriminated against and other material rewards are redistributed in favor of savers. By redistributing income and resources in favor of the entrepreneurial, more educated, and well-established income groups, who are most frequently the discriminating majority, higher savings may be realized. Since higher savings mean higher investment, discrimination may act as a growth factor. There are indicators, however, that the victims of discrimination, because of their insecure economic status, may save more than the discriminating majority.[3]

Some argue that many development and growth opportunities in the New World would have been missed had whites not been able to use cheap labor—slaves, minorities, and women—to expand industry, build roads, develop plantations, and exploit quarries and mines.[4] This theory, however, suggests only that higher profits and savings on wages can be major sources of investment and growth; it does not preclude the possibility that such savings can be realized by means other than discrimination or simply by exploiting all workers regardless of their race, ethnicity, and gender. Or it may be that without exploitation total output will increase and cause savings to increase as well. The fact that blacks, ethnic minorities, and women are often the victims of discrimination means only that they are easier to exploit, or can be exploited at a lower cost to the exploiter, but not necessarily to the social economy. Discrimination may be a growth factor, but that does not mean it is the optimal mechanism to achieve growth.

2. A guaranteed labor supply is another potential growth factor. Labor levies on racial and ethnic minorities can guarantee a labor supply so that production and growth processes are not interrupted because of labor shortages. This argument assumes that other means of recruiting labor, such as material rewards or other forms of compensation, could not guarantee a labor supply that would satisfy demand. If blacks and Indians were not forced to work in the mines, so the argument runs, the mines would have been underutilized. Yet, there is no evidence that other forms of fair compensation were tried before forced labor was imposed. Workers are rational beings and therefore should be willing to offer their services at the right price, though the price may be paid in different forms. This is true even of the blacks who were captured in Africa to be used as items of trade and sources of profit in the growing market for labor in the New World. Having arrived in the New World, they were *forced* to work rather than recruited according to a transaction mechanism or system of payment and reward they could understand. They simply were considered the property of their owners. In one sense, it may be said that their enslavement pushed the production possibility frontier outward and thus raised potential aggregate output, but it is not certain that the same could not have been done by some other means such as the importation of white wage labor to satisfy market demand.

3. Sociopolitical stability may be a social benefit as a cost-minimizing mechanism achieved through control of racial, ethnic, and gender groups. The argument is that in the absence of assimilation of the minority, the power majority must remain in control of the minority and "keep them in their place" to maintain stability. Keeping them in their place usually means keeping them as a source of cheap labor, as noncompetitors and a material benefit to those in power; there is no evidence that this creates a net social economic benefit. True, if racial and ethnic minorities and women were to enjoy equality with the majority and with men, there would be a costly disruption of existing institutions, but it would be costly only in the short run. The long-run benefits of nondiscrimination would be much greater than the costs. The stability argument is not well supported either in the short run or in the long run.

The stability argument also maintains that keeping women at home is a source of family stability because they can better socialize their children and cater to the welfare of the family and the men as breadwinners. Here, too, the costs of disrupting existing institutions that discriminate against women by excluding them from the marketplace may be high in the short run. But weighed against the benefits of eliminating discrimination against women and letting them choose their goals, such costs become insignificant.

To summarize, while private benefits from discrimination may be indisputable, social benefits are not. If they do exist, it is only by tolerating or accepting constraints imposed on the economy by tradition, the majority, or men. If we accept the idea that the constraints are not immutable, or that a woman's place is not necessarily in the home, such benefits become illusory and indefensible. It is not evident that discrimination is the optimal way to increase the labor force and shift the frontiers of the production possibility curve outward. The same results could be achieved by applying a nondiscriminatory reward system to encourage immigration and work in either a market or a planned economy. It is true, however, that expansion of the frontier by discrimination may accrue a private benefit to the traders and employers at the cost of society; hence, discrimination persists.

Social Costs

In a pioneering study of the impact of racial discrimination on economic development, Joan Hoffman has established a strong case that racial discrimination retards economic development. Development in this case means desirable changes in the economic structure, as distinguished from growth. The degree of development retardation may be considered a social cost of discrimination. Several types of social costs are identified by Hoffman: (1) By increasing inequality of income distribution, racial discrimination reduces the ability of its victims to accumulate their own capital and invest in themselves and in the economy; thus they fail to realize their potential. (2) By sustaining inferior education for a segment of the population, discrimination reduces the supply of skills and trained personnel and assures a large supply of unskilled, relatively cheap labor. This has two contradictory effects: on one hand, the lack of skilled labor could lead to mechanization; on the other, the ample supply of cheap labor could reduce the incentive to move toward mechanization and technical change. Both results may have benefits for the employer, but they entail a social cost by keeping a segment of the population in the low-income, low-skill, or underdeveloped status. (3) Underemployment because of discrimination means depriving the economy of the product of unutilized labor, which cannot be recovered. (4) Racial discrimination may retard development because it incites resistance to change or modification of the discriminatory institutions. (5) Finally, development may be retarded because of a perception that an economy based on unskilled labor may be incapable of development because it lacks the necessary resources.[5]

Though Hoffman's study is related to development, its implications are easily generalizable to growth within the developed economies as well. High social costs may be noted in South Africa, Israel, and the American South, which remains much less developed than the North, most probably because of discrimination. Social costs may be incurred by different forms of discrimination: reduced incentives by enslavement, forced labor, and underrewarding for equal work; reduced productivity because of underendowment and exclusion from economic and social opportunities, including educational, housing, and recreational facilities; and underutilization through underemployment and unemployment. Though some of these points have been discussed above, some elaboration seems in order.

1. Forced labor performed by slaves or in penal institutions implies lack of mobility of resources, little incentive or rational decision making by the worker, and the performance of only the absolute minimum necessary to avoid punishment or a bigger burden. If fear of punishment induces workers to perform, then punishment may be made more frequent or more severe to compensate for the low incentives. However, inflicting punishment or discipline entails costs because resources must be used to monitor and apply the punishment. Labor performance may be improved, but costs will rise and the net result will still be below the potential of the free or decision-making worker.

Interestingly enough, social cost may be incurred also in a planned economy if the plan is imposed on society, if the objective functions do not represent the people's objectives, or if the rewards are not consistent with the expectations of the producers. The result in a planned economy would be failure to fulfill the plan or reach the production possibility frontier; the predicament of the formally planned economies of the USSR and Eastern Europe provide good illustrations.

Another form of the social cost of forced labor is the risk of sabotage, destruction, or at least work interruption. Conflict, especially if it becomes overt, may result in slowdowns, strikes, and the destruction of capital. While some of these costs fall directly on the employer, they also inflict high social costs because some potential output will not be realized and the aggregate capital stock will be destroyed. Both results mean that production will be below the production possibility frontier.

2. Underrewarding for work as a form of discrimination is probably the most common and most often analyzed result of discrimination. Cheap labor is probably the most attractive reason for discrimination. According to Margaret Halsey,

The real reason back of the refusal of some of you to mingle with Negroes at the canteen isn't so romantic and dramatic as you think it is. The real reason has nothing to do with rape, seduction, or risings in the night. The real reason can be summed up in two unromantic little words: cheap labor. As long as you treat Negroes as subhumans, you don't have to pay them much. When you refuse to dance with Negro servicemen at the canteen, you are neither protecting your honor nor making sure that white Southerners won't have their homes burned down around their ears. All you are doing is making it possible for employers all over the country to get Negroes to work for them for less money than those employers would have to pay you.[6]

Cheap labor was the incentive for apartheid in South Africa. While segregation between black and white may have been instituted for social, psychological, and political reasons, placing black settlements close to white industry was intended to assure a supply of cheap labor for white employers. Arabs from the Occupied Territories are employed in Israel, even while violence continues, mainly because they may be employed for lower wages than would be paid to Jews. Arabs from the Occupied Territories are not allowed to reside near their jobs, but given the short distances in Israel, commuting is feasible; hence the labor supply is secure.

Obviously, underrewarding is a benefit to the employer, but is it a benefit to the economy? If we relate rewards to performance, then we must conclude that underrewarding must be due to underperformance, which means less aggregate output than would otherwise be possible. If, on the other hand, performance is related to incentives, which are related to rewards, then underrewarding means reducing incentives and hence performance, which results in production levels below the production possibility frontier. The private benefit to the employer tends to be a social cost to the economy that is not compensated for by any apparent gains.

Probably the best illustration of this social cost is the system of rewards for women, first in the home and then in the marketplace. Since women are not paid for work in their own homes, their contribution to the economy is not even counted. Being deprived of the income that would have accrued had they been paid, they are deprived of the opportunity to build their own capital, make their own economic decisions, and realize their potential for themselves or the economy as a whole.

On the other hand, women in the marketplace are underrewarded when they are paid less than men or receive slower promotions, or both, as shown in Chapter 3. Unequal pay for equal work generates conflict, reduces incentives, and affects team spirit in the workplace. All three of these effects tend to reduce performance in quality and quantity. A social cost is inflicted on the economy when capable women are not allowed to occupy positions commensurate with their capabilities and thus are forced into underperformace. Though the employer may benefit from this policy, the resulting underperformance appears in the social economy as an underutilization of factors of production. Output is thus kept below the production possibility frontier.

One may argue that underrewarding is a relative concept. Lower pay for racial or minority groups or for women may entail social costs only if they perceive it as intended underrewarding. If, however, blacks in the United States, Arabs in Israel, or women everywhere were convinced that they were underqualified, less deserving, or that they were not discriminated against, it is possible that their performance, in the home or in the market-place, could not have been higher, even had they been equally rewarded. According to this argument, social costs will be suffered by the economy only if victims perceive themselves as victims of discrimination and thus reduce their own performance as rational economic decision-makers. For example, the fact that the East Indians and Chinese have been regarded as superior workers in Canada and the United States, even though they have often been underrewarded, does not prove that they were performing at their optimum or that their productivity would not have been higher had they been more equally rewarded.

Furthermore, as far as can be observed, victims of racial, ethnic, and gender discrimination have never truly accepted their "inferior reward" as fair and have rebelled whenever they had an opportunity to do so. Thus, if incentives are functions of rewards, underrewarding on the basis of race, ethnicity, or sex results in a social cost to the economy, both by underutilizing potential talent and skill and by depressing the incentives of victims. Thus total production is bound to fall below the production possibility frontier.

3. Exclusion from qualifying and occupational opportunities is probably the most costly form of discrimination from the standpoint of the aggregate economy. Exclusion from qualifying activities is an act of forced underendowment that tends to institutionalize the gap between the majority and the minority, between genders, and between discriminators and victims. Racial, ethnic, and women's groups deprived of educational and other qualifying opportunities available to the majority and to men experience the most serious form of exclusion. These groups are usually socialized to accept their limited educational opportunities. But whether they believe they are deprived or not, they end up undereducated and undertrained, relative to their natural potentials, and therefore become underperformers. If their underperformance is accompanied by lower wages but the difference between revenues and costs remains high, the employer has no reason to complain.

The fact that underperformance has been institutionalized by the under-education and undertraining of more than half of the population of any given country (women plus discriminated-against racial and ethnic groups) means that large potentials of skill, productivity, and output have been lost by the economy. Many unknown geniuses and many great achievers might have been discovered and nurtured had the victims been free from discrimination. It is true that had women, for example, participated fully in qualifying preparations and activity in the market, their added contribution would not be proportional to their number because their lost contributions in the form of housework would have to be compensated for by employing others to do that work. Nevertheless, the apparent social loss is large, perhaps a quarter or a third of the gross domestic product. The higher the rate of exclusion and the lower the rate of participation of these groups, the higher will be the social cost to the economy, or the wider the gap between the production possibility curve with discrimination and potential production without it.

To get an idea of the social cost of discrimination by exclusion, we may look at the increased output in wartime when full mobilization is implemented. In World War II, when women and minorities were encouraged to take jobs they had been excluded from previously, the national output increased by about 45%. This increase would have been even higher had these new producers not been underendowed by discrimination in earlier years.[7]

Excluding qualified workers from occupational opportunities because of racial, ethnic, or gender features entails social costs in at least two other ways. First, such exclusion means that someone less qualified is occupying a position that could have been filled by a better-qualified person. This means that the economy has lost the difference between output of the higher- and the lower-qualified persons in the form of lower productivity. If a black or Hispanic or female engineer is replaced by a white male engineer who is less qualified or proficient, the loss to society will be the difference between the productivities of the two engineers. Second, given that resources were invested in the education of an engineer who is either unemployed or underutilized, a social cost is incurred equal to the difference between the returns on those resources and the returns that might have been realized had they been used in a capacity that involved no discrimination. If so, the combined social cost of exclusion from qualifying and occupational opportunities would be equal to the difference between the already lowered total production and the output at the potential production frontier had there been no discrimination.

However, exclusion from housing, education, recreation, and other opportunities because of race, ethnicity, or sex may or may not entail a social cost to the economy, depending on the form it takes, the alternative options available, and the degree to which it means deprivation and not simply segregation. If, as has been argued, segregation in the sense of "separate but equal" need not imply discrimination or deprivation, there would be little reason for it to entail social costs. It is easy to determine whether exclusion means deprivation; it is not so easy to determine whether segregation means exclusion, deprivation, or underperformance. Before emancipation, blacks, especially in the South, were deprived of education altogether by law. After emancipation, especially when segregation was legalized, they were excluded but presumably not deprived. However, to the extent that black education in the segregated schools was lower in quality and endowment than white education, segregation in education implied both exclusion and deprivation.

The same analysis applies to female education throughout history. Female students at all levels of education were segregated from male students until recent times. Their schools at all levels of education were usually less well endowed, less advanced, and offered less in terms of subject matter and professionalism than male schools. Girls were allowed less education, were sent to school less frequently than boys, and had less choice of subject matter and training than boys. Women have tended to end up with lower levels of education and professional training than men. They have also been concentrated in fields of study and training that have been termed "women's" specialties, often leading primarily to housework, teaching, and social services. Segregation between men and women in education has led to separate but unequal opportunities, to the disadvantage of women and the economy at large.

Segregation has another social cost, one that affects the scale of production and the overhead cost of providing qualifying and recreational services. When schools, buses, restaurants, or factories are segregated by race, ethnicity, or gender, the scale of production in enterprises is diminished on both sides of the segregated economy. Whether each segregated facility can operate at an optimum scale depends on the size of the community served by each facility. There are not usually large enough minorities in each segregated area to support separate schools, sports clubs, housing projects, and communication systems. Underpopulated segregated areas are unable to provide equal services at costs similar to those paid by the majority. Traditionally the result has been to cut services, which means deprivation of certain groups, or to charge more for services, which wastes scarce resources and thus increases social cost to the economy.

The history of segregation between blacks and whites and between men and women provides clear evidence that segregation has always deprived the victims of discrimination of the services and opportunities available to the discriminators. Deprivation resulted either because victims did not have the resources to establish equal facilities or because the discriminating group still allocated resources and defined the objectives of the production system, either by controlling resources or by legislating their prejudices.

Put another way, segregation, with or without equality, raises the overhead costs of providing a service or producing a commodity. Instead of having one gym for an integrated school, segregated schools have to have as many gyms as there are schools. The result often means fewer or smaller gyms and lower-quality and fewer services for minorities and women than for others. Here again, the overhead cost is coupled with deprivation of the victims of the necessary qualifying education and training, thus tending to institutionalize their underqualification, underperformance, and vulnerability to underpayment and discrimination. Whether it is by deprivation through segregation or by raising the overhead costs, the production possibility frontier is pushed inward toward the origin, thus reflecting a social cost to the economy equal to the difference between the product realized with segregation and what it could have been without segregation.[8]

SOCIAL BENEFITS AND COSTS OF POSITIVE DISCRIMINATION OR FAVORITISM

Discrimination can go both ways—against or in favor of certain racial, ethnic, or gender groups. So far we have dealt with the negative, but what about the positive forms, sometimes called reverse discrimination, favoritism, or protectionism toward certain individuals or groups? Our concern is with favoritism toward any of the three groups we have been studying, both as individuals and as groups. To what extent does such favoritism incur costs or accrue benefits to the economy as a whole?

If positive discrimination or favoritism is accorded to certain individuals or groups, its social economic effects would be the same as those of negative discrimination, since certain groups and individuals are given benefits at the expense of others with better qualifications and higher merits for the positions in question. If a favored engineer is placed in a position that requires higher qualifications than he/she has, even though better-qualified engineers are available, the total output would be less than the potential output had the better-qualified engineer been hired. The social costs would be equal to the difference between what is accomplished and what could have been accomplished without favoritism, computed for all such situations of favoritism.

The issue, however, becomes a little more complicated when favoritism takes the form of affirmative action intended to redress the grievances of discrimination victims. Such action is sometimes described as "reverse discrimination" because it "favors" former victims at the expense of new victims from among the groups previously practicing discrimination. When a black or a Native American, or a woman, is given a job in preference to a white, or a male, respectively, even though he or she is less qualified than the latter, the potential output will not be realized and society will lose because output will be within and not at the production possibility frontier. Regardless of the reasons, allowing a less-qualified person to take the job of a more-qualified person will entail social economic costs. It is possible, of course, that the objective function or target of economic policy is not to achieve the maximum output but the maximum social utility, which may include a combination of commodities, social justice, political stability, or redress of previous injustices, in which case affirmative action will accrue sociopolitical gains that offset the social economic costs. Such "reverse discrimination" may lower these costs if the alternative to affirmative action is extensive litigation, labor unrest, or claims for compensation for past discrimination.

Favoritism to less-qualified individuals from among victimized groups may have other effects on the dynamics of change in minority-majority relations and consequently on the economy as a whole. To place minority persons in positions above their qualifications would not only create a gap between the realized and potential outputs, but could also reduce their incentives to push hard or to achieve on their own merits.[9] Placing a few minority or women candidates in key positions through affirmative action could create the impression that discrimination has been eliminated, even though only a few individuals may be benefited, and thus perpetuate discrimination and the social costs generated by it. Inasmuch as affirmative action may affect only the results and fail to reach the roots of discrimination, it may perpetuate discrimination and compound the social costs attached to it.

On the other hand, if minority or female candidates are placed in positions for which they have full qualifications but which would not have been available to them without affirmative action, then affirmative action will not only redress the grievances of the victims and prevent discrimination, but also replace the social economic costs that would have been incurred through discrimination with social economic gains by pushing total output closer to the production possibility frontier

MEASURES OF BENEFITS AND COSTS

We have seen above that because of discrimination, wages of minorities tend to be lower than those of the majority, and wages of women tend to be lower than those of men almost across the board, regardless of occupation, education, historical period, or economic system, though the gap is not equally evident in all economic systems. The wage gap, however, a cost to the victim, is not necessarily a gain to the discriminator. If there were no discrimination, the forces of the market might bring about an adjustment of wages such that the private costs may not be fully offset by the private benefits. The aggregate effects, however, will always be negative, even if the private costs and benefits offset each other, since the forgone output, because of undertraining, underutilization, and reduced incentives, cannot be recovered.

The aggregate impact may be assessed by resorting to micro measures of discrimination, or by aggregating the private effects to arrive at social or aggregate results. Therefore it may be helpful to look at some of the approaches used to estimate the costs and benefits of discrimination to different groups in society. As noted above, social costs may be incurred by four different mechanisms. (1) Forced labor, as in slavery, leads to reduced incentives and lower output, waste of resources needed to impose discipline, and destruction of capital and suspension of work through sabotage. (2) Underrewarding, whether by payment below marginal product or below wages paid to others for similar performance, leads to reduced incentives and loss of output. It could also restrict participation in the labor force by workers who anticipate underrewarding. (3) Underutilization leads to loss of output in various ways. Exclusion of women from the labor force is one major source of reduced output. Underemployment or employment in jobs below a worker's qualification is another. Equally costly is the employment of favored groups in jobs above their qualifications, which results in inefficiencies and loss of output. (4) Underendowment is probably the most obvious source of social costs. Minorities and women deprived of education and investment in human capital are less qualified and therefore less productive than they could be. They lose and society loses.

It may be best to measure these social costs by applying counterfactual analysis, on the assumption that in the absence of discrimination, output would be higher than it actually is. The social costs would be equal to the difference between the actual output of minorities and women and the output they could produce in the absence of discrimination. That gap can be estimated by assuming that in the absence of discrimination, minorities and women would have similar incentives and be as productive as the majority and men, in which case their levels of output or average marginal products would be similar, since there is no compelling reason to assume otherwise. An illustration of this method will be presented below after a survey of the methods that have been used to estimate the effects of discrimination.

One approach is to use descriptive statistics such as means, medians, and standard deviations of wages received by different groups, rents and prices paid, and frequencies of facilitation and obstruction these groups face, as noted in Chapters 2 and 3. The assumption behind this approach is that by analysis of variance, these measures may help to decompose and thus explain the impact of race, ethnicity, and sex on the costs and benefits of discrimination.[10]

Another method of measuring the impact of discrimination is the field survey. One version, the "fair housing audit," calls for investigators of different racial or ethnic (could be gender) backgrounds to visit housing units advertised for rent and record the facilitation or obstruction they met with on the visits. The data collected are then analyzed to see whether the different racial or ethnic features of the investigators may have affected the difficulty or ease of renting. According to a study of fair housing in Boston in 1981, discrimination was quite evident and statistically significant. Black auditors were invited to inspect 36.3% fewer apartments than were whites. The brokers acting in a discriminatory manner were apparently complying with the wishes of their customers.[11]

To make it possible to explain income and earning differences among different ethnic and gender groups, regression analysis has been almost a standard approach. To illustrate, Kathy Connings has used various regression models with gender as one of the independent variables, trying to isolate and assess the impact of sex on earnings. Gender is found to be significant in determining earnings in all the models.[12]

Regression analysis has also been applied in a British setting to measure earning differences between colored and white workers, using schooling, experience, industry, and "other" as independent variables. The results indicate that schooling is the "variable that contributes most to the earnings difference" and that "the rates of return to years of schooling are substantially higher for whites" than for colored people.[13]

In a variation of this method discrimination is measured by use of a reverse regression model, which compares job qualifications among different racial and gender groups with similar earnings. The argument is that if there is discrimination against blacks or women, these victims would have to have higher qualifications than whites and men, respectively, to earn similar incomes. A study of 4,542 individuals from the University of Michigan for 1976 indicates that no discrimination existed and that qualifications were rewarded equally regardless of race or gender.[14] One should wonder, however, whether those employed at a university subject to affirmative action regulations would be an unbiased sample to test for discrimination by reverse regression.

Regression analysis has also been used to test for discrimination as a violation of the principle of comparable worth. This is done by regressing earnings, actual and expected, in the absence of discrimination, on job and worker characteristics, including gender (or ethnicity and race). The results of one such study indicate a large disparity between earnings in male- and female-dominated occupations, with male-dominated occupations paying much higher rates than mixed or female-dominated occupations.[15] Comparable worth measures, however, apply only within firms and not between firms or industries; hence they are of limited use, especially for aggregate assessments of costs and benefits.[16]

A broader set of independent variables has been used to explain racial posttax earning differences. The independent variables include qualifications, occupational data, amenity variables that measure quality of life values, and residence, with differentiation between city center and suburb. The data are taken from *Current Population Survey,* 1976. The results indicate that when all differences are accounted for, blacks in the suburbs earn 15.6% less than whites and blacks earn 21.62% less than whites in the central city.[17]

One problem that complicates regression analysis has to do with the specific model used and the assumptions made to test that model. For example, in the absence of discrimination should workers, potential renters, and buyers or sellers be considered perfect or imperfect substitutes regardless of race, color, or gender? If they are to be considered imperfect substitutes, different standards of measurement will have to be used, one standard for each individual or group of perfect substitutes. Aggregate measurement is virtually impossible because of the large number of variations among individuals and groups. A way out of this dilemma is to assume that the members of these groups are perfect substitutes so that in the absence of discrimination the distribution of occupations and earnings among the various groups would be similar to each other and to the total population. This is implied in a study of wage differentials over time by Low and Villegas, who questioned the "traditional approach" because it ignores differences in productivity arising from unequal levels of employment, which may result from discrimination and lead to unequal marginal products among workers from different groups. To rectify the bias, Low and Villegas apply a "hedonic wage perfect substitution model" in which workers from different racial groups with similar training are considered equally productive if no discrimination is encountered. Though this model was not empirically tested by its authors, it has merit, as my attempt to measure discrimination in the Middle East will show.[18]

Now we shall turn to the aggregate or social effects of discrimination on the economy. In an attempt to measure the impact of other forms of discrimination, Jerome C. Rose found that Afro-Americans suffered a much higher frequency of skeletal lesions than the rest of the population because of inadequate food provisions and poor diet. The dietary deficiencies and lower immunity to infectious diseases resulting from dietary inadequacy led to higher infant mortality and Afro-American population decline.[19] What is not clear is whether this higher infant mortality and population decline were confined to black people who had suffered from segregation and deprivation. In other words, did they result from discrimination or from class distinction and poverty? However, assuming that discrimination and deprivation were the cause, the loss to society would be equal to the loss of lifetime incomes of the lost population and the depleted production capacity of the survivors. As far as can be ascertained, no aggregate measure of this loss is available.

Another attempt to measure the effects of discrimination views income gaps between blacks and whites as due to gaps in education between the two groups. It has been accepted that education is an important determinant of income, but this human capital theory attributes only a part of the difference in income between blacks and whites to the gap between their levels of education, about 30% and 35% of that difference. The rest of the income gap has usually been attributed by institutional or structural theory to several factors, including policies dealing with crisis situations such as the Depression in the United States and World War II. Margo includes among other factors that may have reduced the gap in income the "movement of blacks out of the low-wage South; changes in the labor force brought about by agricultural mechanization, the growth of manufacturing, and unionization; re-enfranchisement of the southern black population after World War II; various court decisions reaffirming the Fourteenth Amendment and outlawing racial segregation; the Civil Rights movement; and especially the anti-discrimination legislation of the 1960s."[20] Not content with findings based on census data, because they underestimate the educational gap, Margo measures educational achievement in terms of months spent in school, rather than years or grades completed. The results show that the educational gap between blacks and whites is twice as significant as had been previously thought.[21] One may assume that the income gap is a measure of the additional output that would have been produced had those deprived populations been allowed to attain equivalent-to-white education. Furthermore, one may assume that the educational gap explains between 30% and 60%—anywhere between Margo's estimate and previous estimates—roughly 45% of the income gap. In other words, if income or lost output data are not available, it may be possible to estimate the loss of aggregate output by estimating the educational gap for the total population over the period during which it existed as a proxy for the lost output.

Such measures apply to "integrated" situations only; they do not apply to situations where deprivation includes segregation, or exclusion from employment, ownership of property, access to credit, and freedom of occupational, geographic, and residential mobility. Even if the loss due to restricted opportunities were accounted for, it is still not obvious that estimates of private costs and benefits would tell us how much the social costs and benefits were. For example, in an attempt to build a case for reparations to Afro-Americans, Browne found that slaves were always willing to buy their freedom for a higher price than the market value placed on them by their owners, presumably because of a subjective value they attached to freedom. It is also possible that they would have paid a higher than market value for their freedom because they knew that their productivity and income earning potential would go up once they were freed. Their market value and income earning capacity under slavery could be underestimates of the opportunity cost suffered by society because of their enslavement.

Browne includes the value of unpaid slave labor, the value of unpaid labor before emancipation and after, compensation for the share of the national wealth that would have belonged to blacks had they been accorded equal opportunity to reclaim land or stake claims to underground minerals and water resources, etc., and compensation for lost opportunities in education and the improvement of black human capital. He arrives at a figure between $448 and $995 billion as of 1972.[22] A similar estimate of costs has been applied to the removal and internment of Japanese Americans in the United States during World War II. The private losses to the 120,000 Japanese Americans are estimated at $400 million.[23] Internment of the Japanese, however, also entailed a social cost to the economy because it deprived the aggregate economy of output they could have produced, in addition to expending resources to implement the internment program.

Regardless of the reliability and justifiability of these estimates, it is not obvious that the loss to blacks was a loss to the economy. For example, the land not reclaimed by blacks was presumably reclaimed by others, and the resources not utilized by blacks were presumably utilized by others. It is not evident either that had the blacks had these opportunities, their output would have been any higher than it was when they were exploited by others. A private cost is not necessarily a social cost, nor would a private benefit automatically constitute a social benefit.

The only obvious social cost is the cost to society because segments of its human resources have been underendowed or underdeveloped, restricted from seeking the opportunities for which they are best suited, or underrewarded and discouraged by dampened incentives. In this case, the human capital resources of the blacks, other minorities, and women that have been underdeveloped, underutilized, and underrewarded form the basis for estimating social cost. The social cost, if it can be computed, would equal the lost output of all racial and ethnic minorities and of women denied opportunities to develop their human capital, biologically and educationally, and restricted from applying their knowledge and skills fully in the production process. Unfortunately, no measures of these social costs are available, though some rough estimates may be made.

Interest in measuring the costs of discrimination, especially those suffered by blacks in the United States, has increased in recent years, though few new approaches have been devised.[24] The predominant conceptual framework and method remain the neoclassical approach, which estimates differences between the marginal product and the wage as a measure of discrimination.[25] However, there have been attempts to estimate the costs of deprivation of blacks from capital, education, and job opportunities, as well as of losses to the economy because of their underutilization. Marketti estimates the income lost by the slaves as the lost return on their market value, or the income they would have earned had they not been slaves. Applying different combinations of rates of return and different estimates of prices and wages, Marketti provides a range of estimates of lost incomes to blacks because of slavery but none to indicate the social costs to the economy. Marketti's estimates range from $147 billion to $53.1 trillion through 1983, in 1957 and 1959 prices, but these estimates do not allow for added training or higher qualifications the slaves might have acquired had they not been enslaved. These losses to the slaves and their posterity were diverted as benefits to the slave owners and their posterity.[26]

Probably the most comprehensive concept of the costs of slavery and discrimination has been proposed by Swinton, who assumes parity between the races as normal. Swinton maintains that any disparity in incomes or output due to slavery or discrimination can be measured by estimating the lost opportunities and lost values, as follows:

Costs of Slavery = Value of labor expropriated + value of lost opportunities to acquire capital + value of lost freedom + pain and suffering.

Costs of Discrimination + Segregation = Reduced value of labor due to discrimination + reduced value of capital due to discrimination.

These are calculated for each year in which slavery and discrimination have been practiced. All are to be calculated in present value.[27] Swinton concludes that as long as a gap exists in initial capital endowments between the races, income gaps between them will continue to exist.[28]

In an attempt to estimate the private benefits derived by discriminators in the labor market, a Berkeley group has calculated benefits from wage and occupation discrimination as well as from employment discrimination between 1929 and 1984. Their estimated benefits come to $1,277.7 billion in present value.[29] These, however, are transfer payments, whose impact on the aggregate economy is not known.

ESTIMATES OF SOCIAL COSTS IN THE MIDDLE EAST: A CASE STUDY

So far, however, there has been no estimate of the aggregate effects of discrimination on the economy as a result both of underutilization of ethnic and gender resources and of their underendowment and the resulting lower productivity. This is what I have tried to do with regard to discrimination against ethnic and gender groups in the Middle East, mostly as a way of illustration.[30]

My hypothesis is that if there were no discrimination and economic behavior were guided either by a perfect market or by a perfect plan, economic performance would be at the production possibility frontier, and any deviation from those conditions would create a gap between the optimal and the realized results. If a gap existed between output without discrimination and output with discrimination, the gap would be equal to the lost output, which is the cost of discrimination. It is my hypothesis that economic discrimination against ethnic minorities and women inflicts sizable social costs on the respective economies of the Middle East, which I use as a case study. I further propose that such costs have become so institutionalized that few policy-makers pay attention to their existence.

To measure the lost output or the social cost, I resorted to an estimate of the aggregated private losses that affect the economy at large. Private costs and benefits may be measured as the gap between what a person or group would receive or pay with and without discrimination. Such costs and benefits could accrue from transactions involving wages and salaries, interest, rent, and profits. Private costs can be caused by underrewarding or by underendowment or both, as reflected by the gap between the average marginal products of different groups, and between the marginal product and the wage. In the absence of discrimination the average marginal product should be the same for the majority and the minority, and it should be equal to the average wage for both groups; any gap between one level of reward and the other, or between one marginal product and another, would indicate the private costs of discrimination.

The Arabs in Israel, like most other minorities, and women in all Middle Eastern countries, are discriminated against by underendowment, underutilization, and underrewarding. Their rates of participation and choices of occupation are interfered with by the more powerful groups—the ethnic

Jewish majority and men, respectively. Both groups are undereducated, undertrained, and less economically mobile because of restrictions imposed on them by the ethnic majority and men. They have fewer specialization opportunities, control less capital, land, and other resources, and face more difficulties in acquiring credit or aid to industry and business. Women receive smaller inheritances than men, and both groups suffer relatively higher rates of unemployment at all times than do the Jewish majority or male workers, respectively. If so, then the Israeli economy and the economies of the other countries in the region must be functioning below their potential without discrimination. The question is, how much do the respective economies lose because of existing discrimination? Given the limitations of data and the complexity of measuring the effects of discrimination, the following crude estimate is presented for illustrative purposes only.

To simplify estimation we shall look at the Arab minority household in Israel as the earning unit. The relevant measures are the differences between current earnings and the estimated marginal product, and also between the estimated marginal product and the counterfactual potential marginal product in the absence of discrimination. Since there are no data showing that Arabs receive less than Jews for comparable work, and since it is evident that they are less endowed with human and material capital and therefore have lower productivity than the Jews, we may assume that their lower earnings are commensurate with their lower marginal product. However, we also know that they are underutilized and underendowed and therefore their marginal product is below their potential marginal product in the absence of discrimination. In other words, discrimination is applied by underendowment and underutilization, rather than by underrewarding. Since in the absence of discrimination the potential marginal product of Arabs should be similar to that of the majority, we shall consider the marginal product and average wage of the Jewish majority as the measure of the potential marginal product and wage for the Arab minority. Accordingly, the total cost or the difference between the estimated output and the potential output without discrimination may be measured as follows: .

$$Cd = T[st \ (1 - et/ej)] \tag{1}$$

where Cd = Costs of discrimination or loss of potential output; T = total potential output; st = size of minority in the population or the potential labor force (assumed proportional); et = minority earnings; ej = majority earnings; et/ej is the ethnic minority/majority earnings ratio.

Since the Arab labor force is about 0.10 of the national labor force, and its earnings per household of 1.5 earners is 60.4 on a scale of 100, compared with the national earnings of 88.7 of a household of 1.6 earners on that scale, an Arab minority earner's earnings are 60.4/88.7 x 1.6/1.5, or 72.6% of the national average earnings. In other words, the Arab minority is apparently producing only 0.727 of what it could produce if there were no discrimination by underutilization or underendowment. Given the size of the Arab minority in the labor force, and assuming that its contribution to the total output would be proportional to its size, then the loss in total output would be equal to 0.10 (1 - 0.727) or 0.027 of the total output. In other words, the total Israeli output would be higher by 2.7% if there were no discrimination against the Arab minority.

Assuming that women are 50% of the potential labor force, but given their underendowment and that their participation in the labor force is much lower than that of men, the loss because of discrimination against them would be

$$Cd = T[(sf \times rf)(1 - ef/em) + sf(rm - rf)] \qquad (2)$$

where Cd = costs of gender discrimination or loss of potential output; T = total potential output; f and m indicate female and male (equivalent to minority and majority in the ethnic context above); r = rate of participation in the labor force; e = earnings

Since women in Israel participate only at a rate of 40.1% and earn about 60% of what a male earns, and since they would be expected to earn as much as men do were they not underendowed and underutilized, the loss because of discrimination against them would be:

$$Cd = T[(0.50 \times 0.40)(1 - 0.60) + 0.5(0.65 - 0.40)]$$
$$= T[(0.20 \times 0.40) + 0.125] = 0.205 \, T$$

In other words, the Israeli economy loses about a fifth of its total output because of discrimination against women. Combining the two estimates, the total loss due to discrimination against the Arab minority and women could amount to 23.2% of the potential GDP, as an upper limit, with full participation, full employment, and no discrimination. According to this approach, the loss to the Israeli economy in 1984 ranged between 10.7% of GDP, as a result of discrimination in the form of underendowment against Arabs and women actively participating in the labor force, and 23.2% because of discrimination against them in the form of underendowment and underutilization.[31]

In Egypt females earned between 65% and 75% of male earnings in 1976, and their rate of participation was 18.64%, compared with a rate of participation for males of 77.39%. Assuming that females form 50% of the potential labor force, and those who are working earn an average of 70% of male earnings, the cost of discrimination to the economy would be about 3% of the GDP because of underendowment, and another 29% because of underendowment and underutilization.

In the Gulf area, where the rate of participation of women is much lower than in Egypt and Israel, the potential loss would be much higher as a result of underendowment and underutilization, but it would be much lower as a result of overall male and female underendowment or low productivity of those active in the labor force. Assuming a rate of female participation of 5% and a female/male earning ratio of 70%, the costs of discrimination due to underendowment, and the resulting low marginal product of those working, would be about 1% of the total potential output. However, the loss due to underendowment and underutilization would amount to another 30% of the potential output.

Similar estimations of lost output because of discrimination should be feasible for other countries, depending on the availability of data and our ability to justify assumptions of similarity regarding incentives and rational economic objectives regardless of ethnic origin or gender.

It should be stressed that the estimates above have been based on certain assumptions, but if those assumptions do not hold, the potential output still may not be realized for reasons other than discrimination. For example, women may choose to stay out of the labor force more frequently than men. Minorities may, for reasons of their own, decide to work less or retire sooner than the majority. The return on investment in human and material capital or endowment of minorities and women may be at rates different from the rates of return to endowment realized by the ethnic majority or by men. Or full employment may not be feasible because of bottlenecks that are not related to discrimination. In any of these cases the loss of output would not be a cost of discrimination, and the actual cost of discrimination would have to be lower than the estimated cost. These problems, however, are only complications and that should not affect the conceptual or methodological framework of our analysis.

If we were to apply similar techniques to estimate the social costs of discrimination in the developed countries in which there are vast gaps between ethnic minority and majority levels of endowment and rates of utilization, the costs could exceed 10% of the GDP annually.

CONCLUSIONS

Several observations may be made regarding the social benefits and costs of discrimination. On the social benefit side, lower wages could result in higher savings and lower consumption; sociopolitical stability could result from keeping minorities "in their place" through discrimination; and discrimination could guarantee a relatively cheap labor supply. None of these benefits, however, is certain, nor is it evident that similar benefits could not be secured by the market or other cooperative means that may be less costly than discrimination.

The social costs are more obvious. While much of the literature has concentrated on the measurement of private costs, little has dealt with macro economic effects. The methods used to compute costs have ranged from comparative descriptive statistics to regression analysis, reverse regression, and counterfactual analysis. As far as can be ascertained, no empirical studies of the macro effects of discrimination have been previously undertaken.

Though the data and the tools are rather crude, by applying counterfactual analysis to the effects of discrimination, in the form of underendowment and underutilization, against the Arab minority in Israel, and against women in Israel and Egypt, we discover that the Israeli economy probably lost anywhere between 10.7% and 23% of its potential output in 1984. Similarly, losses to the Egyptian economy came close to 31% of its potential, assuming full employment and no discrimination. These upper-limit cost estimates, however, depend on the availability of complementary factors of production and the feasibility of full employment. Finally, these illustrative results indicate that the methodology is generally applicable, and the need for social cost studies of discrimination is acute.

NOTES

1. See Denny Braun, *The Rich Get Richer: The Rise of Income Inequality in the United States* (Chicago: Nelson-Hall, Publishers, 1991), especially Chs. 5 and 6, and bibliography.

2. Ansel M. Sharp, Charles A. Register, and Richard H. Leftwich, eds., *Economics of Social Issues*, 9th ed. (Plano, Tex.: Business Publications Inc., 1988), 295-96.

3. Marcus Alexis, George Haines, Jr., and Leonard S. Simon, *Black People's Profiles in the Inner City* (Ann Arbor: University of Michigan Press, 1980).

4. See quotation from *Virginia Examiner* above, Ch. 2, p. 27.

5. Joan Hoffman, *Racial Discrimination and Economic Development* (Lexington, Mass.: Lexington Books, 1975), 5-11.

6. Margaret Halsey, *Color Blind: A White Woman Looks at a Negro* (New York: Simon and Schuster, 1946), 56-57, quoted in Sharp et al, eds., *Economics of Social Issues*, 291.

7. There is no doubt that patriotism and wartime psychology had much to do with the

increased output, which may not be equally achievable in peacetime, but the increase does indicate the high unutilized potential in the economy.

8. Though segregation may be interpreted as satisfying the "taste" for discrimination and other noneconomic objectives, it does accrue economic gains to the discriminators. Employers, for example, would not have to compensate "prejudiced" workers for having to mix with those against whom they are prejudiced.

9. Stephen Coate and Glenn Loury, "Will Affirmative Action Policies Eliminate Negative Stereotypes?" (mimeo), May 1991.

10. For an illustration, see Donald Cox, "Inequality in the Lifetime Earnings of Women," *Review of Economics and Statistics* (August 1982): 50-54.

11. J. Yinger, "Measuring Racial Discrimination with Fair Housing Audits: Caught in the Act," *American Economic Review* (December 1986): 881-93.

12. Kathy Connings, "The Earnings of Female and Male Middle Managers: A Canadian Case Study," *Journal of Human Resources* 23, no. 1 (Winter 1988): 34-56.

13. Robert McNabb and George Psacharonpoulos, "Racial Earnings Differentials in the UK," *Oxford Economic Papers*, 33, no. 3 (November 1981): 413-25.

14. Richard F. Kamalich and Solomon W. Polacheck, "Discrimination: Fact or Fiction? An Examination Using an Alternative Approach," *Southern Economic Journal* 49, no. 2 (October 1982): 450-61.

15. Donald J. Treiman, Heidi I. Hartmann, and Patricia A. Roos, "Assessing Pay Discrimination Using National Data," in Helen Remick, ed., *Comparable Worth and Wage Discrimination* (Philadelphia: Temple University Press, 1984), 137-55. For other studies that illustrate this methodology, see Naomi T. Verdugo and Richard R. Verdugo, "Earning Differentials Among Mexican Americans, Black and White Workers," *Social Science Quarterly* 64, no. 2 (June 1984): 417-25; Jeremiah Cotton, "Discrimination and Favoritism in the U.S. Labor Market," *American Journal of Economics and Sociology* (January 1988): 15-27.

16. G. Johnson and G. Solon, "Estimates of the Direct Effects of Comparable Worth Policy," *American Economic Review* 76, no. 5 (1986): 1117-25.

17. Richard Price and Edwin Mills, "Race and Residence in Earning Determination," *Journal of Urban Economics* 17, no. 1 (January 1985): 1-18.

18. S. A. Low and D. J. Villegas, "An Alternative Approach to the Analysis of Wage Differentials," *Southern Economic Journal* 54, no. 2 (October 1987): 449-62. "The hedonic wage equation is fundamentally a relationship between wages and the human capital characteristics....It measures the income potential of...present stock of human capital and the potential rewards of additional investment" (p. 454).

19. Jerome C. Rose, "Biological Consequences of Segregation and Economic Deprivation: A Post-Slavery Population from Southwest Arkansas," *Journal of Economic History* XLIX, no. 2 (June 1989): 351-60.

20. Robert A. Margo, "Race, Educational Attainment, and the 1940 Census," *Journal of Economic History* XLVI, no. 1 (March 1986): 190.

21. Ibid., 191-92.

22. Robert S. Browne, "The Economic Case for Reparations to Black America," *American Economic Review* LXII, no. 2 (1972): 39-46.

23. John Lescott-Leszczynski, *The History of U.S. Ethnic Policy and Its Impact on European Ethnics* (Boulder, Colo.: Westview Press, 1984), 31-32.

24. Recent publications include Richard F. America, ed., *The Wealth of Races* (New York: Greenwood Press, 1990); Gerald David Jaynes and Robin M. Williams, Jr., eds., *A Common Destiny: Blacks and American Society* (Washington, D.C.: National Academy

Press, 1989); Steven Shulman and William Darity, Jr., eds., *The Question of Discrimination: Racial Inequality in the U.S. Market* (Middletown, Conn.: Wesleyan University Press, 1989); Walter E. Williams, *South Africa's War Against Capitalism* (New York: Praeger, 1989); Just Faaland, J. R. Parkinson, et al., *Growth and Ethnic Inequality: Malaysia's New Economic Policy* (New York: St. Martin's Press, 1990); Irene Tinker, ed., *Persistent Inequalities: Women and World Development* (New York: Oxford University Press, 1990).

25. Richard Vedder, Lowell Gallaway, and David Klingman, "Black Exploitation and White Benefits: The Civil War Income Revolution," in America, *Wealth of Races.*

26. America, *Wealth of Races,* 118, compare with Browne's estimation above.

27. Ibid., 155.

28. Ibid., 155.

29. Ibid., 168.

30. "Economic Costs of Ethnic and Sex Discrimination in Middle Eastern Society—Exploration." Paper presented at the Middle East Studies Association Meetings, San Antonio, Texas, 13 November 1990. This is the source of data for this section unless otherwise noted.

31. The potential output might be higher if a separate calculation were made for Arab minority women, whose rate of participation is quite low in relation to the rate of participation of Jewish women.

5

Theories of Economic Discrimination

So far we have focused on and established the existence, variety, ubiquity, and costliness of racial, ethnic, and gender discrimination, nationally and internationally, over long periods of history. Now we must concern ourselves with explaining economic discrimination.

Economic theories of discrimination, which are relatively sparse and of recent origin, relate mostly to the labor market, wages, and prices. Theoretical formulations and models of discrimination as economic behavior did not receive much attention before the second half of this century. A lack of theoretical interest in discrimination may be attributed to at least three factors: the young age of economics as a discipline, the common misperception of economic discrimination as a product of noneconomic forces, and the historical acceptance of discrimination as expected, normal behavior, just as slavery seemed generally acceptable well into the nineteenth century.

Economics as a discipline goes back in history only a short time. Until the twentieth century, economics was intertwined with philosophy, politics, and social or moral subjects. To establish economics as a discipline, the tendency has been increasingly to concentrate on obvious economic behaviors and phenomena as fields of study and modeling. It also has seemed more convenient or efficient to stay away from issues of causality in trying to explain economic behavior. Instead, interest has focused on decomposing structures on the premise that knowing the components of a structure will explain its existence. Economics has also drifted toward abstract and quantitative issues that are difficult to apply to discrimination. Accordingly, discrimination has been seen as a "normal" form of behavior in an imperfect market, which therefore should be analyzed as part of the market mechanism. Inasmuch as economic analysis has emphasized models of perfect markets, homogeneous labor, income or utility maximization, and equilibria achievable through the forces of competition and demand and supply, there has been little room for the imperfections associated with the heterogeneity of a multiracial, multiethnic, and bi-gender labor force.

A second possible explanation for the apparent lack of theoretical interest is that discrimination is generally considered a sociological or psychopolitical phenomenon, which should be explained by sociological and psychological, rather than economic, theories and models. Given the increasing interest in specialization, specificity, and precision in the study of economic phenomena and behaviors, economists have little incentive to deal with such imprecise topics as discrimination.

Finally, economists, like most other people, are influenced by the social and institutional environment in which they live. The extent to which discrimination had, until recently, been legislated and accepted as normal behavior may have precluded any particular interest on the part of economists in trying to explain it. Slavery and the segregation of the blacks, exclusion of the Chinese, and underpayment to Chicanos in the United States were for a long time consistent with the laws of the land and with accepted norms of ethics and morality. Similarly, women in all cultures, as we have observed, have been treated as less than equals as a matter of course. Therefore, until discrimination became a target of political criticism as a violation of civil rights and a destabilizer of economic life, economists had no special reason to use their resources to study it. However, as soon as discrimination became a subject of controversy, challenged by civil rights movements, especially during the last half century, economic efficiency and racial/ethnic labor relations became legitimate topics of economic analysis. Several attempts have been made in the meantime to formulate theories and build economic models of discrimination.

ECONOMIC THEORIES OF DISCRIMINATION

Most existing theories of economic discrimination relate to the market or capitalist economy. Yet discrimination has prevailed in feudal, precapitalistic, and socialist economies, as well as in capitalism. The prevailing theories do not deal directly with those systems, although one may argue that economic theories and principles are universal concepts and instruments of analysis that apply to all situations at all times. However, to make such assumptions would betray doctrinal or ideological convictions rather than scientific truths or established empirical findings. It would also indicate a certain degree of preconditioning or prejudice on behalf of any scholar making those assumptions in a way that could bias the analysis. Actually such prejudice is implicit in the common tendency to classify theories of discrimination and their authors as conservative, liberal, or radical—all ideological categories with serious implications.

Our approach is different. We shall study economic discrimination within different economic systems in an attempt to explain it within each respective system, avoiding, to the extent possible, all value-loaded classifications. Accordingly, we shall try to explain discrimination as it relates to various economic systems and historical periods. To facilitate the analysis, we shall divide these systems into capitalist and noncapitalist systems. Inasmuch as theories dealing with the capitalist economies have been predominant, we shall begin with the capitalist system.

Economic Discrimination in a Capitalist Economic System

The capitalist economy is one in which capital is a prominent factor of production, profit-making is an ideal goal, and competition, private ownership of means of production, and wealth accumulation are legitimate and admired values. Various models of this economy may be specified, according to their degree of acceptance of the market mechanism as the dynamic force in the economy. Three main variations may be distinguished: market-orientation theories, market-regulation theories, and market-rejection theories.

Market-Orientation Theories

The theme of these theories is that the competitive market and rational behavior do not tolerate discrimination in the labor market for long. If certain employers, buyers, or sellers discriminate against certain racial, ethnic, or gender economic agents by refusing to deal with them, even when their replacement by others entails paying higher wages or other costs, their competitors who do not discriminate and are willing to hire lower-paid workers regardless of race, ethnicity, or sex, will be able to undersell them and drive them out of the market. Thus, competition should put an end to discrimination, as long as there are nondiscriminators who are willing to hire workers at lower wages regardless of race, ethnicity, or sex. This is the theory formulated by Gary Becker and expanded by Kenneth Arrow and others.[1] As Becker explains it, discriminators are assumed to have a "taste" for discrimination at the starting point, which they try to satisfy by excluding those to be discriminated against from the market, even though they may have to forgo potential profits in the process. However, they may satisfy their taste for discrimination by putting a value on it and then seeking compensation for not discriminating, either by underrewarding those whom they wish to discriminate against, or by obtaining some other form of compensation.

Becker estimates the value of the taste for discrimination, or "discrimination coefficient," to be equal to the difference between the wages of the favored and the wages of the discriminated-against workers. Thus, the discrimination coefficient may be represented as

$$DC = \frac{Wf\text{-}Wd}{Wd}$$

where w, f, d represent wages, favored, and discriminated-against, respectively.

An employer who discriminates will compensate the favored worker by paying him a higher wage than his/her marginal product (MP) to induce him/her to work with the workers he/she discriminates against, while penalizing the discriminated-against by paying him/her less than marginal product, so that $wf + wd = MPf + MPd$.

Becker also looks at the capital and labor markets of two groups, one favored and one discriminated against. Assuming that the favored community has relatively abundant capital and relatively scarce labor, and that the discriminated-against community has the opposite, so that

$$\frac{Cf}{Lf} > \frac{Cd}{Ld}$$

then $MPCf < MPCd$ and $MPLf > MPLd$, where C and L represent capital and labor respectively. If there is free trading of labor and capital, capital moves from the favored market in which it is abundant to the market in which it is discriminated-against but relatively scarce, and labor moves in the opposite direction. Assuming that Cx is the transferred capital, at equilibrium

$$\frac{Cd + Cf}{Ld} = \frac{Cf - Cx}{Lf} = \frac{C}{L}$$

where $C = Cf + Cd$ and $L = Lf + Ld$.

If there is discrimination against the movement of capital and labor so that the favored capital can receive more than its marginal return, and the disfavored labor can receive only less than its marginal return, mobility of both inputs will be discouraged and the economy in both markets will suffer because an efficient equilibrium will not be achievable. However, discrimination combined with mobility of capital and labor from the abundance to the scarcity market would generate higher marginal productivity to the mobile factor, with benefits to its owner and the loss of benefits to the owners of the nonmobile factor.

Discrimination, however, may emanate from workers who may have a taste for discrimination against workers from other racial, ethnic, or gender groups. If so, these discriminating workers will interact or transact with members of those other groups only if they are compensated for the psychic costs of being with them. For example, they may expect higher wages, lower rents, or lower prices for their purchases than they would have had to pay in order not to discriminate.

In all these cases, according to the market-orientation theory, if the market is allowed to function perfectly, discriminators who put a premium on psychic costs will eventually be driven out of the market, because nondiscriminators who hire lower-paid members of the groups whom the discriminators will not employ or deal with, will be able to produce at lower costs and make more profits than the discriminatory competitors. Put differently, potential discriminators may have a disincentive to discriminate because they know that they cannot bear the resulting losses for long.[2]

Becker's theory has been criticized and modified by a number of people. For example, Anne Krueger has pointed out that employers or decision-makers who take into consideration the welfare of their ethnic group as a whole, rather than their own self-interest, may discriminate regardless of compensation, and thus discrimination will continue. This, however, violates the market theory, in which individual self-interest is the driving incentive.[3]

Marcus Alexis raises a different question: How does Becker's theory explain discrimination by certain people against others with whom they do not associate physically? In this case one can hardly speak of a "psychic cost" for which one is to be compensated. Alexis suggests that discrimination may be based more on an "envy-malice" motivation than on "aversion" to association with the discriminated-against group. In such a case an employer may be willing to sacrifice profits by discriminating in order to enhance the welfare of his or her own favored group.

Barbara Bergmann sees the possibility of discriminating among equally qualified people by means of "occupational segregation," or division of labor by race, ethnicity, or gender, in such a manner that "overt" discrimination will not be "overt" or obvious, though discrimination will be just as real as if it were overt.[4]

Another attempt to explain why discrimination persists in the market-orientation economy suggests that the economic costs of labor to the discriminators, if any, tend to be slight because employers are able to offset them through modernization and technological innovation, which reduce dependence on labor. The less labor employed, the fewer instances of discrimination to be faced, and the lower the costs entailed tend to be. Even if the majority workers discriminate against members of a minority and refuse to work with them at first, employers may convince them to work together by paying the majority workers a little more than they otherwise would earn as compensation for the psychic hurt they suffer by violating their own taste for discrimination.[5] Given a reduced dependence on labor, these costs would still be bearable, and therefore discrimination could persist. This explanation, however, is consistent with Becker's theory because in the long run, even a slight cost could be sufficient to give the competitor an edge that would put the discriminators at a disadvantage and force them out of the market.

A two-part critique and elaboration of the market theory of discrimination comes from Kenneth Arrow: First, discrimination may persist because of rigidities built into the investment structure. Inasmuch as employers who discriminate may have invested heavily in an economy based on discrimination, they may find it too costly to dismantle the existing structure and erect a new one free of discrimination. In other words, they may get trapped, unable to eliminate discrimination on their own even if they wanted to. Eventually, their discriminatory behavior becomes institutionalized and expected. Second, certain groups may discriminate against others or treat them less equally because they honestly believe them to be inferior and therefore undeserving of equal treatment. In other words, because of a different "perception of reality," people who act rationally may discriminate because their rationality begins with a value system that includes prejudice.[6]

Ray Marshall raises many questions about the market-orientation theorists. First, they seem to be preoccupied more with theory than with reality. Second, they treat discrimination as an exogenous factor and hence fail to analyze it. Their results, therefore, tend to be mechanical; they hardly treat the causes of discrimination and hence reach "misleading policy suggestions."[7] Marshall, however, sees discrimination as related to status, not necessarily to wage rates—though he provides no evidence for this claim—and many of his criticisms are addressed to the omissions rather than to the contents of market-orientation theories. Unfortunately, Marshall does not propose an alternative theory, though he attempts to explain discrimination in terms of "an industrial organization or bargaining model," even though the discriminated-against workers rarely have options or bargaining power.[8]

Another bargaining theory of discrimination is Amartya Sen's interesting attempt to explain discrimination against women. According to his "cooperative conflict" model, parties in conflict sometimes find it to their advantage to cooperate with rather than oppose each other. Cooperation at least minimizes the loss or results in a lesser evil to the weaker party. Women within the household, seen by Sen as in conflict with men, cooperate by accepting a smaller entitlement because refusing to cooperate could put them in a worse bargaining position, cost them more of the entitlement, and possibly jeopardize their existence. This bargaining model is based on the following precepts: (1) A "breakdown well-being response" suggests that if a person feels that a breakdown of the cooperative game could lead to a worse-off position than the cooperative one, it would be rational to cooperate even at lower terms to avoid a breakdown. This means that the limited options available to women may force them into submission. (2) A "perceived interest response" suggests that by attaching "less value" to one's own well-being, one assumes a weaker bargaining position and thus would be willing to accept a lower entitlement. This means that socialization leading to self-deprecation is a factor in accepting discrimination. (3) A "perceived contribution response" suggests that those who are perceived as making larger contributions to the well-being of a group should be entitled to larger entitlements. Conversely, those who are perceived as contributing less, as women usually are, come to accept a relatively smaller entitlement than they deserve, as in marginal product/wage distribution models.[9] In all three situations, women are seen as weaker than men, and men take advantage of that position and try to gain wealth and power at their expense. How men and women acquire these precepts is a matter of education and socialization, which begin with the parents before a child is born.[10]

It may be noted that Sen's model is equally applicable to minority/majority discrimination situations as long as cooperation and bargaining are permissible. However, his assumptions regarding the male/female relationships apply more to the special than to the general case. Women are never in danger of losing all entitlement; losing it from one man, as in a divorce case, may be offset by gaining it from another, including a male relative in traditional societies; nor do they lose their knowledge, experience, and ability to earn an income. Furthermore, it is misleading to assume that conflict over entitlements is a normal condition in the home. In most situations there is an understanding upon marriage regarding the distribution of wealth and power, either by tradition, culture, or by contract. One has only to remember how mothers traditionally try to prepare their daughters for entering into a marriage relationship with acceptance and expectations of fulfillment rather than conflict. In other words, the model, though logical and theoretically useful, hardly applies to the inherent discriminatory behavior that characterizes male-female relationships.

A number of questions may still be raised with regard to the market-orientation theory. First, it is not clear whether compensation for psychic cost should be a higher economic benefit in absolute or relative terms. For example, suppose there is no discrimination and wages are equal to marginal product. Here comes agent A, who discriminates and would like to be compensated for working with agent B, a member of the group subject to discrimination. Will agent A insist on having a wage higher than the value of marginal product, or will he/she be satisfied if his/her wage remains equal to the marginal product, so long as agent B receives a wage lower than the value of the marginal product?

In the former case, agent A would be insisting on an absolute advantage; in the latter case, a relative advantage would be sufficient. In the former case the employer may have to reduce the wage of agent B in order to compensate agent A; in the latter he may have only to lower the wage of agent B and pocket the difference between that wage and the marginal product. The answer will determine whether an employer who discriminates does or does not benefit materially from discrimination. I propose that the prejudiced worker has no choice but to accept a relative advantage and let the employer pocket the surplus of marginal product over the wage of the worker subject to discrimination. In that case, the employer and the favored worker have incentives to practice discrimination.[11]

Another more general question is: If the market is capable of eliminating discrimination by driving the discriminators out, why has discrimination persisted? The simplest and most difficult hypothesis to test is that discrimination persists because the market is not perfect or because governments interfere in it. Because no market has ever been perfect or perfectly free from intervention, it is difficult to test any hypothesis based on this theory.

There are, however, other problems with the Becker-Arrow theory. For instance, it assumes rational decision-making in the labor and goods market, based on merit and negotiation among equals, which is never true in society or in the market economy. Economic agents that enter the market are neither homogeneous nor equals. Their differentiation includes both their inherited and acquired merits. Their inherited economic merits give them advantages or disadvantages and reinforce acquired differences so that their bargaining power becomes distorted and the gap between the favored and the disfavored is not only tolerated, but often increased and perpetuated. Minorities are most often among the disadvantaged at the starting point, and their falling behind tends to be sustained and lasting, as can be seen in various parts of the world. In other words, the perfect market theory may be logical and consistent, but it is not free of bias, nor is it operational or applicable in the real world. Racial, ethnic, and gender differences, presumed and enforced, tend to preclude equality of opportunity long before a worker's entry into the market, as will be argued in more detail in Chapter 6.

Market-Regulation Theories

Proponents of market-regulation theories are generally not in conflict with market-orientation theorists regarding the main principles, but they differ from them by noting that the market is not perfect and that imperfection allows discrimination to continue. Hence, they argue, it is necessary to regulate the market to correct the deficiencies and compensate for the discrimination. Gunnar Myrdal probably was the first to observe that poverty and discrimination are parts of a vicious cycle. Those who are discriminated against and deprived of opportunities for education, training, health, etc., stay poor and therefore cannot overcome the obstacles that stand in their way. Thus they continue to lack qualification and stay behind. The same theme has been echoed by Paul Samuelson, Arthur Okun, Lester Thurow, James Tobin, Michael Piore, and others. The argument centers around the fact that once members of racial and ethnic minorities (and women) are deprived of qualifications similar to those of the majority, members of the majority give the impression—and the expectation—that such minorities are less qualified than others. Therefore, they are passed over in employment, business opportunities, credit facilities, and other pre-conditions for economic advancement and equalization, and their poverty is perpetuated, because those attitudes, or what Kenneth Arrow has called "the perception of reality," become institutionalized and self-fulfilling.

There are, of course, variations among these scholars with regard to remedies. James Tobin, for example, sees discrimination as an "aberration" inconsistent with the market economy. Therefore, he emphasizes the importance of strengthening the economy and increasing employment so that even minorities will have employment. Michael Piore sees discrimination against women as a function of the belief that women are not career-oriented and therefore are not given equal opportunities with men, who are considered career-oriented. Over time women begin to act accordingly, and thus the vicious cycle is institutionalized. This cumulative process, however, can be changed, Piore suggests, if governments discourage discrimination and start a process in the opposite direction.[12]

It is important to note that the arguments of these theories are based on the belief that differences in merits and capabilities between minorities and majorities, or between men and women, are acquired and not genetic. They are created by society and its institutions. The individuals demonstrating those differences have little choice in the matter. The institutions of society and the economy tend to encourage the continuation of unequal opportunities, which undermines the capabilities of minorities, and discrimination against them continues on the assumption that merit is the criterion for reward and that minorities are less meritorious and therefore must be rewarded at a lower rate than the majority. One argument bolstering this explanation is that the institutions of education, health, and employment tend to foster unequal opportunities and amenities and thus perpetuate discrimination. Therefore, only through the transformation of these institutions by the authorities will discrimination be overcome.

Probably the most explicit of these theories is presented by Lester Thurow. According to this theory, racial discrimination usually occurs within a given society because of the monopoly or monopsony powers of the discriminators. The inability of disfavored groups to gain entry into certain economic sectors gives the discriminators advantages inconsistent with competitive markets. The enforcement of discrimination "comes from the interlocking nature of the different types of discrimination" in different sectors of the economy and from community and social pressures. To end discrimination, therefore, government action may be necessary to break the monopoly powers of the discriminators.[13] While such theories are not in conflict with the market-orientation theories, they and the policies based on them tend to be more realistic and more applicable in dealing with discrimination.

Market-Rejection Theories

Usually called radical theories of discrimination, market-rejection theories are sometimes associated with leftism, socialism, and Marxism. The main idea of these theories is that racial discrimination is caused by and is inherent in market capitalism because discrimination is profitable to capitalists. In that sense, discrimination is economically motivated. Market capitalists, according to these theories, tend to separate people (workers) according to race, ethnicity, or sex, in order to divide their ranks, weaken their bargaining power, and realize extraordinary profits by underrewarding all workers. In contrast to majority employers, majority workers tend to lose as a result of discrimination because it separates them from minority workers, thereby weakening their bargaining power, and thus reduces their potential earnings. In essence these theories see discrimination as motivated by class conflict and profit expectations, both of which are nurtured by capitalism and market forces. Therefore, the way out for workers of both minorities and majorities is to unite against the discriminating capitalists and deprive them of the power to discriminate.[14]

It is not clear at this point whether, according to the market-rejection theories, a perfect capitalist market would preclude such exploitation of workers, since the market does little to remove the inequalities existing at the starting point. On the other hand, these theories seem to confuse class exploitation with racial, ethnic, and gender discrimination. Observations of various societies suggest that discrimination against minorities exists within economic classes and not between them. For example, white employers discriminate against black employers, even though they both belong to the same income group or economic class. Likewise, workers from majorities discriminate against workers from minorities, even though they both belong to the same economic class.

Noncapitalist Theories of Discrimination

The theories discussed so far say little regarding discrimination in precapitalist or postcapitalist economies, especially regarding discrimination in socialist or communist economies. Yet, there is little doubt that discrimination predates capitalism, and it has existed in socialist economies of the twentieth century in which the market has virtually been nonexistent. Therefore, to be able to explain discrimination in other and more general situations, we need to look elsewhere for a theoretical foundation. First we shall look at socialism and economic discrimination, then at a more general statistical-positivist theory, and then at my "gain, accumulation, and power" theory of discrimination.

Socialism and Economic Discrimination

As an economic system, socialism ideally is a nonmarket system in the sense that economic decisions are made by plan, not in the marketplace. Under socialism all individuals are equal, given the slogan "from each according to ability, to each according to contribution," or to "need" under communism as the last stage of socialism. In this system there is no private property, no profit-making, no private accumulation of wealth, and therefore no material basis for a private economic power structure. People cannot gain power over others through income and wealth distribution. Thus, while planned socialism is similar to the ideal market system, being blind to racial, ethnic, or gender differences, and therefore intolerant of economic discrimination, it differs from the market system by not allowing one person to profit by discriminating against another. Individuals, being neither employers nor profit-makers, have no chance to realize material gains by discriminating against others, nor can they make profit at the expense of the aggregate economy. They may steal from the economy or cheat the public employer, but they have no incentive to discriminate against racial, ethnic, or gender groups for economic reasons. If exploitation prevails, it is due to imperfections in implementation of the socialist system, and it takes the form of class exploitation, regardless of race, ethnicity, or gender.

This doctrinal or philosophical nondiscriminatory position can be enforced or compromised by the economic plan. A socialist economic plan may, of course, have biases such as favoring industrial against agricultural workers, urbanites against rural people, or party members against others. But racial, ethnic, or gender affiliation cannot be a cause for discrimination, given the principles or philosophy of the system. Another view of Marxian socialism is that discrimination can be overcome by class solidarity, which is inherent in socialism. To permit discrimination would undermine class solidarity and jeopardize efforts to abolish classes, which is a major objective of Marxian socialism. Hence, discrimination cannot be tolerated.[15]

Yet, some might ask: how is it that the Soviet politburo has always been a male institution? How is it that the Jews have been discriminated against? In one sense, positions on the politburo do not involve economic power, and therefore exclusion from them does not entail economic discrimination. Furthermore, there is no indication that Jews are discriminated against in economic terms. On the other hand, the biased treatment of women in Soviet Russia may be explained either as a survival of past (presocialist) traditions or by imperfections in the system, but not because of material objectives. Even more important, the Soviets never achieved the stage of communism, nor did they apply the socialism model fully.

The Israeli kibbutz or collective settlement is another good illustration of socialism in practice in which the basic principles of equality were applied but have been corrupted over time. Interestingly enough, as soon as the economies of Soviet Russia, Eastern Europe, and the Israeli kibbutz started to lean toward the market system—private ownership, profit-making, and the accumulation of wealth—discrimination became evident, especially against women, as has been illustrated above. One should note, however, that the kibbutz community compromised the philosophy of equality by failing to apply equality to other ethnic groups interacting with them. Arabs working in the kibbutz, for example, were never given equal treatment compared with Jewish workers.[16]

An interesting attempt to study discrimination in Soviet Russia is a survey of Jewish émigrés in Israel who came from different parts of the Soviet Union. According to 82% of those interviewed, people were conscious of their ethnic affiliation. When they approached an official for a service, ethnic origin seemed to make a difference. Two-thirds of the respondents said that managers and supervisors tended to favor their own nationality. Two-thirds felt that people were treated "less well" outside their home republics, although this was contrary to the feeling of an equal number of respondents who felt that Jews were not treated differently outside their area of residence. In contrast, nationalities were proportionally distributed in the workplace, and none seemed to have a disproportionate representation among managers and supervisors, although overall, directors may have come mostly from the majority nationality in the state or locality. Whether these directors were any less qualified for the job than others is not indicated.[17] What we observe in these experiences is a contradiction between the principles of a socialist economy and their application in the treatment of minorities and women.

Statistical-Positivist Theory

According to this theory, discrimination is not a question of market or plan, but a matter of fact. What appears as discrimination is simply due to evident features of minorities and female groups. To the extent that certain minority groups or women are observed to be less meritorious than majority groups and males in the marketplace, discrimination is a shortcut mechanism to minimize costs while screening for better-qualified workers, more responsible tenants, or more promising students. Choosing members of the majority groups or males in preference to minority groups or females may thus be seen as discrimination, even though it is just a way of cutting costs, reducing risks, and augmenting the viability of an economic activity.

In other words, discrimination in this case is explained as a matter of economic efficiency and not of prejudice. For example, if blacks or female workers are considered less skilled or productive than white or male workers, employers will automatically seek white or male workers in the belief that such action is rational and profit-maximizing. However, for minority groups and females, such behavior must be considered prejudicial and discriminatory, since the individual member of the minority is judged not by merit but by the behavior of a statistical average or the frequency of occurrence of the phenomenon under discussion.[18] That the distribution of merit among minorities and women may resemble that found among majorities and men is not given sufficient consideration, nor is it acknowledged that each individual is a unique person who cannot be judged accurately on the basis of an average. On the contrary, this theory leads to the conclusion that the mean scores on merit or the norms among minorities and women are definitely lower than those among the majority and men and therefore justify differential treatment, which in itself is a biased and prejudicial judgment.

Gain, Accumulation, and Power Theory of Discrimination

In his attempt to explain ethnic stratification, Donald L. Noel identifies three factors that are necessary for discrimination to take place: ethnocentrism, competition for resources, and differential power. "Without ethnocentrism the groups would quickly merge . . . without competition there would be no motivation . . . without differential power it would simply be impossible for one group to achieve dominance."[19] But where do these factors originate? There should be a reason for the existence of ethnocentrism, competition, and differential power. In the rest of this section I shall attempt to answer this question through a theory of economic gain, accumulation, and power as the motive for discrimination.[20]

According to this model, economic discrimination exists only if economic benefits accrue to those who discriminate. Such benefits are indicators of success in societies in which the dominant philosophy of society considers self-interest and competition legitimate means to realize gain, accumulate it, and utilize it as a source of power. In a society where scarcity is avowed and the gain of one person is the loss of another, it is generally legitimate for one to acquire gain and accumulate it, secure power as a result, and use it to achieve further gain and accumulation. Furthermore, to realize these objectives by the least costly method, it has been considered legitimate and rational to use power against the less powerful and least resistant. Since females and certain racial and ethnic groups are traditionally perceived as less powerful and are easy to identify, they become the target of discrimination by the more powerful groups.

The philosophy of gain, accumulation, and power is sustained by those in power, who establish institutions, make laws, formulate regulations, and create precedents so as to legitimize behaviors consistent with that philosophy. The laws of property, ownership, and inheritance are the most conspicuous of these institutions. Furthermore, these institutions are usually reinforced by an administrative machinery or government that implements the laws and regulations. It is important to note that government itself is both an institution that reflects the predominant philosophy on which society is based and a mechanism that enforces the laws and sustains the institution. Enforcement depends on the field workers or on those who carry out the day-to-day affairs of government, presumably because they also agree with that philosophy and its institutions. Therefore, society functions effectively through the process of socialization, which prepares its members to accept its philosophy, respect its institutions, and make the enforcement of its laws and regulations by the government and field workers possible. As long as these four components—the philosophy, the institutions, the administrative machinery, and the field workers—are in harmony with each other, the expected behaviors will be exercised by members of society. Disharmony between these components will cause conflict to erupt and the expected behavior will cease until harmony is restored.

The gain, accumulation, and power theory of discrimination suggests that discrimination has been embedded in the philosophy of our society, which admires the realization of economic benefits, even if obtained by discrimination against weaker members of society. This philosophy has been sustained because it accrues benefits to powerful segments in society, and because our socioeconomic and political institutions support and reinforce the philosophy of discrimination by rendering the behavior based on it as normal and by taking its control out of the hands of individuals. Those who oppose it, even among the majority group, often find themselves under socioeconomic pressure that makes them incapable of changing even their own behavior without incurring heavy penalties.

To illustrate how this model explains economic discrimination, let us look at three major institutions: government and the law (including the systems of tenure, private ownership, and inheritance), the credit system, and the educational system.

Government and the Law

Regardless of the economic system, government, both as an institution and as an instrument of enforcement, usually represents the majority in society in the sense of power and control distribution. In a feudal system or in a multiparty democracy, government reflects the philosophy of the majority in power terms. It pools the policy-makers from the majority, and it protects the privileges of those whom it represents. Most governments, however, declare it their responsibility to protect the rights of minorities, but only as those rights are formulated and interpreted by the majority itself. If the majority opposes change in the institutions and their accepted interpretation, the executive branch of government will continue to enforce the guidelines of behavior dictated by those institutions. The legislative branch of government passes the laws that formalize the philosophy of society and establish the basis on which those institutions are built.

Slavery was legal because it was approved and legitimized by the governments of the countries in which it existed. Had the Civil War in the United States not taken place, it is doubtful that slavery would have been voted out when it was. Segregation in the United States and apartheid in South Africa were legalized by the (power) majority governments. The laws of inheritance and the laws protecting private ownership and wealth are passed by the majority. Restrictions on ethnic and alien minorities and limits on entitlements to women are the work of government and of the majority. Women's rights of inheritance in Islamic countries are half of those of men, and they are enforced by the government.

The government is an employer, a producer, and a consumer. Its behavior sets the pace for society. To the extent that key positions in government are held by members of the majority, the private sector finds it convenient to comply, or at least to resist change as long as its interests are protected. Even where the letter of the law may be against discrimination, the spirit of the law has to be expressed by interpreting and enforcing it. The interpreters and enforcers are parts of the machinery of government, which represents the majority. Thus members of the minority are either excluded from public positions, as were the Jews throughout Europe for centuries, or restricted to lower and menial jobs, as are blacks and Hispanics in the United States, Arabs in Israel, North Africans in France, and Indians and Pakistanis (coloreds) in Britain.[21] All these minorities have usually been legal residents of the countries in which they face discrimination. The government, which is based on the philosophy of the majority and serves its interests, enforces, or at least tolerates, discrimination against minorities, and thus makes it possible for discrimination to continue.

The laws of tenure and inheritance, whether by exclusion or by restriction of the size of the entitlement of certain groups, tend to augment the interests of those with economic power and perpetuate their dominance. In many countries, minorities have been prohibited from owning property, as were black slaves in the United States and Jews in Europe, or they have been excluded from ownership in certain areas, as were the blacks of South Africa under apartheid and aliens in most of the Middle Eastern countries, even though they may be legal residents of those countries. Such restrictions are legalized by the institutions and enforced by the government. Thus the privileges or rights of the majority to gain, accumulate, and sustain power are denied to minorities simply because they are ethnically different or because they are aliens, such as Arabs from one Arab country residing in another Arab country.

Women, on the other hand, are often left out of inheritance by custom, which is an important institution, even though the laws of their country may not deprive them of the right of inheritance. For example, in most Middle Eastern countries, women are expected to surrender their inheritance to their male siblings, in order to keep the family wealth intact "within the family," for a woman married to a different family is considered lost to her nuclear family. On the other hand, as noted aabove, Muslim law limits the inheritance of women to half that of men and such law is enforced by the courts. The British system of primogeniture shares this discriminatory feature against women. By definition such limitations perpetuate the power of men over women because women's control over resources is limited for no reason other than their gender. The power majority and the government that represents its philosophy are the most solid foundations on which discrimination survives.

The Credit System

Whether we go back to medieval Europe and the Middle East or we come to contemporary Europe and the New World, we find that ethnic minorities and women have had limited access to credit. Even Jews, who are historically known to include major financiers and bankers, have had difficulty securing credit from banks, and financial institutions other than their own. The method of restricting access is simple: the terms and conditions for lending are usually set beyond the reach of minorities. Women are often restricted by laws and regulations classifying them as minors and requiring male cosigners to approve loans or conclude contracts for them. Limited access to credit means limited access to earning opportunities, and it discriminates against minorities and women solely because of their ethnicity or gender. These restrictions, which exclude potential borrowers, tend to reduce the demand for credit, keeping the rates lower than they would otherwise be, thus favoring majority borrowers. Even majority creditors, who may lose customers and profits in the short run by practicing discrimination, gain in the long run by catering to the majority that controls wealth and power. The impact of a biased credit system is cumulative, because it tends to sustain and expand the gap between the economic opportunities of the majority and those of minorities.

The System of Education

Education within the family, at school, or in society at large is the most important institution to reinforce or deinforce discrimination. As long as children are brought up to believe that gain, accumulation, and power are legitimate and worthy aspirations, that aliens and minorities are less than equal, or that males are more capable and deserving than females, discrimination in society will be perpetuated. In fact, a member of a minority or a female child may grow up to believe that he/she is less deserving and less capable than a member of the majority or a male child. In these circumstances minority and female children grow up to expect discriminatory behavior, and even to accept it as "fair" in a given society, just as those who accept inequality of income and wealth distribution as normal have no difficulty accepting and revering the rich in their societies.

Because educational socialization is probably the most important cementing factor in society, those who control the educational institutions control social and economic behavior for generations to come. The traditional impact of education on discrimination has been to perpetuate it, as is illustrated by the movie "Separate but Equal," which shows how American black children attending segregated and inferior schools grow up to believe that white children are more beautiful and more desirable than black children. It also shows how these children's feelings of inferiority generate an acceptance of discrimination against them as normal behavior.

Another illustration of the process by which socialization leads to an acceptance of discrimination is presented by Hanna Papanek, who shows that by receiving less than their male siblings, female children grow up to expect and accept less than male children.[22] This pattern of socializing females to accept less than males is still common in the Arab world, especially in distributing access to school, if girls are lucky enough to be sent to school at all. The reward system in society is itself a part of the educational institutions that reinforce and perpetuate differential rewards in favor of males and majorities.

In an elaborate discussion of female education in developing countries, Ester Boserup argues that the design of education by families and educational institutions tends to bias business and employment opportunities against females. On one hand, females are directed into certain economic activities and given fewer opportunities to acquire skills. On the other hand, their expectations are directed away from industrial, highly skilled, and highly rewarded activities. As a result, their levels of productivity tend to be lower than those of male competitors. They also tend to become more accepting of masculine bias as a normal condition with which they have to live. They even grow sometimes to defend it and make room for male workers to occupy jobs they themselves might be equally capable of filling. Hence, discrimination becomes accepted as a normal behavior, with chronic and self-sustaining effects on future generations.[23] These various institutions are sustained by an enforcement mechanism. For instance, the schools or educational institutions have their own reward and punishment mechanisms, which serve to enforce conformity, especially among those who may not be true believers in the philosophy that sustains or tolerates discrimination.

The family is once again a major player in the drama of preparing for stability in the economy and society on the basis of differential treatment of ethnic minorities and females. Punishment rather than reward is the common practice by which one growing up in the family is harmonized with the philosophy of the larger society and the economy. The family prepares a child for his or her place in the market and business (or out of it) and on the accepted scale of distribution of opportunities for gain, accumulation, and power. Those who refuse to conform are often the objects of scandal or ridicule. Children of ethnic minorities are thus prepared for "their place" in the economy and society. Some, such as Jews, Asians, and Arabs in the United States, are geared to high education, finance, and the professions. In contrast, smaller percentages of blacks and Latinos are prepared for these specializations. This difference may be due largely to differential wealth and income distribution, but it is also due to the perceptions of each of these minorities of their status in the economy and society. Thus, the pattern of occupational distribution and differential treatment of minorities and females tends to be enforced by the family, and violations are preempted by parents while their offspring are still dependent minors.[24]

To illustrate the relationship between expected economic gain, accumulation, and power and the existence of discrimination against weaker groups, or those who have been described as minorities, let us look at some representative historical experiences.[25]

The enslavement of the weak and alien is an old practice, sometimes applied to those of the same racial affiliation, as when blacks enslaved blacks, but only to those who are aliens (of a different ethnic origin), as can be observed in the ancient world and in medieval and early modern Africa. In all these cases enslavement was usually practiced for material gain.[26]

Discrimination against aliens was common in the cities of medieval Europe. Merchants who came from other cities or countries to trade and conduct business were usually restricted in terms of economic activities, location, and residence. They usually had to pay special fees to be able to trade outside their own cities, because each city discriminated against aliens in favor of its own people, regardless of merit, quality of merchandise, or level of prices. In fact, the history of the medieval and early modern periods, especially in Europe, is replete with evidence of the differential treatment of alien merchants by the citizens and authorities of the host cities and countries to which they traveled. The histories of the Hanseatic League of German cities and of the capitulations within the Ottoman Empire leave little doubt that discrimination was associated with ethnic origin, differential power distribution, and the expectation of material gain as a result. As the Hanseatic League became stronger, its merchants started to enjoy preferential treatment abroad. Similarly, European merchants in the Ottoman Empire at first sought permission to trade in the empire, which was often given to them as a favor by the Ottoman sultans. However, as the power of European countries increased and the power of the Ottoman Empire declined, the favor conferred became an expectation and eventually an imposition, so that European merchants often received more economic benefits than the native merchants.[27]

The story of discrimination against aliens for economic gain is repeated and crystallized in Europe in the period known as mercantilism or the early modern period, 1500-1700 A.D. The budding nation-states made it their business to give preferential economic treatment to their citizens and nationals against other ethnic or national groups. Such treatment was reflected in trade protectionism in favor of nationals, prohibition or restriction of imports, exclusion of aliens, and even endorsed piracy against "aliens" on the high seas. Those affected were usually private merchants, and they were treated badly just because of their alien origin, as clearly illustrated by the Navigation Acts and similar laws of the seventeenth century enforced by Britain, France, Spain, and other countries. A classic case of discrimination against Jews is illustrated by their treatment in Poland in the early modern period. They were blamed for the successes and failures of the economy, for the implementation and viability of the Second Serfdom, for good management of the economy and for its failure to develop along Western patterns of the period. After being encouraged to deal with money and finance, they were fined and their wealth was confiscated, with little reason other than their being Jews.[28]

The climax of discriminatory behavior because of racial and ethnic origin and weakness of the "other" party was reached in the reinvention of slavery of the African black peoples by the whites of Europe and the New World. The ethnic and racial differences, the differential power distribution between the slavers and the slaves and their national protectors, and the expected material gain were sufficient incentives for slavery to flourish. The severity of discrimination against blacks far surpassed any experience of discrimination in Europe and the West since the decline of the Roman Empire. Blacks were not considered human beings worthy of human treatment and compassion. They were regarded as barbaric and savage, to be used as chattels, capital, and a source of gain. Any care or attention given to blacks in that period was mainly in the form of charity or to protect the capital investment they embodied. The story of black slavery is well known, but what is not easily recognized is that it was the culmination of a long period of cumulative experiences of racial and ethnic discrimination extending over centuries, stimulated largely by the expectation of economic gain, accumulation, and power. In fact, slavery was not considered inconsistent with the principles of democracy, equality, and freedom professed by the enslaving majority and the institutions of society that catered to their welfare. Such discrimination was in harmony with the philosophy of gain, accumulation, and power.

To sum up, we may conclude that economic discrimination against racial and ethnic groups in the precapitalistic economies of Europe was widespread and supported by the authorities. Such discrimination was usually associated with or dependent on the existence of ethnic differences, differential power distribution, and high expectations of material gain by those practicing discrimination.

Since early times discrimination against racial and ethnic minorities and women for gain, accumulation, and power has been a standard form of behavior in most countries of the world as demonstrated in Chapters 2 and 3. The treatment of the Chinese and other Asians in the United States, the North Africans in France, and the Indians and Pakistanis in Britain is a clear illustration of such discriminatory behavior in the "most democratic" countries in the world. However, the most sinister forms of racial discrimination in recent times have been the Nazi philosophy of Aryan superiority and that practiced by the whites of South Africa. The former led to the extermination of the Jews in Europe and the confiscation of their properties; the latter led to apartheid, which transferred most of the wealth of the country to white hands at the expense of the minority blacks.[29] The discriminators in both instances had gain, accumulation, and power incentives, in addition to the psychological and social gratification they derived from discrimination.

Similarly, the discrimination against women by men has been based on institutions and authorities that were created by men. By restricting women's freedom of choice and decision-making, their education and training, and their choice of occupation, and by distributing to them lesser rewards for performance in the economy, society has consistently treated women as inferior to men. Such discrimination has been possible because men have had the power, control of the material resources, and the expectation that discrimination against women will sustain and enhance male privileges. The philosophy of discrimination against women or of the fictitious superiority of men is entrenched in the institutions of society.

Ironically, discrimination against black female slaves in favor of male slaves was not practiced by slaveholders and traders. Males and females were equally dehumanized, reduced to the level of chattels, and traded only in accordance with the prospects of earning income or profit for their owner. A female slave, being a human breeder, might have been sold for a higher price than a male, or she might have been better protected by her owner because of the expected high value of her offspring. In any case, once dehumanization had been imposed, gender discrimination became unnecessary: both male and female would be traded for the highest possible price. However, within the black slave community, women might have been discriminated against by black male slaves.[30]

These observations indicate that while discrimination in the modern period has been associated in economic literature with capitalism, racial, ethnic, and gender discrimination predate capitalism. However, in the capitalist period it has been easier to identify discriminatory behavior, to speak against it, and thus to increase awareness of its existence. In the shop and in the economy at large, against racial and ethnic minorities and against women, precapitalist as well as capitalist economic discrimination has been closely associated with material gain and higher profits, both of which have been highly valued by society.

CONCLUSIONS

Economic theory has not been forthcoming in trying to explain economic discrimination against racial, ethnic, or gender groups. Most available theories have been related to market capitalism, either directly or indirectly. On one hand are theories that claim that a capitalist market economy has no tolerance for discrimination. Elaborations of this theory suggest that market imperfections, including monopoly and monopsony power, render the market incapable of eliminating discrimination. Hence, government intervention becomes necessary to cope with it.

In contrast, radical or political economy theories tend to explain discrimination as a result of capitalism, primarily as a form of class conflict, even though racial, ethnic, and gender discrimination is evident within classes and has predated capitalism.

Other theories discussed include a statistical existential approach, which says simply that differential treatment of minorities is a fact, differences between ethnic groups in performance are a fact, and differential treatment is consistent with observed differences in efficiency and performance. Accordingly, no theory is necessary to explain these facts, since the evident differential treatment is rational, not prejudicial.

Another theory that tries to explain the treatment of women by men is a bargaining theory that proposes a conflict-cooperation model. Women, or the weaker party, fearing that by not cooperating they may lose more, tend to cooperate as a way of coping with the conflict and assuring themselves a part of the entitlement, or they simply accept the inevitable. The assumptions on which this theory is based, however, are not entirely realistic.

None of these theories delves deeply enough to explain why discrimination exists in the first place. That a "taste" for discrimination exists is a convenient assumption, but it does not help to explain the motives or reasons for discrimination or the origins of that taste. To deal with this problem I have introduced a "gain, accumulation, and power" theory, which states that discrimination originates in the incentives sanctioned by the philosophy of society, is bolstered by institutions that support that philosophy, and is upheld by an administrative machinery that implements policies based on it. The motives are material gain and the acquisition of power. Where material gain and accumulation are not inherent in the philosophy of society, as in a socialist system, economic discrimination becomes impossible, though other forms of discrimination may prevail as means of power acquisition. This theory also suggests that a purely economic theory may not be capable of explaining discrimination. An interdisciplinary model seems more capable of such an explanation. The question, however, remains as to what sustains discrimination and why it does not go away, even when policymakers say they are trying to abolish it. To that we shall turn next.

NOTES

1. Gary Becker, *The Economics of Discrimination*, 2d ed. (Chicago: University of Chicago Press, 1977), Chs. 1-2; Ray Marshall, "The Economics of Racial Discrimination: A Survey," *Journal of Economic Literature* XII (1974): 850-52, provides a comprehensive bibliography.

2. Michael L. Wyzan, ed., *The Political Economy of Ethnic Discrimination and Affirmative Action* (New York: Praeger, 1990), xxii.

3. Marshall, "Economics of Racial Discrimination," 851. Anne O. Krueger, "The Economics of Discrimination," *Journal of Political Economy* 71 (October 1963): 481-86.

4. Marshall, "Economics of Racial Discrimination," 852-53.

5. Barbara Bergmann, "The Effects on White Income of Discrimination in Employment," *Journal of Political Economy* 79, (March-April 1971): 295.

6. Kenneth J. Arrow, "Models of Job Discrimination," in Anthony H. Pascal, ed., *Racial Discrimination in Economic Life* (Lexington, Mass.: Heath, 1972); Stanley Masters, *Black-White Income Differentials: Empirical Studies and Policy Implications* (New York: Academic Press, 1975), Ch. 1.

7. Marshall, "Economics of Racial Discrimination," 859.

8. Ibid., 866-71.

9. Amartya Sen, "Gender and Cooperative Conflict," in Irene Tinker, ed., *Persistent Inequality: Women and World Development* (New York: Oxford University Press, 1990), 135-36.

10. For more on this, see Hanna Papanek, "To Each Less Than She Needs, From Each More Than She Can Do: Allocations, Entitlements, and Value," in Tinker, *Persistent Inequality*, 162-81.

11. Arrow, however, considers the effects of discrimination on the employer's profits. Applying the discrimination coefficient measure, he shows that the employer will realize profits to the degree to which the discrimination coefficient paid to the favored workers is equal to or less than the discrimination coefficient suffered by the disfavored workers. If the two coefficients are equal, there will be zero profits, but if the discriminating coefficient suffered by the disfavored exceeds that received by the favored, the employer will realize profits from discrimination.

12. Gunnar Myrdal, *An American Dilemma: The Negro Problem and Modern Democracy* (New York: Harper 1944); James Tobin, "On Improving the Economic Status of the Negro," *Daedalus*, reprinted in Paul Samuelson, ed., *Readings in Economics* (New York: McGraw-Hall, 1973); James Coleman, *Equality of Educational Opportunity* (Washington, D.C.: U.S. Department of Health, Education, and Welfare, 1966); Robert Cherry, *Discrimination: Its Economic Impact on Blacks, Women, and Jews* (Lexington, Mass.: Lexington Books, 1989); Ch. 3 summarizes what he calls the liberal view.

13. Cherry, *Discrimination*, 124-30.

14. David M. Gordon, ed., *Problems of Political Economy: An Urban Perspective*, 2d ed. (Lexington, Mass.: Heath, 1977); Part 3, which focuses on race, is probably the most comprehensive representation of this school of thought on discrimination. See also Cherry, *Discrimination*, Ch. 4, on the radical view.

15. Wyzan, *Political Economy*, xxiii.

16. I have interviewed Arabs working in a *kibbutz* in the Galilee in Israel. I remember one worker in particular who was paid the highest possible wage in the *kibbutz*. He was not allowed a vote in policy-making nor was he given the same rights of retirement or other benefits accorded to Jewish members. In fact, he was not allowed to become a member of the collective, although he was the most skilled technician in the metal factory.

17. Zvi Gitelman, "The Politics of Ethnicity and Affirmative Action in the Soviet Union," in Wyzan, *Political Economy*, 167-81.

18. Edmund S. Phelps, "The Statistical Theory of Racism and Sexism," *American Economic Review* 62 (1972): 659-61; Cherry, *Discrimination*, 37.

19. Donald L. Noel, "A Theory of the Origin of Ethnic Stratification," in William Barclay, Krishna Kumar, and Ruth P. Simms, *Racial Conflict, Discrimination, and Power* (New York: AMS Press, 1976), 64.

20. For a general view of the model, see E. H. Tuma, "Why Problems Do Not Go Away: The Problem of Inflation," *Journal of European Economic History* 11 (Fall 1982), especially 473-82.

21. For the story of Britain, see Sheila Rule, "Black Britons Describe a Motherland that has Long Held Them as Inferior," *New York Times*, 31 March 1991.

22. Papanek, "To Each Less."

23. Ester Boserup, *Women's Role in Economic Development* (New York: St. Martin' Press, 1970), especially Ch. 12.

24. Certain individuals break away from this constrained framework, but the majority among those discriminated against remain trapped, and thus discrimination is perpetuated.

25. Some of this material may overlap slightly with contents of Chapter 2.

26. D. Lange, "The Kingdoms and Peoples of Chad," in D. T. Niane, *General History of Africa*, IV, UNESCO (London: Heinemann, 1981), 250; M. Adamu, "The Hausa and Their Neighbors in the Central Sudan," in Niane, *General History*, 299.

27. On the Hanseatic League, see my *European Economic History: Tenth Century to the Present* (Palo Alto, Calif.: Pacific Books, Publishers, 1979), Ch. 8; on the capitulations see my "The Economic Impact of the Capitulations: The Middle East and Europe: A Reinterpretation," *Journal of European Economic History* 18, no. 3 (Winter 1989): 663-82.

28. Hillel Levine, *Economic Origins of Anti-Semitism: Poland and Its Jews in Early Modern Poland* (New Haven, Conn.: Yale University Press, 1991); see also my *European Economic History* on interpretation, Chs. 11-14. Though some may question the validity of Levine's interpretation, the facts of discrimination and economic gain as a result can hardly be disputed.

29. Apartheid is being dismantled as an institution today, but its economic effects are still intact.

30. In the absence of adequate information on male-female economic relations within a slave community, in which neither could achieve economic gain or accumulate wealth, it is not feasible to address this point in any detail.

Dealing With Discrimination

The political-economic problem of minorities has been a constant in state affairs almost throughout history. Treatment of a minority, whether its distinguishing characteristics are racial, ethnic, religious, or sexual, has often had an economic impact. Most frequently the "special" treatment of minorities has had negative effects in at least two ways: it has disrupted economic activity, leading to waste and inefficiency, and it has biased the distribution of opportunities and rewards in favor of certain groups.

Concern for the individual members of minorities has been a recent phenomenon, dating back only to the Enlightenment, the Age of Reason, and the American and French revolutions. Such concern has been most notably associated with the Industrial Revolution in Europe, as competition, self-interest, and materialism made exploitation of the weak a dominant mode of behavior in the expanding economies of the West.

Awareness of the problems facing individual members of society did not always translate into action, improve conditions of those individuals, or remove prejudice against them. The dissociation between awareness and positive action can best be illustrated by the treatment of women (as a minority in terms of power). As groups and as individuals, women and their concerns were not taken seriously until recent decades. Only then did they begin to vote, participate in the labor force, and expect to be rewarded on more equal terms than they had been in past years.

Both awareness of and action against discrimination are related directly to the role minorities play in the economy and to their resistance to discrimination, especially as civil rights action groups. Measures to remove discrimination have been stimulated mainly by internal forces such as sociopolitical movements, changes in market conditions, or opportunities to realize benefits or reduce costs to the discriminating majority. The external forces against discrimination have had only a slow and indirect impact.

The message of the Enlightenment, for example, was too abstract to directly affect social and economic minority relations. The American and French revolutions resulted in idealistic documents favoring the majority. To apply to the minority, these documents needed reinterpretation, because they seemed to be racio-ethno-andro-centric. They represented the interests of white males, the dominant majority in the Western world. That is why forces against discrimination were inadequate to protect minority rights, such as those of Jews in Europe and the United States, blacks in the United States before and after emancipation, and women in most countries.

Furthermore, these new philosophies had few positive effects for minorities until they were invoked by minority demands and actions. Indeed, until such demands and actions became intensive and threatening to the majority, little improvement in the position of minorities and women could be discerned. The twentieth century, largely the second half of it, has been the era of fighting against discrimination in various parts of the world.

A significant feature of the "fight" against discrimination is the variety of approaches pursued by the authorities in public policy and action, which will be the focus of our present analysis. Whether discrimination is legal (as in slavery or gender treatment), or illegal, its reduction has resulted largely from formal action by the authorities. Laws to end discrimination may be passed, but they will have little impact on the status of minorities, or on discriminating behavior of the majority, unless they are enforced and reflected in public and interpersonal relations. We shall be concerned in this chapter with public policy toward discrimination, as well as with its interpretation and enforcement, especially in economic relations between majorities and minorities and between men and women. Though our concern is mainly with economic discrimination, we shall look also at its legal, social, and political dimensions to put economic relations in the right perspective, nationally and internationally.

MEASURES AND POLICIES

The impact on minorities and women of measures against discrimination have ranged from extremely negative to extremely positive. Certain measures have been international in scope and relevance, but most have been national and internal. It is my impression that most of these measures, the national and international, have hardly dealt with the motives for economic discrimination, and therefore their impact has been limited; thus economic discrimination has survived.

International Treaties, Declarations, and Conventions

Probably the most common type of treaty dealing with minorities since medieval times has been the capitulations system practiced by the

European countries in their relations with the Ottoman Empire and the Middle East. The capitulations, discussed briefly above, were forms of extraterritoriality devised to protect the political and civil rights of their European beneficiaries, but they went beyond that to grant them economic and trade privileges. The protected minorities, usually Christians under Muslim rule, were often treated more favorably than the nationals as a result of the capitulations. Because the capitulations made victims beneficiaries and beneficiaries victims, they institutionalized rather than removed discrimination.[1]   Eventually an unwritten form of capitulations was imposed by the colonial powers on their colonies or spheres of influence, which gave their nationals—the French *colons* in North Africa, the Dutch in Indonesia, the British in India, the Middle East, and the New World— economic opportunities and privileges unavailable to the natives of the dominated countries.

Following World War I the victorious countries tried to establish minority protection principles to be applied largely in Europe. The United States, under President Wilson, mostly favored self-determination by national groups. Britain, in contrast, favored more assimilation of minorities within the ranks of the majorities.[2] The end result was a combination policy that was flexible enough to fit the short-run interests of the triumphant countries.   A commentary on the principles agreed to at the Paris Peace Conference in 1919 concluded that:

all in all . . . the minority treaties largely satisfied the British and great power view. They were confined to Eastern Europe and were not universal. Protection was defined almost entirely in legal, political and linguistic terms, and most of the protection was in negative form. There was no concept of economic protection or privilege. The clauses infringed as little as possible [on] the concept of national sovereignty, and they were almost exclusively concerned with guaranteeing that the citizen who was a member of a national or religious minority was not treated worse, as an individual, than a citizen of the majority nationality.[3]

However, the equality of citizens, regardless of religious or ethnic affiliation, was to be guaranteed, though no mechanism was created to enforce such guarantees. On the contrary, the tendency after World War I was to consider such rights and issues as internal or domestic affairs of sovereign states not subject to foreign intervention, thus removing all but the moral power of the treaties and the principles upon which they were based.

This policy of ambivalence was well reflected in the reluctance of Britain to protect its East Indian subjects residing in various parts of the British Empire from discrimination on the assumption that no one can dispute "the right of the self-governing dominions to decide for themselves who, in each case, they will admit as citizens of their respective dominions."[4] Thus, the declared principles were more rhetoric than grounds for action on behalf of minorities. As Section III of the Treaty of Lausanne (July 21, 1923) shows, concern for minorities concentrated on how Turkey, a defeated country, would treat minorities under its sovereignty. At the same time, states created by the dissolution of the Ottoman Empire were expected to comply with these same principles regarding their minorities. The essence of these principles was to assure that minorities were fully protected against mistreatment based merely on their minority characteristics, and that they were allowed to enjoy the rights of citizenship specified by the laws of the respective country. The Treaty of Lausanne guaranteed equality before the law but did not protect against discrimination in the marketplace or the economy.

These same principles were reaffirmed in the United Nations Charter and in the General Assembly's Universal Declaration of Human Rights, which guarantees that "everyone has the right to take part in the government of his country" (Article 21). Article 25(1) guarantees that "everyone has the right to a standard of living adequate for the health and well-being of himself and of his family, including food, clothing, housing and medical care and necessary social service, disability, widowhood, old age or the lack of livelihood in circumstances beyond his control." Article 26(2) guarantees that "education shall be directed to the full development of the human personality . . . ."[5] The Declaration of Human Rights, thus, protects minimum rights for all, but not equal rights for minorities.

The UN Charter has been supplemented by three documents, the International Labor Organization (ILO) Convention (107) Concerning the Protection and Integration of Indigenous and Other Tribal and Semi-Tribal Populations in Independent Countries of 1957, the United Nations Covenant on Civil and Political Rights of 1966, and the International Convention on the Elimination of All Forms of Racial Discrimination of 1966.

The ILO Convention is of particular interest because it touches most closely on the economic aspects of discrimination, especially with regard to landholding and employment. The Convention calls for recognition of the rights of tribal and semitribal people to the lands they traditionally occupied. However, it also allows for their removal from that land as long as they are provided with substitute lands of at least equal quality, or with adequate compensation in money or kind for the land expropriated. According to Article 15, which deals with employment, "each member state shall, within the framework of national laws and regulations, adopt special measures to ensure the effective protection with regard to recruitment and conditions of employment of workers belonging to the populations concerned so long as they are not in a position to enjoy the protection granted by law to workers in general." Each member state is urged to "do everything possible to prevent all discrimination between workers in the population concerned and other workers, in particular to (a) admission to employment . . . ; (b) equal remuneration for work of equal value; (c) medical and social assistance . . . ; (d) the right of association and freedom for all lawful trade union activities . . ." Article 21 guarantees that "members of the populations concerned have the opportunity to acquire education at all levels on an equal footing with the rest of the national community." The respective governments are responsible for implementation of these provi-. sions.[6]

These provisions are powerful, but they are two-edged. If used carefully, they cut both ways: on one hand, they serve to protect minorities; on the other, they leave enough loopholes to undermine their potential positive effects. For example, while land rights are guaranteed, expropriation is permissible if compensation in money or kind is offered. What is to prevent the majority from using the loopholes to its advantage, as has been the case in most situations involving natives, as in the United States, Canada, and Israel? Another positive provision calls for protective and equalizing measures, or what is now called affirmative action, if the tribes and semitribes are not in a position to enjoy the general protections of the law. But who decides that? The government that establishes the laws can hardly be expected to turn around and say that these laws do not offer enough protection, and it may not be easy for the deprived minorities to show that they cannot enjoy those protected rights.

A similar loophole exists in the provision protecting equal education. On one hand, it may be difficult to show inequality from a technical standpoint. On the other hand, the provision allows for separate education for the concerned peoples, or for segregation as long as the principle of equality is respected. Yet, the principle of separate but equal has never been feasible to apply. Finally, neither the UN Charter nor the ILO Convention has any means of enforcement or control. The respective sovereign states have the authority to keep these issues in the domain of domestic affairs. In other words, the power of these documents is mainly a moral one, which so far has not been very effective.

The International Convention on the Elimination of All Forms of Racial Discrimination adopted in 1966 gives the United Nations a direct role in combating discrimination. Article 1 (4) states that measures taken to protect and advance certain racial or ethnic groups or individuals will not be considered discriminatory as long as such measures are intended to bring these groups up to a level of equality, but also as long as they do not "lead to the maintenance of separate rights for different racial groups." The Convention provides for protection of economic, social, and cultural rights, including equal rights to work, union membership, unemployment pension, equal pay for equal work, housing, public health, and education and training. It also provides for a committee to monitor violations or discriminatory behavior, to report annually to the secretary-general of the United Nations on such violations, and to make recommendations regarding actions that may be taken.[7] The UN can go as far as to recommend to member countries the imposition of sanctions against the violating country, as has happened against South Africa and is currently taking place against Iraq.[8] However, the power of the Convention is primarily in moral suasion. It should be noted further that not all countries have ratified the UN Declaration on Human Rights or the Convention against discrimination.

The trend charted by the League of Nations and by the United Nations has been adopted by individual countries and groups of countries on a regional basis in the form of regional conventions. Individual countries have tended to include appropriate provisions in their constitutions or bodies of laws, as in the constitutions of Bulgaria, the USSR, the People's Republic of China, and the United States. Regional and subregional conventions include the European Convention on Human Rights and Fundamental Freedom, which provides only that the enjoyment of rights shall be achieved without discrimination. The main provisions of the European Convention, which have come to be known as the Helsinki Accord, provide for some protection of minorities but simultaneously encourage the incorporation of minorities into the life of the nation— meaning that of the majority.

The specific group conventions, including the Helsinki Accord, have served as tailored alternatives to ratification of the more general UN documents. This became evident in the comprehensive African Charter on Human Rights and Peoples' Rights adopted in July 1981. The African Charter draws on the major UN documents relating to rights but reformulates those principles to fit the African context. The African context, however, emphasizes the equality of all peoples, the right to self-determination and independence, and the rights and duties of the individual within the framework of the respective nation. The Charter also establishes a Commission on Human Rights to gather information, monitor for violations, and make recommendations, and cooperate with other African and international institutions regarding the promotion and protection of rights.[9]

Finally, an important instrument for protecting minorities has been the bilateral agreement between countries or between the majority and minority within a given country. For example, India and Pakistan concluded an agreement regarding their respective minorities in 1950. India and Sri

Lanka concluded an agreement in 1987. Unfortunately neither agreement has been effective in removing discrimination and promoting equality. Middle Eastern countries have reached agreements with their minorities, sometimes formally and other times informally, as with the Kurds, Berbers, Copts, and others. Because these bilateral agreements have been less than fully respected, however, their impact has not always been as positive as had been hoped for.

National and Domestic Measures

The various instruments discussed above have been concerned with group rights. The rights of individuals have been considered an internal concern of the state. Therefore, protection against discrimination and measures of equalization must depend on national policies of individual countries. Some of these measures deal with discrimination in a negative way; others deal with it positively; and still others are ambivalent in their potential impact on discrimination. We shall look at each of these separately.

Negative or Passive Measures

It is not uncommon to hear policy-makers declare that there is no problem with minorities in their country and that all citizens there are equal. Denying the existence of the problem is a common way of dealing with discrimination against minorities and even more so against women. Not long ago the prime minister of Turkey expressed this opinion strongly, saying: "We accept no other nation as living in Turkey, only the Turks. As we see it, there is only one nation in Turkey, the Turkish nation. All citizens living in different parts of the country are content to be Turkish."[10] Once it is declared that minorities do not exist, the problem is supposed to vanish. The fact that the Kurds, Greeks, and Armenians in Turkey feel like and are treated as minorities does not seem to matter to the prime minister. Negation of the problem is a standard policy.

Another version of this "decreeing" away of the discrimination problem is to legislate equality but do nothing to enforce it. This is one of the most prevalent approaches in the world today; policy-makers emphasize the form or letter of the law and ignore the spirit or substance of the law. Such an approach usually satisfies international monitors, unless a given country happens to be a target of criticism on other matters, in which case its failure to respect human rights and minority rights becomes an excuse to bring it to account, as happens to be the case currently with Iraq. Though Iraq is no more cruel to the Kurds than Iran and Turkey, it is the target of Western powers in the name of the UN and minority rights. Ignoring the problem has been a fairly effective way of avoiding the conflict without resolving it, especially in situations in which the minority is too small to be a threat or reluctant to resort to protest or violence in pursuit of equality or nondiscrimination.

A third approach is to explain differential treatment as a function of unique situations. In Western Europe, for example, migrant workers are deprived of certain benefits enjoyed by other workers because their jobs are "temporary." Their employment may last for years but still be designated temporary to avoid extension of benefits, including social security benefits, family allowances, and security of employment, long after a standard probation period has elapsed. When certain jobs are reclassified as temporary, discrimination against the relatively "weak" migrant minority workers is legitimized and perpetuated, since it is deemed consistent with the law.[11]

Reclassification of workers and residents as a way of dealing with discrimination is more common when treating problems faced by indigenous peoples. They are usually reclassified as minors and thus automatically deprived of the ability to claim equality with other adults in the marketplace, land ownership, property management, and the other economic rights of citizens. Though such reclassification is supposed to be for the protection of these people, it tends to subject them to discriminatory measures, presumably with their consent. This has been the pattern throughout the New World, including the Americas, Australia, and New Zealand.[12]

Another common case of thinking away the problem of discrimination is the treatment of women in modern society. Women have been considered inferior to men for so long that when the issue of discrimination against them is raised people are shocked and readily deny that they suffer from discrimination. In the name of tradition, religion, or some other value system, keeping women in the kitchen, thinking of them simply as a means of reproduction, or exploiting them in unpaid and less rewarding labor seem normal, expected, and not at all discriminatory. That women have no say in the choice of their status, or that they may wish a different role in the economy and society, is rarely considered or is dismissed as silly, irrelevant, radical, or subversive. Some policy-makers go as far as to claim to answer such questions on behalf of women, asserting that they are privileged, satisfied, and happy with their place in society. All these scenarios can be illustrated in Middle Eastern countries, in which the treatment of women ranges from almost full participation in the economy, as in Israel, to total seclusion and dependence on and subservience to men, as in Iran and Saudi Arabia.

Another negative form of dealing with discrimination is to decree away the problem by legalized segregation of the races, ethnic groups, or genders in the marketplace, shop, residence, and educational institutions. The idea of segregation takes two main forms: separate but equal, and separate and unequal. Separation with presumed equality has been a way of avoiding the issue of racial and ethnic discrimination by insisting on one's freedom to be with one's own kind, as long as it is not at the expense of others. Hence, if equal public facilities and services are provided to each of the segregated groups, then segregation is said to be nondiscriminatory and not in violation of civic or human rights. Segregation of the sexes in education in Saudi Arabia and of the races in the United States in all walks of life up to the 1960s are and were supposed to be based on the principle of separate but equal. The fact that equality is not attained is blamed on misinterpretation or on imperfections in the system, but not on intentions or on the acceptance and institutionalization of discrimination. Actually the issue does not arise in Saudi Arabia because women there are not supposed to expect equality with men in the first place. On the other hand, the fact that the minority has no say in the matter of segregation is not considered discrimination, the facts to the contrary notwithstanding.

There is, however, the principle of separate and unequal, which is based on the conviction that the races or ethnic groups are not equal and therefore should not be treated as equal. The most critical and lasting examples have been the segregation of the untouchables in India, of the blacks of South Africa, and of women in societies in which culture, political philosophy, or religion sets the rules of behavior, as in theocratic Islamic countries, or Orthodox Jewish communities. In all these situations, minorities and women are considered less deserving than the majority of men and therefore, in the eyes of the majority, should not expect equality. It is argued further that all people in these countries are treated according to their "natural" abilities or worth. Those who are less equal in physique, mental capacity, achievement, or spiritual valuation must be treated less equally than others as a matter of logic, justness, and efficiency. The fact that the untouchables of India, the blacks of South Africa, or the women of Saudi Arabia and Napoleonic France may be as capable as the majority and men is dismissed quickly without concern for fact or evidence.

Prejudice plays a major role in sustaining the practice of separate and unequal segregation. The separate and unequal policy may be observed in its modern form in the housing policies of various European countries. In France, Germany, Switzerland, and Britain, ethnic minorities, especially non-Europeans, tend to be grouped in ethnic compounds, because of both economic and administrative forces. The relatively lower cost of housing and the attraction of ethnic compatriots draw the members of individual ethnic groups together into separate zones or compounds. Public policy tends to enhance that segregation. In Germany, for example, where the government subsidizes minority housing, ethnic minorities are grouped in segmented compounds, presumably to avoid their social isolation but also to reduce ethnic concentration that might threaten social or political stability. Although no legal segregation is imposed, the subsidy and housing access policies lead toward separate and lower-quality housing for ethnic minorities than for the ethnic majority.[13]

Probably the best examples of separate and unequal, and the most negative way of dealing with discrimination, have been associated with slavery and apartheid. Under these institutions, public policies dehumanized minorities and legalized and mandated both segregation and inequality. Black Americans were considered outside civil society, and it was not considered discrimination to treat them differently, since they had no legal or human rights to protect. Such dehumanization is severe because it ignores the problems of minorities and precludes any attempts to deal with them by policy-makers. Apartheid in South Africa, which has been recently dismantled, has been the most recent example on a national scale to apply the unequal and separate policy toward blacks and coloreds.

Negative measures concerning discrimination have often been more oppressive than supposedly benign neglect. They have been used to eliminate the problem in one barbaric way or another, such as genocide or decimation of the minority. The dismal fate of Native Americans in the Western world and the aborigines in Australia and New Zealand is illustrative. Ironically, however, no people has been so completely eliminated in modern times that no traces remain of the tragedies they suffered because of racial or ethnic conflict. Enough members of the targeted minority groups have always survived to remind the discriminators of their actions and sometimes to haunt them. Enough Native Americans in the United States, Maoris in Polynesia, Armenians from and in Turkey, and Jews from Nazi Germany have survived to remind us of the costs of racial and ethnic discrimination.

Another negative way of dealing with discrimination without annihilating minorities has been to transfer, relocate, or expel them from a country altogether. Transfer and relocation were most common after World Wars I and II in Europe and Southeast Asia. The idea was presumably to help both minorities and the majorities by creating more homogeneous national and ethnic groupings and thus reducing the potential for conflict between them. Given that the minorities had few options, relocation has been the most efficient way of dealing with them, but it could not be a permanent or stable solution. Furthermore, inasmuch as population transfers usually fail to transfer every single member of the targeted minority, those who remain behind often continue to be subjected to discrimination, especially because most such relocations take place within the national boundaries of a state.

The expulsion of minorities has long been used to resolve racial and ethnic conflict. The Jews have been a common target of expulsion from the days of the Babylonians to the very recent past. Expulsion of Jews and Moors in the late fifteenth and early sixteenth centuries left Spain without its most skilled artisans, financiers, and business people. The Gypsies are another group often subjected to expulsion. During the second half of this century, expulsion has been motivated by policies of nativization and nationalization of sectors of the economy, expropriation, and removal of vestiges of colonialism. The *colons* of Algeria were forced to leave Algeria after independence. Western minorities and Jews were forced to leave Egypt after the 1956 war with Britain, France, and Israel. While these episodes of expulsion were political in nature, they also represented attempts to redress the discrimination exercised against the natives by nationals of the colonial powers. Those who were expelled, had they remained and retained power, would presumably have continued a system of discrimination and hierarchical socioeconomic relations, with themselves at the top and the natives far below them.

Expulsion measures, however, have always been imperfect and they have never succeeded in eliminating ethnic discrimination, though they may have reduced it. The current and most recent episode of forced relocation of minorities has been termed "ethnic cleansing." More than two million people, including Serbs, Croats, Macedonians, Albanians, Hungarians, and Muslim Slavs, have been driven out of their homes in order to create ethnic homogeneity, regardless of the impact on the victims and of UN and individual country protests.

It should be noted that these measures seem negative only from the standpoint of the minorities. The power majority, as a group and possibly as individuals, has tended to reap economic benefits from them, at least in the short run. Elimination of controversy, reduction of security costs, confiscation of property, avoidance of competition for scarce resources, and the exploitation of minorities have all been sources of private economic gain. However, the net effects have been negative from the standpoint of society, especially in the long run, because of loss of human resources, dislocation, and continuation of ethnic conflict.

Positive Measures

One of the oldest approaches to minority discrimination has been to take the minorities under the wing of the sovereign, prince, or other member of the ruling elite for protection, either because they are needed for their skills, wealth, and resources, or simply for humanitarian reasons. However, it has not been demonstrated that in such cases the minorities were treated equally with members of the majority, as a *right*, although they may have more than equal benefits by virtue of the protection they received from their patron. In fact, there is no evidence of any attempts to guarantee equal treatment of minorities as a right anywhere prior to the modern period or, more accurately, before this century. While Muslim powers gave the "believers," Christians and Jews, the right to safe and secure existence upon payment of a special tax, there is no evidence that they were treated as equals with Muslims in the marketplace, government administration, or with regard to property ownership and personal security. On the other hand, though all Muslims are supposed to be equal, regardless of ethnic origin, there are Muslims who are aliens as nationals of other Muslim countries. These aliens are not considered equal, and their protection is derived from treaties or the benevolence of a given ruler.

The Jews of medieval and early modern Poland enjoyed various degrees of security, depending on the mood of the sovereign. Sometimes they were fully protected and other times they hardly knew what hit them. These arbitrary instances of protection and abuse by the sovereign demonstrate the vulnerability of minorities prior to the modern period.

Concern for the individual rights of citizens may be traced back to the Greeks, Romans, Arabs, English, and French of the modern period. However, these rights did not include the members of minorities, as illustrated by the exclusivism and anti-Semitism practiced by the British and French until very recent times. The United States Constitution, the French Revolution, and the Code of Napoleon, which emphasized individual rights in the modern period, guaranteed equality before the law only for male citizens; they did not preclude separatism or the segregation of minorities or women. Before emancipation the United States census counted a black as three-fifths of a white person. Even after emancipation, segregation of blacks in the United States, presumably with equality, was considered legal until ruled unconstitutional by the Supreme Court in 1954, *Brown v. Board of Education of Topeka,* because it was shown not to be segregation with equality. Protecting the minorities in a positive way, or by removing the shackles of discrimination and providing minorities with opportunities to offset the inequality to which they had been subjected, came first through political pressures and court rulings, rather than through special legislation on their behalf. Thus, the attack on discrimination required constitutional protection for all individuals, as well as the legal and political forces to give to the minorities the rights they never had as individuals.

Legislation and rulings by the courts in favor of equal rights have proved to be inadequate to overcome discrimination, because minorities in the United States and elsewhere have been so far below equality with the majority that simply to outlaw discrimination and segregation was not enough to enable minorities to enjoy equal opportunity, escape discrimination, and feel equal to others in theory and practice. Hence, implementation of positive measures in the form of affirmative action was deemed necessary to equalize opportunities.

Affirmative action has come to mean different things to different people, ranging from the prevention of discrimination to the preferential treatment of minorities over the majority in matters of employment, promotions, educational opportunities, business, housing, etc. Our concern is with positive measures that could be interpreted as affirmative action. We will also be concerned with evolution of the concept of affirmative action, which has come to include positive measures to remove discrimination against minorities and women and give them opportunities to acquire equal levels of endowment, exercise equal utilization of their potential, and enjoy equal rewards for their labor, which are otherwise not available to them in spite of their qualifications.

Before the 1917 Soviet Revolution, Russian Jews were legally barred from government service, work on the railroads, and jobs in the postal service. "After the revolution, these laws were wiped off the books. Affirmative action placed 150,000 Jews in industrial jobs in the 1920s .... With the organization of state farms, the proportion of Jews earning a living in agriculture rose from 2 to 11 percent in the years before World War II. Anti-Semitic quotas in education were abolished, and the possibility of education in one's native language was provided everywhere."[14]

Women have also been affected by affirmative action in the Soviet Union. Following the revolution, "they almost immediately received the right to vote (a pioneer right for women at this time); the right to inexpensive, easy divorce; the right to hold jobs that had formerly been reserved almost exclusively for men; and, in 1920, the right to inexpensive abortion. As early as 1923, over half of the Soviet university students specializing in medicine and the arts were women."[15] Some of these rights, however, were modified or suspended before, during, and after World War II until 1956 to combat the loss of population. But, as mentioned above, legislation is one thing and implementation is another. Discrimination against women still prevailed in the Soviet Union, although to a lesser degree than in other countries.

Few countries other than the United States have any history of affirmative action in favor of ethnic minorities that is not assimilative in nature. Recently Malaysia introduced what has come to be known as the New Economic Policy (NEP) to combat discrimination against the majority Malays by the minority Chinese and other foreign Malaysian citizens who represent economic power in the country. Since winning independence from the British in 1957, a Malay numerical majority government has been in office, but the Malays have continued "to see themselves as the victims of discrimination."[16] The Malays constituted a disproportionate percentage of the poor, a relatively smaller percentage of capital owners, and a relatively smaller percentage of professionals and skilled workers in comparison with their size in the population. Chinese Malaysians and other aliens dominated the economy.

After the riots of 1969, however, the government introduced its NEP, a set of affirmative action programs with two main targets: to eliminate poverty for all Malaysians and to restructure the economy and society to bring about equalization or proportional distribution of opportunities and incomes according to the ethnic composition of Malaysian society. Poverty was to be eliminated by "improving the access of the poor to the land, physical capital and infrastructure, and training." Employment was to be restructured by sector so as to reflect the ethnic composition of the population, so that "by 1990 Buminputera [i.e., Malays and other indigenous people] should own and manage firms that have at least 30 percent of the value of corporate equity." Ironically, "all these objectives were to be achieved without explicitly shifting already existing resources among the ethnic groups. The 'process of restructuring is to be undertaken in the context of a rapidly expanding economy.'"[17]

To implement these policies, various agencies were established: the Federal Land Development Agency (FELDA), the Majlis Amana Rakayat (MARA or National Trust for Indigenous People), the Urban Development Authority (UDA), the Perbadan Nasional (PERNAS or National Corporation), and the National Equity Corporation (PNP or Permodalan Nasional Berhad). FELDA specialized in the development of large areas on which new settlers, mostly Malays, were to be settled. MARA was to issue loans at relatively low rates of interest to allow Malays to purchase securities and also to train Malays in vocations. PERAS focused on controlling large enterprises with both commercial and social objectives. It delved into joint ventures with foreigners as well as into aggressive takeovers. PNP concentrated on the takeover of foreign corporations, such as those that dominated Malayan banking.

The activities of these organizations were facilitated by legislation, the most important of which was the 1975 Industrial Coordination Act (ICA), which provided roughly for the following:

1. 30 percent of equity had to be set aside for Malay interests; 2. Malaysian citizens had to be trained and employed to the extent possible; 3. Malay distributors had to be used to the extent possible, with a minimum set of 30

percent turnover;   4.   prices could not be increased without ministry approval, and price limits were set based on the prices of equivalent imports and on cost factors;   5.   companies had to use local materials, components, and parts to the extent possible; and 6.   all agreements on starting up and shutting down operations, employment of expatriates, technical know-how, trademarks and royalties, and marketing and to be approved by the ministry in writing; an existing license could not be transferred without such permission.[18]

Implementation proceeded while the economy was expanding, but as soon as an economic crisis hit in the mid-1980s, the NEP was suspended. The results have been positive but limited. Many obstacles stood in the way: economic expansion came to an end;   certain groups that were directly affected in a negative way objected;   functions of the different groups overlapped; government bureaucracy did not work smoothly; and most significant of all, the NEP had internal contradictions of its own. It seems to be a contradiction in terms to use scarce resources to promote the welfare of the Malays without reducing benefits of other groups, as the legislation stipulated.   Furthermore, the new regulations tried to reconcile conflicting economic and social objectives, which is not easy.

Implementation has now been resumed in the form of quotas especially in government offices and educational institutions.   Often top posts are given to Malays, with Chinese and Indian deputies who have more experience or training working under them.   This has led to charges of "Ali Babaism," according to which the Chinese and Indians do the work while the Malays receive "rent" benefits.   Nevertheless, the NEP seems to be the institutionalized way of Malaysia to overcome racial and ethnic inequality.[19]

An interesting approach to the economic status of women has been that of France.   During the nineteenth century women were protected in the workplace by special legislation, which often equated them with minors, especially with regard to the number of hours to be worked, the type of work that could be done, and exclusion from night shifts. The rationale was that women were more vulnerable than men and needed protection.

Since World War II, however, women in France and elsewhere have sought equality, not protection.   As a result, equalization with men in France has often come to mean the repeal of protective laws.   For example, legislation passed in 1975 and 1979 repealed the "employers' moral guardianship over women" and the prohibition against the "employment of women in the production or sale of writings, drawings, etc., whose sale is subject to strict controls as being liable to offend morality."   Another law repealed the prohibition against women's employment "in the repair of machines, mechanical appliances or parts in motion."[20] By the end of the 1980s legislation to establish the equality of women with men was virtually complete. However, little effort has apparently been made to implement the law and realize equality in the sense of affirmative action. Whatever benefits may have been extended to women have been related to concern for the family, such as the protection of maternity, paternity, and the welfare of the children. Discriminatory attitudes and prejudices toward women have yet to be changed.[21]

Women in India have benefited from legislation passed over the last century and a half to improve their condition. *Sati* (widow burning) was prohibited as far back as 1829, and female infanticide was prohibited in 1870. A Widow Remarriage Act was passed in 1856, and an Age of Consent Act raising the age for sexual relations to 12 was passed in 1891. Passing legislation and implementing it, however, are two different things. Attitudes did not change with the passage of the laws. Educational facilities for girls were not expanded as they were for boys. Literacy among women was about 0.7% in 1901 and only 6% in 1946. Access to employment outside the home was also restricted by the *purdah* (veil or segregation). Furthermore, salaried work for women was frowned upon, although teaching and medicine were areas of concentration for women professionals.[22]

Indian women gained the franchise in 1930 on limited terms only. They had to have property to vote; since few women owned property, the British government of India allowed the wives of property owners and of military personnel to vote. It remained for independent India to give legal equality to women. The 1950 Constitution gave them the right to vote and made them equal to men such that discrimination against them would not be possible, since they would have the opportunity to share equally in decision-making. In 1954-55 new legislation was passed abolishing polygamy and basing divorce on mutual consent. However, this legislation excluded the Muslims of India, who continued to apply the *Shari'a* laws, which subordinate women to men in economic and sociopolitical rights and activities.

Affirmative action in the United States must be seen as a supplement to the legislation that aims at equalizing citizens and thus indirectly prohibits discrimination on account of race, ethnic origin, or gender. Though interpretations of affirmative action in the United States have varied, in application it has come to mean that opportunities otherwise unavailable to qualified women or members of minority groups because of their racial, ethnic, or gender status would be made available to them, even on a priority basis if need be. Thus, jobs may be given to minorities, presumably in preference to equally qualified members of the majority, though such action is not explicitly mandated.[23]

Affirmative action has existed in the United States for half a century. Often it has been introduced in the form of executive orders based on existing legislation. The first such executive order was E.O. 8802 issued by President Roosevelt in June 1941 to establish a committee on fair employment practices in all companies holding defense contracts.[24] In May 1943 E.O. 9346 extended such coverage to the rest of the war industry and specified nondiscrimination to apply to hiring, tenure, conditions of employment, and membership in unions. In 1951 President Truman issued E.O. 10308, which created a Committee on Government Contract Compliance. President Eisenhower issued E.O 10479 in 1953 and E.O. 10557 in 1954 expanding the responsibilities of contractors to observe nondiscrimination in rates of pay, layoffs and terminations, and selection of candidates for training and apprenticeship. The vice-president was made chair of the committee in charge in order to give it more credibility. In 1955 E.O. 10590 established a President's Committee on Government Employment Policy. All these executive orders were of the passive type of affirmative action; they were intended to prevent discrimination, but not to redress past results or equalize citizens through positive action.[25]

Positive affirmative action began with E.O. 10925, issued in 1961 by President Kennedy, whose Committee on Equal Employment Opportunity became responsible for removing discrimination in federal employment, by government contractors, and in unions working on government contracts. The major legislation, however, was the 1964 Civil Rights Act, which covered, among other provisions, voting rights, discrimination in public accommodations, education, and equality of employment opportunity. It also dealt with implementation and administration. Title IV on Education and Title VII on Equal Employment opportunity are the most relevant in this context. Both titles prohibit discrimination, but they do not offer any remedies or redress for the effects of existing or past discrimination except indirectly by way of preventing discrimination. For example, the Commissioner of Education was authorized to expend funds to provide technical assistance and training as a way of abolishing segregation in schools.

Title VII prohibits segregation and discrimination, but it also prohibits "preferential treatment" even "for the purpose of curing an imbalance in the racial composition of a given body of employers and apprentices." The commission created to implement Title VII was authorized "to investigate, make conciliation attempts, and . . . prosecute."[26] It was a preventive authority, not a curing one. Curing measures were more a function of the executive orders.

E.O. 1114 extended the same coverage to the construction industry. These executive orders were supplemented by E.O. 11246 of 1965 and E.O.

11375 of 1967, issued by President Johnson, and E.O. 11478, issued in 1969 by President Nixon. These executive orders are still considered the basis for affirmative action, having established the mechanisms for compliance with federal law against discrimination in both public and private industry. The Office of Federal Contract Compliance, established in 1966, was absorbed in 1971 by the Employment Standards Administration of the Department of Labor. Before then, however, it issued guidelines on affirmative action to help contractors and departments with compliance. Before hiring, a contractor is supposed to consider the following factors in his or her analysis:

(i)   The minority population of the labor area surrounding the facility;

(ii)   The size of the minority unemployment force in the labor area surrounding the facility;

(iii) The percentage of the minority work force as compared with the total work force in the immediate labor area;

(iv)   The general availability of minorities having requisite skills in the immediate labor area;

(v)   The availability of minorities having requisite skills in an area in which the contractor can reasonably recruit;

(vi)   The availability of promotable and transferable minorities within the contractor's organization;

(vii) The existence of training institutions capable of training persons in the requisite skills; and

(viii) The degree of training which the contractor is reasonably able to undertake as a means of making all job classes available to minorities.[27]

To cover discrimination against women, article (i) was modified to add the "availability of women population. . . ." However, confusion and misinterpretation of affirmative action continued to be rampant. Therefore in 1971 Revised Order No. 4 (a revision of the 1968 "goals and timetables" of the Office of Federal Contract Compliance) gave a more precise meaning to affirmative action on the establishment of goals and timetables for affirmative action, as follows:[28]

(a)   The goals and timetables developed by the contractor should be attainable in terms of the contractor's analysis of its deficiencies and its entire affirmative action program. Thus, in establishing the size of its goals and the length of its timetables, the contractor should consider the results which could reasonably be expected from its putting forth every good faith effort to make its overall affirmative action program work. In determining levels of goals, the contractor should consider at least the factors listed in Â60-2.11.

(b) Involve personnel relations staff, department and division heads, and local and unit managers in the goal-setting process.

(c) Goals should be significant, measurable and attainable.

(d) Goals should be specific for planned results, with timetables for completion.

(e) Goals may not be rigid and inflexible quotas which must be met, but must be targets reasonably attainable by means of applying every good faith effort to make all aspects of the entire affirmative action program work

(f) In establishing timetables to meet goals and commitments, the contractor will consider the anticipated expansion, contraction, and turnover of and in the work force.

(g) Goals, timetables, and affirmative action commitments must be designed to correct any identifiable deficiencies.

(h) Where deficiencies exist and where numbers or percentages are relevant in developing corrective action, the contractor shall establish and set forth specific goals and timetables separately for minorities and women.

(i) Such goals and timetables, with supporting data and the analysis thereof, shall be a part of the contractor's written affirmative action program and shall be maintained at each establishment of the contractor.

(j) A contractor or subcontractor extending a publicly announced preference for Indians as authorized in 41 CFR 60-1.5(a)(6) may reflect in its goals and timetables the permissive employment preference for Indians living on or near an Indian reservation.

(k) Where the contractor has not established a goal, its written affirmative action program must specifically analyze each of the factors listed in Â60-2.11 and must detail its reason for a lack of a goal.

(l) In the event it comes to the attention of the Office of Federal Contract Compliance Programs that there is a substantial disparity in the utilization of a particular minority group or men or women of a particular minority group, OFCCP may require separate goals and timetables for such minority group and may further require, where appropriate, such goals and timetables by sex for such group for such job classifications and organizational units specified by the OFCCP.

(m) Support data for the required analysis and program shall be compiled and maintained as part of the contractor's affirmative action program. This data will include but not be limited to progression line charts, seniority rosters, applicant flow data, and rejection ratios indicating minority and sex status.

(n) Copies of affirmative action programs and/or copies of support data shall be made available to the Office of Federal Contract Compliance Programs upon request for such purposes as may be appropriate to the fulfillment of its responsibilities under Executive Order 11246, as amended.

While compliance was supposed to be voluntary, Title VII of the Civil Rights Act of 1964 made it possible for the courts to mandate compliance. As stated in Section 706 (g) of Title VII,

if the court finds that the respondent has intentionally engaged in or is intentionally engaging in an unlawful employment practice charged in the complaint, the court may enjoin the respondent from engaging in such unlawful employment practice, and order such affirmative action as may be appropriate, which may include, but is not limited to, reinstatement or hiring of employees, with or without back pay . . . or any other equitable relief as the court deems appropriate.[29]

Thus, affirmative action has come to include legislation by Congress, executive orders by the president, and interpretation and enforcement by the court. The machinery of implementation has always been complex and duplicative, involving various federal agencies with rather inadequate coordination between them.[30] Litigation has been an important instrument of implementation in the sense that court decisions have usually become established precedents in interpreting and applying affirmative action.

Federal affirmative action programs became models for state and local public employment. State and municipal departments began to create their own programs and offices to monitor compliance with federal law, probably in part because they were beneficiaries of federal grants and in part because it became "politically correct" to do so. In 1972, all state and local public offices were required to follow that policy under the Equal Employment Opportunity Act. Furthermore, Title VII gradually acquired a new interpretation making it mandatory for all employers to comply with the nondiscriminatory employment rules.[31] Thus, the voluntary character of affirmative action became somewhat less voluntary by court interpretation. According to one such interpretation by Herbert Hill, employers were willing to institute affirmative action programs for a number of reasons: First, the plaintiff can be almost anyone who has any connection with the employment practices of the employers. Second, the range of complaint can be as broad as the employer's total enterprise. Third, the proof may be accomplished on the basis of statistical data. Fourth, the relief given by courts may involve substantial amounts of money and serious alteration of established business practices. It is the growing awareness of this risk which currently gives most promise of a meaningful change in discriminatory policies.[32]

Interestingly enough, there is no mention of a change in social, humanitarian, or philosophical attitudes toward discrimination as a possible reason for the change.

The federal government, however, has done more than pass legislation and try to monitor compliance. It has created incentives for the various constituencies to comply by establishing programs that accrue material benefits to those who comply. For example, in accordance with the Manpower Development and Training Act, special funds were created to help finance economic opportunities for the poor, including those who are members of minorities. Students at universities were admitted under these programs as part of the apprenticeship and training programs. Work study and internship programs fell under that category, for which the federal government pays up to 75% of the cost, though both programs are open to the majority, both male and female. Private employers could also be reimbursed for training minorities and disadvantaged people. Such subsidized programs are usually voluntary. The incentives, however, have often been high enough for employers to "make up" jobs rather than train workers in order to reap the benefits.[33]

Another approach to affirmative action has been the voluntary "hometown" plan, according to which "unions, contractors, and the minority community negotiate voluntary plans to increase minority participation." Though a large number of cities have gone on record as participating in such plans, the results have been nominal.[34]

Some efforts have been made to increase affirmative action effectiveness by increasing the number of minority students in universities and helping them to complete their programs as a way of increasing the pool of qualified minority members who could hold jobs on an equal basis with the majority. Such programs, however, have run into serious problems for supposedly promoting reverse discrimination, which will be discussed below.[35]

The impact of affirmative action in the United States has been felt in Europe, especially in Britain. Though Britain's policy toward ethnic minorities and women has been influenced by its membership in the European Economic Community and as a signatory to the Treaty of Rome, in application the example of the United States has had the most significant impact. British policy toward discrimination remained passive until Britain was required to comply with the Treaty of Rome, which mandates equal pay for equal work. Accordingly, an equal pay amendment was passed in 1984. However, though British policy-makers have since the 1970s monitored U.S. approaches to discrimination as reflected in affirmative action, executive orders, and enforcement mechanisms, no political commitment has been made by British authorities to implement the legislation.

Debates have continued, centering around interpretations of the law, the principle of meritocracy, the impact of government affirmative action on the rights of "citizenship," the possible effects on affirmative action of partial measures that may be feasible, and the common aversion to quotas as "demeaning and unfair." Consequently, the effects of British legislation and action have remained limited, and the courts and tribunals have been reluctant to get involved. Thus, minorities and women in Britain continue to suffer from discrimination far more than they do in the United States.[36]

REACTIONS TO AFFIRMATIVE ACTION

The most extensive affirmative action program in the world exists in the United States, so a look at the reactions to anti-discrimination policies and measures there will illustrate the uphill struggle such policies still face, there and elsewhere. The first and most crippling reaction has been a "counterattack" by many whites against what they consider "reverse discrimination." Whites who traditionally enjoyed disproportionate privileges suddenly felt abandoned by the federal, state, and local governments that passed laws establishing affirmative action. Whites who had always wanted a mainly white society, as reflected by the school systems, curricula, language requirement, and methods of student evaluation, felt threatened by measures of integration and assimilation, by increasing competition from highly qualified minorities, and by the preferential treatment accorded underprivileged minorities. Their resentment went beyond verbal protest and lobbying all the way to the U.S. Supreme Court, as in the Bakke case, which concerned admission to medical school at the University of California, Davis. Such reaction has apparently dampened the effects of affirmative action.[37]

Another protest has been expressed by lower-income whites—primarily Italian, Irish, Greek, or East Europeans—who need help but cannot get it because they are not discriminated-against minorities. They may be recent immigrants or longtime residents who have faced hard times. Affirmative action does not apply to them. Though other programs are supposed to serve them, they resent the preferential treatment accorded minorities by affirmative action as if it were given at their expense.

Another type of reaction has come from certain members of the disadvantaged minorities themselves who object on principle to affirmative action and the preferential treatment of any group. A number of influential blacks and Hispanics, liberals and conservatives, have argued against preferential treatment of their own communities. They argue that people should take responsibility for their own situations and that diligent individuals can succeed. According to this view, the market is the best guarantor of equal opportunity and no other action by government is necessary. On the contrary, they argue, government intervention could reduce the effectiveness of the market in providing equal opportunities.[38]

One other argument has been raised against affirmative action, namely, that preferential treatment tends to sustain stereotypes inimical to minorities and reduce their incentives to invest in themselves enough to be able to compete for the positions to which they aspire. If they are assured of appointments and promotions on the basis of affirmative action regardless of their qualifications, it would be economically rational for them not to invest in themselves to acquire additional qualifications. Thus, affirmative action does not eliminate employers' stereotypes of minorities; it may even worsen them. Furthermore, by reducing incentives, affirmative action may be a debilitating mechanism rather than an equalizing mechanism.[39]

At this juncture, in 1995, affirmative action in the United States is at a crossroads. A conservative Congress, pressures for a balanced budget, and protests by the white majority against affirmative action are threatening its effectiveness, if not its existence. The next two years may tell a different story from what is hoped for by proponents of measures to eliminate discrimination.

GENERAL OBSERVATIONS

In spite of the attempted precision in the language of the executive orders, the apparent need for interpretation and reinterpretation of what is expected of affirmative action persists. The multiplicity of agencies in charge has made enforcement especially difficult, and the bureaucratic nature of these agencies has added to the difficulty. The laws and executive orders themselves have sometimes been sources of confusion. For example, compliance has continued to be voluntary, especially in the private sector, although violators may be prosecuted. While some preference may be given to minorities and women in hiring and firing, the law strictly prohibits the imposition of quotas in establishing a "fair" distribution of employment and opportunities, which exposes affirmative action to legal challenges and extended and costly litigation. Yet, the courts have sometimes mandated quotas, or the creation of a specified number of positions for minorities, in training and apprenticeship programs.[40] Universities, often grudgingly, have also set aside a certain number or percentage of positions for minority and women students. However, such allocations have usually been far below the proportional size of the respective minority in the population at large on the assumption that is both logical and expected and does not violate the quota restriction.

In the overall picture, direct positive action on behalf of minorities and women has been recent, concentrated mostly in the second half of the twentieth century. Indirect action as part of a general concern for the poor, regardless of race, ethnicity, or gender, has been more common, partly because it benefits members of the majority as well.

International concern for minorities has been primarily politically motivated, focusing on national minorities and their treatment by national majorities. Concern for economic welfare and individual rights has remained in the domain of domestic affairs. International actions have consisted mainly of international conventions, charters, treaties, and political and moral suasion.

Domestic action has included legislation, the creation of administrative machinery to monitor implementation, and court procedures to enforce the law when challenges are made. Funds to support implementation have been made available (in the United States as the most important example) on a limited basis. Economic incentives for the majority and male employers have been the most important factor inducing implementation by the private sector. Compliance with its own laws has been the driving force in the public sector.

Finally, virtually all the measures illustrated have been so flexible and imprecise that they are vague and difficult to enforce. Even when such measures are enforced, as in the Soviet Union, the motives for enforcement were national political objectives, rather than concern for minorities or women. These observations cast doubt on the true goals of policy-makers toward minorities, the efficacy of the measures utilized, and the feasibility of removing discrimination as long as certain benefits accrue to certain groups and individuals in positions of power. These are the issues to be addressed next.

NOTES

1. E. H. Tuma, "The Economic Impact of the Capitulations: The Middle East and Europe: A Reinterpretation," *Journal of European Economic History* 18, no. 3 (Winter 1989)

2. Donald L. Horowitz, Foreword in Robert G. Wirsing, ed., *Protection of Ethnic Minorities* (New York: Pergamon Press, 1981); see also Robert G. Wirsing, "Dimensions of Minority Protection," in Wirsing, *Protection of Ethnic Minorities.*

3. Alan Sharp, "Britain and the Protection of Minorities at the Paris Peace Conference," in A. C. Hepburn, ed., *Minorities in History* (New York: Edward Arnold, 1978), 198.

4. T. G. Fraser, "Imperial Policy and Indian Minorities Overseas, 1905-23," in Hepburn, *Minorities in History,* 157.

5. Minority Rights Group, *World Directory of Minorities* (Chicago: Longman, 1990), Appendix 1.2, 391.

6. Ibid., Appendix 2.1, 395-98.

7. Ibid., Appendix 2.2, 399-400.

8. George W. Shepherd, Jr., ed., *Effective Sanctions on South Africa: The Cutting Edge of Economic Intervention* (New York: Greenwood Press, 1991).

9. *World Directory,* Appendix 6.1, 408-11.

10. Wirsing, "Dimensions of Minority Protection," 6.

11. W. R. Böhning, "International Migration in Western Europe: Reflections on the Past Five Years," *International Labour Review* 118, no. 4 (July-August 1979): 404-6.

12. For highly representative illustrations see Lee Swepston, "Latin American Approaches to the 'Indian Problem,'" *International Labour Review* 117, no. 2 (March-April 1978): 179-96.

13. Elizabeth Huttman, ed., *Urban Housing Segregation of Minorities in Western Europe and the United States* (Durham, N.C.: Duke University Press, 1991).

14. Lynn Turgeon, *State and Discrimination: The Other Side of the Cold War* (New York: Sharppe, 1989), 62.

15. Ibid., 64.

16. Michael L. Wyzan, "Ethnic Relations and the New Economic Policy in Malaysia," in Michael L. Wyzan, ed., *The Political Economy of Ethnic Discrimination and Affirmative Action* (New York: Praeger, 1990).

17. Ibid., 54-55.

18. Ibid., 63-64.

19. Richard Basham, "National Racial Policies and University Education in Malaysia," in William C. McCready, ed., *Culture, Ethnicity and Identity: Current Issues in Research* (New York: Academic Press, 1983), 58-76; Margaret Scott, "Where the Quota is King," *New York Times,* 17 November 1991, 62.

20. Marcelle Devoud and Martine Levy, "Women's Employment in France: Protection or Equality?" *International Labour Review* 119, no. 6 (Nov.-Dec. 1980): 744.

21 .Ibid., 25.

22. Barbara N. Ramusack, "Women in South and Southeast Asia," in Organization of American Historians, *Restoring Women to History* (Bloomington, Ind.: Organization of American Historians, 1988).

23. The only way minorities and women can be guaranteed jobs without preferential treatment is to guarantee full employment, which has not prevailed.

24.   *Affirmative Action: The Unrealized Goal* (Washington, D.C.: Potomac Institute, 1973), 5; the following brief history is based on this reference and on Herbert Hammerman, *A Decade of New Opportunity: Affirmative Action in the 1970s* (Washington, D.C.: Potomac Institute, 1984). See also John Lescott-Leszczynski, *The History of U.S. Ethnic Policy and Its Impact on European Ethnics* (Boulder, Colo.: Westview Press, 1984).

25.   *Affirmative Action*, 5-7.

26.   Lescott-Leszczynski, *History of U.S. Ethnic Policy*, 142-47.

27.   Hammerman, *Decade of New Opportunity*, 13.

28.   Quoted in Hammerman, 13-14.

29.   Quoted in Hammerman, 12.

30.   Hammerman, Decade of New Opportunity, 18.

31.   Affirmative Action, 15.

32.   Ibid., 18.

33.   Ibid., 88, 117-18.

34.   Ibid., 103, 107.

35.   Ibid., 128-29.

36.   Jeanne Gregory, *Sex, Race and the Law: Legislating for Equality* (London: Sage Publications, 1987), 49-68, 17.

37.   Lescott-Leszczynski, *History of U.S. Ethnic Policy*, 58-66, 136-40.

38.   Thomas Sowell, Markets and Minorities (New York: Basic Books, 1981).

39.   Glenn Loury, Seminar at the Department of Economics, University of California, Davis, December 1991.

40.   *Affirmative Action*, 1973, 17.

7

Why Discrimination Does Not Go Away

Major efforts have been made in the United States and other countries to reduce or eliminate discrimination against racial, ethnic, and gender groups, particularly during the last few decades. Policy-makers and citizens often have expressed interest in creating discrimination-free economies and societies. Experts have investigated, diagnosed, and prescribed; some have even become activists in movements dedicated to fighting discrimination. One crisis after another preventing the guarantee of civil rights for all has motivated special attempts to promote equality and harmony. Internal conflicts, sometimes violent, have prompted immediate actions to relieve the tensions. Resources have been used in efforts to remove discrimination in both the public and the private sectors.

Though some progress may be observed in the United States, Malaysia, and a few other countries, discrimination has not been eliminated, nor has it been substantially reduced. It is true that few efforts have been expended in Europe and Asia to deal with discrimination. Where attempts have been made, there has been little success, although the forms of discrimination may have changed. Even slavery, which has been formally abolished throughout the world, is said to be practiced in various parts of the world today. These mixed results force us to question whether it is reasonable to expect the elimination or serious reduction of discrimination in the modern economy or society. Inasmuch as efforts are being expended to fight discrimination, the apparent answer must be yes, in view of the partial successes realized and the belief that discrimination is costly to society and should be eliminated. If so, why has not discrimination gone away? Stated simply, because there are more reasons for it to stay than for it to go away. These reasons involve economic theory and perceptions, incentives, behavioral structures, and the nature of the remedies that have been applied. Let us look at each of these separately and then look at the future and propose steps to deal with discrimination.

ECONOMIC THEORIES AND PERCEPTIONS OF DISCRIMINATION

Impractical Implications

The logical conclusion of both the market-oriented theories and the radical political economy theories of discrimination seems to be that attempts to eliminate discrimination are bound to fail because the conditions for its elimination do not exist; therefore, unless those conditions can be created, discrimination is here to stay. The market-oriented theories consider discrimination to be inconsistent with a market economy, assuming the market is perfect and the economy is guided by economic rationality. By the same token, to the extent that the market is imperfect and economic rationality is not fully implemented, discrimination is bound to exist. Since no one has even suggested that a perfect market exists or that it is more than an ideal structure, there is no reason to expect discrimination to go away.

The fact that the market is imperfect does not mean that nothing can be done about discrimination. This is where liberal economic theorists enter the picture. Liberal economic theory recognizes imperfections of the market and suggests ways to moderate these imperfections by government policy and intervention in the market to reduce the incentives to discriminate. The degree of success depends on comprehensiveness of the reforms and the thoroughness with which they are implemented.

The radical theories, in contrast, explain discrimination as a function of capitalism and class conflict. The implication is that as long as capitalism and class conflict persist, discrimination is bound to persist. Therefore, it is not surprising that discrimination has continued to prevail in the modern economy, since the measures dealing with it are the wrong measures. Applying the same logic, inasmuch as the present trend has been in the direction of more widespread capitalism and privatization within a market economy, we probably should expect discrimination to continue or perhaps to increase, rather than go away.

A more subtle factor that tends to dampen expectations for the elimination of discrimination is implied by the statistical theory, which explains discrimination as a function of observed differences in performance and capabilities by different racial, ethnic, and gender groups. Accordingly, what is observed is not discrimination but justifiable rewarding according to differential performance. The proponents of this view, however, ignore the standards of measurement and the explanations of differential performance. For example, little attention is paid to the starting points of the different groups to see whether they have an opportunity to give equal performance. It is not evident either that equality of opportunity, if it exists at all, prevails in early stages of growing up so that a minority individual can enter the market with an endowment comparable to that of a majority individual. The fact that the statistical theory looks at results, whereas discrimination begins with opportunities and not with results, may be a good reason to doubt whether it addresses the issue of eliminating discrimination at all. To summarize, economic theory leaves one with the perception that as an integral part of an imperfect economy, discrimination can hardly be expected to go away.

ECONOMIC INCENTIVES

If we ask why discrimination does not go away, we get indirect, speculative, and interpretive answers. However, if we ask why discrimination should be expected to continue, we get answers that are directly related to the economic costs and benefits of discrimination. More specifically, one can argue that economic discrimination has continued because it accrues private benefits to certain groups and individuals, and because its elimination would incur costs that neither private nor public agents are willing to bear. For example, removing imperfection in the market by fighting monopoly, enforcing antitrust laws, or facilitating mobility are costly efforts. Inasmuch as fighting discrimination has not been a top priority of policy-makers, they have usually hesitated to incur costs to fight discrimination. Furthermore, for the sake of public relations and political objectives, they have tried to contain costs by expending as little on fighting discrimination as seems economically efficient or the minimum acceptable to their constituents, in this case the discriminatory majority. This is the macrocost disincentive to fight discrimination or the incentive to leave it alone.

A similar argument, however, applies in the micro sense. An investor who may have to incur costs to restructure a business from being discrimination-based to discrimination-free has little incentive to bear that cost if it can be avoided. On the contrary, the incentive will be to avoid the transformation cost and let discrimination continue so long as the cost of allowing it is lower than the cost of disallowing it. Furthermore, since private benefits accrue from discrimination, it is more likely to be sustained as long as the benefits exceed the costs. That is probably why many private business and public sector employers let discrimination continue in spite of the laws against it.

Another cost factor that may have been a disincentive to eliminating discrimination or provided incentives to continue it is the relatively low estimated cost of discrimination to the discriminator, assuming there is a cost at all. The employer tends to reduce the burden of higher wages to the prejudiced workers by substituting as much capital for labor as possible. By this means, even if the employer wants to remove discrimination, it may be economically rational to substitute capital for labor, rather than embark on dismantling discrimination.

There are reasons that more directly favor discrimination. If, for example, employers choose to integrate their labor force by paying compensation to prejudiced workers to induce them to work with those they are prejudiced against, they provide workers with incentives to hold on to their prejudices, which causes discrimination to continue.

Another incentive to continue discrimination is the economic benefit employers realize by paying wages to their minority or women workers that are lower than their marginal product, or lower than the wages they pay to other workers with similar estimated marginal products. Landlords do not have to offer the same benefits to their discriminated-against tenants, even though they may charge them the same or higher rents than they do others. Creditors charge higher interest rates to minorities than to others on the assumption that they carry higher risks or simply because of their oligopolistic command over the market. In other words, given imperfections of the market, a business person would be acting rationally to continue to discriminate as long as there are benefits to realize. Though such behavior may entail waste and costs to society, the burden falls on someone else, not on the individual discriminator. Thus, while the incentive to discriminate continues to exist, the disincentive to discriminate is weak or nonexistent.

PHILOSOPHY, INSTITUTIONS, AND NORMAL BEHAVIOR

A major incentive for discrimination is embedded in the philosophy of gain, accumulation, and power that has dominated our modern society and economy. Though this is not purely an economic incentive, it has economic implications and effects. People derive security from conforming to tradition, the accepted doctrine, or philosophy by which their society is guided. Accepting the philosophy of gain, accumulation, and power, however, is not only a source of security, but also a potential source of material benefit. On one hand, conformity means complying with the institutions that support that philosophy and being on the side of the law. On the other hand, conformity condones, even reveres, the behavior representative of the competitive market economy that aims at gain and accumulation, even at the expense of others in a competitive market economy. In fact, conformity may be a way of reducing costs by avoiding conflict, even if one objects to certain behaviors such as discrimination. Still another way of realizing security is to "keep others in their place," that is, below one's own.

The philosophy of gain, accumulation, and power has not been affected by attempts to remove discrimination. In fact, it has been enhanced in recent decades in the name of freedom of enterprise, private initiative, and freedom of choice. Even socialist economies, based on a different philosophy, have been inclined toward the philosophy of gain, accumulation, and power. While the socialist experiment may have succeeded in reducing economic discrimination, that experiment has not been influential enough to bring about lasting effects or to extend its influence to the market economies.

Our argument is that as long as the predominant philosophy and institutions do not prohibit discrimination, and as long as they do protect gain and accumulation, in effect they condone discrimination. Even when the philosophy and institutions condemn discrimination in the rhetoric and letter of the law, they do little to raise the costs of discrimination or to reduce its benefits to discriminators. This subtle or implicit condoning of continued discrimination is accomplished by passing laws and adopting regulations that are not comprehensive enough, not precise enough, not strict enough, or that are not expected to be enforced thoroughly enough to eliminate discrimination. Such behavior should not be surprising, because the people who make the laws are themselves the beneficiaries of the existing philosophy and institutions, which are in harmony with discrimination.

REFORM MEASURES AND PARTIAL IMPLEMENTATION

Reform is supposed to reduce the negative effects of discrimination by modifying the laws and extending help to the victims without removing its causes. Thus reform tends to reduce the pressure for a change in philosophy or institutions or the removal of discrimination. Specific reform measures may function as pacifiers, thus prolonging the life of the philosophy and institutions that condone discrimination. These processes are easily observable in the attempts to deal with discrimination in the United States and in other countries.

Looking back at the Enlightenment, the American and French revolutions, the United States Constitution, and the Code of Napoleon, we find that all of these systems of thought and philosophical and sociopolitical and economic forces tolerated discrimination against women, enslavement of blacks, and decimation of American Indians. They were not opposed to the unequal treatment of minorities and aliens in Europe and the New World. In Europe and in the United States, when equality before the law was first decreed or legislated, women were excluded, and so were blacks and Indians. While individual initiative and free enterprise were hailed, wealth was being accumulated and inherited at the expense of minorities and women. While equal opportunity was praised, it never applied to minorities or women, especially at the critical stages of growing up, building character and personality, or acquiring training and qualifications to take full advantage of market opportunities.

Even the revered Founding Fathers of the United States were willing to compromise on the principles they signed into the Constitution, at the expense of blacks, Indians, and women. As Justice Thurgood Marshall has expressed it, "The record of the Framers' debates on the slave question is especially clear: The Southern States acceded to the demands of the New England States for giving Congress broad power to regulate commerce, in exchange for the right to continue the slave trade. The economic interests of the regions coalesced: New Englanders engaged in the Carrying trade would profit from transporting slaves from Africa as well as produced in America by slave labor. The perpetuation of slavery ensured the primary source of wealth in the Southern States."[1] The economic gain, accumulation, and power of whites triumphed at the expense of blacks. The philosophy of compromise on account of material gain has persisted in such a way that it still favors the majority at the expense of the minority and thus perpetuates discrimination.

The international conventions and treaties of the twentieth century, especially those following the two world wars, focus on political stability, rather than on ethnic or national rights, and they have enough loopholes to allow discrimination against minorities to continue. The best illustration is the ILO Convention, which presumably protects minorities but allows their removal from their traditional land as long as they are compensated at equal value. Interestingly enough, a government representing the majority would determine the "equal value," while the minorities lose the land.

Compromise and partial reform have characterized the implementation of legislated change. Upon emancipation, the former black slave in the United States was left without property, education, or qualifications to enter the market on an equal footing with the white. The next generation of blacks was not in a better situation, having been brought up under harsh inequality, deprivation, and segregation. Though segregation was supposed to be accompanied by providing equality in education and other benefits and services, such equality never existed. Hence families of the former slaves could hardly offer equal opportunity to their future generations. Yet, the philosophy and institutions of society and the economy tolerated inequality and supported it by protecting the beneficiaries whose behavior was presumably legal.

The story of the American Indians is well known: they lost most of their people and land. The Indians did not believe in land ownership; they recognized only the right to use the land. The U.S. Constitution, the philosophy of the Enlightenment, the principles of free enterprise, and the market did little to protect them against the loss of that right.

Racial, ethnic, and women's groups have had to wait for the present century to see any serious attempts to improve their conditions and rid them of discrimination and inequality. However, the results have been far less than hoped for by those groups. This should not be surprising, given that their hopes and expectations were overoptimistic, that the philosophy of gain, accumulation, and power has prevailed, and that they still are the relatively weaker groups in society.

First, it was not until almost two hundred years after adoption of the Constitution that serious attempts to bring about the equality it espoused were made by policy-makers, although there was always a minority of reformers who were willing to bring about change.

Second, when change came, it was in the form of decrees and legislative acts that were difficult to enforce, as has been the case with affirmative action. The legislation was subjected to interpretation and reinterpretation that often involved litigation in the courts which incurred costs in time and money. The legislation was fashioned by representatives of the majority, and the courts were usually representatives of the majority. Once a final interpretation was arrived at, implementation often fell to members of the administration who did not believe in reform or affirmative action in the first place.[2] Therefore, such small incremental changes could be realized over long periods of struggle that they had little impact on the conditions of racial and ethnic minorities.

Third, as reform movements have shifted from repealing discriminatory laws, such as those upholding segregation, to positive measures such as affirmative action, which would not only remove inequalities but also prevent new ones and redress some past inequities, new obstacles have been created. For example, questions have been raised as to how consistent the new measures are with the Constitution, what the Founding Fathers meant in the first place, or how to implement these measures without resorting to the imposition of quotas, without harming other groups (namely the majority), or without creating inefficiencies that inflict high costs on business, government, and society. In other words, the new measures of affirmative action have been quickly stripped of any real effect on the pattern of discrimination they are supposed to eliminate.

Fourth, the implementation of affirmative action has no doubt benefited certain women and members of minorities in education, employment, housing, government, and wealth accumulation. These successes, however, have been used almost like pacifiers to keep up the hope that improvement through such measures would remove discrimination. Yet, these minor successes cannot hide the fact that the economic bases for discrimination have remained intact, namely the possibility of gain, accumulation, and power through discrimination. Affirmative action measures as applied in the United States and Malaysia deal mostly with symptoms and cause only slight modifications of the institutions, but they do not question or challenge the philosophy on which discrimination is based. In a way they protect it by serving to calm the activists and opponents of discrimination through immediate partial gratification. Furthermore, to the extent that these reforms do not make the costs of discrimination to the individual prohibitive, nor prevent the realization of gain from such behavior, discrimination can hardly be expected to go away. On the contrary, it should be expected to continue as long as the basic philosophy of society that condones discrimination remains unchanged, and as long as inequality of endowment from the early years of growing up remains inherent in the institutions that reflect that philosophy. Even those modest achievements in reducing discrimination are threatened at present by reactionary movements in the name of merit, fairness, and opposition to what is called reverse descrimination.

IS THERE A WAY OUT?

Alternative solutions have been proposed including full assimilation and integration of minorities with majorities; change of philosophy and institutions from within by political action; removal of market imperfections and raising the costs and reducing the benefits of discrimination; or acceptance of discrimination as a fact of life while trying to minimize its negative effects by sociopolitical and economic actions. Let us look at each of these separately.

Assimilation

One often hears it asked: Why do not the Hispanics in the United States learn English? Why do not the blacks become more proficient and competitive? Why do not women stay home and take care of their children? In all these cases assimilation and adaptation mean accepting the rules of society as set by the majority or men and giving up one's racial, ethnic, or gender identity and values. However, to assimilate or adapt requires that one party be willing to give up its distinguishing features, and the other party be willing to accept it within its own ranks. Even assuming that racial, ethnic, and women's groups were willing to assimilate or fit into the culture and philosophy of the majority and men, it may not be feasible for them to do so for at least four reasons. First, physical differences will always identify members of these groups as distinct and, historically, as members of minorities that were and could be exploited. Blacks, Indians, Chicanos, and women are generally easily identifiable and therefore there is no sense in trying to hide these differences.

Second, these groups have been lagging in technology and acquired endowment so much that it would be difficult for them to catch up with and vanish in the crowd of the majority. The facts of underendowment and prejudice are bound to follow them and prevent their assimilation, even if we assume that they have been able to overcome feelings of inferiority they may have developed because of their historical experiences.

Third, there are debates as to whether assimilation will bring about equality, for in this context equality does not mean being identical. It has been argued that programs in education such as Head Start in the United States have missed the whole point of the struggle of the blacks to maintain an independent and different culture. Preparing black students to achieve in a system that is different from what they idealize may be self-defeating and discriminatory, and this argues against assimilation.[3]

Finally, assuming that both of the problems above can be overcome, it is not certain that members of the majority group will be willing to free themselves of the prejudices and feelings of superiority that led to discrimination in the first place. They would probably cling to the easy scapegoat target they find in weaker minorities and in women. Therefore, assimilation can hardly be considered a viable alternative.

Change the Philosophy and Institutions

As explained above, the philosophy of society represents all the internalized values that guide its behavior and hold it together. It includes the agreed-upon guidelines for governance, distribution of benefits and costs, and resolution of conflict. It also indicates who shall govern and how decisions are to be made. Modern society largely accepts majority rule, tempered by measures for minority protection. This is true both of democracies and nondemocracies. Even in countries in which a traditional autocratic monarchy or a dictatorship exists, the assumption is that the government rules on the basis of acceptance and support of the majority. The implication in all these cases is that a society's philosophy can change peacefully only if the majority decides to change it.

By the same token, the extent to which a given philosophy continues to prevail should indicate the degree to which the majority continues to cherish the benefits accruing from that philosophy and the degree to which they support it and the institutions that reflect its philosophy. For example, so long as the institutions of education, ownership, property, gain, accumulation, and distribution of wealth and power are not challenged or rejected by the majority, they must be a true expression of support by the majority for the philosophy on which they are based, that is, the philosophy and institutions are in harmony with each other and with the expectations of the majority. To prescribe changing that philosophy and its institutions in order to abolish discrimination without concurrence or approval of the majority is tantamount to prescribing a violent revolution. In contrast, to make the change peacefully would require approval of the majority, but why would the majority desire or allow such a change?

The majority enjoys the benefits of gain, accumulation, and power and of the institutions that sustain the distribution of those benefits. It faces no serious threat from minorities to its superiority, nor does it stand to realize any perceived gain by allowing a change in its philosophy and institutions. Therefore, there is little reason to expect the majority to abandon the values and ideals it has internalized generation after generation without evident compensation for the loss of benefits.

Let us assume, however, that the majority agrees to give up those benefits and change the philosophy by reeducating the people. Will it be willing to bear the costs of such change? The body of laws governing society will have to be modified. The educational institutions will have to be reorganized. The courts of law will have to be reoriented. All these changes entail costs, directly and indirectly. There is little reason to expect the majority that controls resources to allocate enough resources to underwrite these costs. Such an undertaking has not happened in recent history, and without it the changes cannot be implemented.

Let us assume further that the laws and other institutions are changed so that discrimination will not be tolerated. It will require a long time to reeducate the constituents and implement these laws fully and effectively so that both the majority and the minority and men and women will abide by the new philosophy. The American experience of the last century and a half in the fight for equality is not an encouraging example. Nor is the socialist experiment in Russia and Eastern Europe. After seventy years the Soviet revolution is being reversed and the people are again seeking to live by the philosophy of gain, accumulation, and power. Their socialist reeducation was apparently not basic or comprehensive enough, even after three generations, to sustain the new philosophy and make it work. People seem to want gain. They want accumulation. And they want power. Therefore, to change that philosophy does not seem a viable alternative for eliminating discrimination.

Remove Market Imperfections, Raise Costs, Reduce Benefits

A third alternative is to change the environment by removing market imperfections, making it costly to discriminate and rewarding to dismantle discrimination. This is an ideal solution if it can be implemented. A perfect market, however, is only a theoretical construct. It has never existed and it never will. One might try to approximate it, but even that is a very difficult thing to do, because its preconditions are not easy to achieve: people are not homogeneous; information is not perfect; mobility in and out of the market is not completely free; and the actors in the market are not all small enough not to influence it. To bring about these conditions by government policy means interfering with the market, which itself is a form of imperfection.

Another problem that stands in the way of market perfection is the built-in structural imperfections in the market. Systems of production, worker-employer relationships, and business-government relations are all built on the existing imperfect market. In terms of mobility, scale, and market information, imperfect competition is the rule rather than the exception. Therefore, to perfect the market means rebuilding or restructuring it, and that entails costs. Members of the majority are not likely to impose costs on themselves by restructuring the market in favor of perfection as long as they have the power and the right to refuse to do so.[4]

Government policy, however, can influence the market in other ways. For example, a tax on discriminators could tax away any gains from discrimination and inflict additional costs that would make it prohibitive to discriminate. On the other hand, it is possible to reward those who do not discriminate or who dismantle discrimination. It is possible, for instance, to subsidize such behavior by amounts at least equal to the costs, direct or indirect, they incur by not discriminating. In theory both policies seem promising. However, to adopt tax and subsidy policies against discrimination and implement them would require approval by the authorities, who also happen to represent the power majority in any system. To what extent would members of the majority agree to inflict costs on themselves and offer rewards to members of society who behave contrary to the accepted philosophy and the prevailing institutions they themselves cherish and approve of? Useful on occasion for partial and symbolic implementation to keep the spirit of reform alive, this alternative can hardly be considered a viable, comprehensive, and permanent solution to discrimination.

If Discrimination Cannot be Eliminated, It Can be Tamed

The only remaining alternative, which is promising but difficult, is to try to tame discrimination and minimize its negative effects. This can be done by a combination of four ways: by promoting equality before the law, affirmative action, full employment, and equal opportunity for endowment. The first two are simply a continuation of policies currently practiced in the United States. The other two are new and more effective ways to deal with discrimination in the long run. Let us look at each separately.

Equality Before the Law

The law of the land is the foundation on which coexistence in society depends. If the law permits discrimination, nothing can be done to remove it short of abolishing that law. However, if the law proclaims equality for all, then the victims of discrimination, the reformers, and the authorities will have legal grounds on which to expect equality or nondiscrimination by legal means. Therefore, the United States Constitution, its amendments, and the civil rights acts are basic to the taming of discrimination.[5] Even if the laws are abused, ignored, misinterpreted, or reinterpreted, their existence forms the moral and legal basis upon which to fight discrimination. True, as we have seen, the laws often have loopholes, are vague, inadequate, unenforced, or too costly to enforce. Nevertheless, the first step in the struggle to tame discrimination is to build the foundation for its arrest and eventual breakdown. It is in this respect that treaties, conventions, charters, as well as constitutions and systems of jurisprudence become indispensable. Even if the philosophy and legal institutions of society do not totally preclude discrimination, their proclamations of equality before the law are a powerful force to tame discrimination.

Affirmative Action and Reform

Though affirmative action and reform measures have been inadequate to remove discrimination, they have served at least four functions. (1) They have helped to focus attention on the need to deal with discrimination; (2) They have served as experiments that show what does and does not work; (3) They have benefited certain groups and individuals who were directly involved in actions and programs emanating from affirmative action; (4) They have reduced social costs whenever they reduced economic underutilization resulting from discrimination. In the marketplace, in business and government, and in educational institutions, affirmative action has benefited certain people, employed others, and helped to relocate still others in positions and occupations more fitted to their qualifications. In all these situations, affirmative action has reduced the costs of discrimination.

Although counsereffects may have been suffered, as in what is called reverse discrimination, the net effects are more likely to be positive.

One other presumably positive function of affirmative action has been to reduce conflict and prevent a more serious breakdown of the political and economic system. The stabilizing function of affirmative action as pacifier should not be ignored, especially by the majority that opposes change. It is therefore essential that reform of the laws and affirmative action be continued to directly reduce discrimination.

Full Employment

It is generally accepted that social conflicts become more conspicuous during periods of crisis. People compete more severely, search for scapegoats, and revive old habits including discrimination to offset costs of the crisis. Such behavior is usually seen as a matter of survival in a "lifeboat" with limited capacity. The weaker ones will be the first to let go or be pushed off the boat. On the other hand, in periods of prosperity and full employment, expansionism and the resulting high demand for resources reduce the pressure for competition and allow further expansion and enjoyment of the fruits of one's labor. Furthermore, in periods of full employment public resources become ample, and more can be expended on reducing the ills facing everyone, including the minority. To illustrate, one of the problems facing affirmative action has been the charge of reverse discrimination, that is, that some minority and women members of the labor force have been given work opportunities unfairly, in preference to members of the majority or men, at a time of unemployment when opportunities are fewer than the number of seekers. If, therefore, unemployment did not exist, there will be little reason to accuse anybody of reverse discrimination.

Full employment is a benefit not only to minorities and women, but to all members of the labor force, to business, and to government. This much is usually admitted. The problem is how to create full employment. The debate usually centers around the economic costs of creating full employment by policy because that tends to create inflation and thus impose a cost on society. Yet the costs of inflation with full employment would be more than offset by the benefits of full utilization of resources and the taming of discrimination. The effects of inflation are usually redistributive and reallocative. The redistributive effects can be offset by compensation, but the reallocative effects, which tend to reduce competitive efficiency, are elusive because the market is imperfect and inefficient in the first place. How much inefficiency is added because of inflation is not easy to estimate, since such effects depend on the alternatives. If the alternative is unemployment and reduced output, the net effects of full employment are most likely to be positive. In any case, from the standpoint of reducing or taming economic discrimination against minorities and women, the institution of full employment is indispensable. Full employment in wartime has been one of the major mechanisms by which discrimination has been reduced, by necessity if not by choice. Furthermore, the aftereffect of wartime full employment has been frequent interaction between the discriminators and the victims and less prejudice, and therefore a lower tendency to discriminate.

Equality of Endowment

Probably the most fundamental and effective way of dealing with discrimination is to promote equal opportunity of endowment prior to or at birth so that no racial, ethnic, or gender group will be subjected to "acquired" (in contrast to genetic) underendowment. No group would see its children undernourished, undereducated, or left homeless because of prejudice and discrimination, or because the parents cannot afford the expense of caring for them. If the children of blacks, Indians, and Hispanics and female children of all groups were awarded the same minimum opportunities as the children of the majority and boys, there is every reason to believe that they would face less discrimination and enjoy much more equality of opportunity in the marketplace than they have in the past. This approach dictates that the equalization of opportunities should start at the beginning of life, not at the time one enters school, the labor market, or the world of business. Equalization of opportunity to acquire endowment would remove many of the excuses for discrimination against minorities and women, the rationalizations based on the statistical theory of discrimination, and the arguments that the pool of qualified minorities and women is too small to allow for their equal and proportional participation in the various sectors of the economy. One might argue that equalization of endowment may go a long way toward reducing economic discrimination against minorities, as it has in the case of Jews and Asians in the United States, the Chinese in Malaysia, and the Greeks, Armenians, and Lebanese in Africa.

Finally, one of the most rewarding effects of equalization of acquired endowment is its impact in reducing the social costs of underendowment of minorities and women or failure to develop their inherent capabilities. The taming alternative is the most viable and rewarding feasible approach, both to those subject to discrimination and to society as a whole. It is also the approach with most lasting effects.

WHO SHALL DO IT?

We know the ailment and we have a four-pronged prescription to tame it. Assuming that the diagnosis and the prescription are correct and a cure is feasible, it remains to explore the way to go about it and to determine who shall be responsible for it. Three forces are at work: the victims, or minorities and women; the majority, or the discriminators; and the government, which presumably represents the society as a whole.

There is little doubt that the victims have the major responsibility to seek equality as a right by virtue of the constitutions and laws of their respective country. Where such laws dictate unequal treatment, as is the case in various parts of the world, their struggle has to be directed toward changing the laws themselves. Where equality is embodied in the laws of the country, the struggle will be both to keep the issue of discrimination alive and to pressure the majority and government to make the necessary changes to tame discrimination.

The majority, in spite of positive action by individuals in the market, cannot be expected to change its behavior and remove discrimination. As we have seen, it has benefits to realize from discrimination and costs to incur by change as long as the market is imperfect. The market system has not tamed discrimination because of its imperfection and the ability of power majorities to realize benefits by discriminating against minorities and women. Therefore, if change is to be realized, it has to come by pressuring the majority and by interfering with the market. The only force that can do that is government.

Government intervention to pressure the majority to change its behavior, even though it presumably represents that majority, may be a contradiction in terms. How can the government act against the welfare of the majority it represents? The contradiction, however, disappears once we recall that discrimination entails social costs, benefits only certain members of the majority, and its continuation in the face of the struggle for equality threatens the whole society with instability and higher costs. Therefore, since the government has the obligation to maintain stability and try to maximize social benefits and minimize social costs, it must enforce the laws that guarantee equality and protect all citizens against discrimination.

Finally, the government is the only authority that has control of the resources needed to effect change on the societal level. Intervention in the market to guarantee full employment can be done only by government. It is also the only authority that can create the institutional framework to equalize opportunities for acquired endowment for all from the beginning of life regardless of race, ethnicity, or sex, and regardless of the economic status or ability of the parents. The government is the only force that can guarantee the equality of legal, social, economic, and political protection, as well as acquired endowment for the individual. To shirk that responsibility renders the taming of discrimination as remote from realization as its removal has been.

CONCLUSIONS

It has been shown that discrimination is ubiquitous, wasteful, and persistent. It does not seem to go away in spite of the efforts expended to remove it. The reasons for its stickiness are not difficult to trace. All the theories and models of economic discrimination reach the same dismal conclusion: discrimination will not go away, because the ideal environment does not and cannot exist, or because there are few incentives to discourage discrimination, because many incentives exist to encourage it. The discriminators suffer few costs, though society does, and they realize material benefits at the expense of their victims or society at large.

Prescriptions to abolish discrimination have centered around assimilation, perfection of the market, or change of the philosophy and institutions that tolerate or encourage discrimination. None of these, however, seems practical, either because of the potential opposition of the parties concerned, or because of the immensity or high cost of the expected change. These findings lead to the conclusion that discrimination will not go away by peaceful or organizational means. However, if discrimination cannot be eliminated, it can be tamed and rendered almost benign.

Taming discrimination involves four major approaches. First, it is essential that equality before the law be guaranteed to minorities and women as well as to all other citizens. Affirmative action is the second measure to ensure that no discrimination is tolerated in daily interaction in the economy. Though a short-run measure, it is indispensable to keep the issue of discrimination in view and to reduce its practice as much as possible.

The two major recommendations of this study are a guarantee of full employment, and a guarantee of equal opportunity to acquire endowments from the time of birth of the individual. The former reduces the pressure of competition and the grounds for charges of reverse discrimination. The latter guarantees that minorities and women will be equipped to compete in the market on equal terms with others on the basis of merit.

Finally, it is evident that the market, especially because of its imperfection, will not remove discrimination. It is also highly unlikely to expect the majority and men who benefit from discrimination to alter their behavior willingly and cease to discriminate, for to do so would be economically irrational. Therefore, the only mechanism to tame discrimination, in addition to a sustained movement by the victims in pursuit of equality, is for the government to apply affirmative action and to guarantee equality before the law, equality of opportunity for acquired endowment, and full employment.

NOTES

1.   "Justice Marshall's Constitutional Critique," *Focus,* June 1987, 5.

2.   How often have university administrators formulated job descriptions that automatically preclude women from applying!

3.   Stephan S. Baratz and Joan C. Baratz, "Early Childhood Intervention: The Social Science Institutional Racism," *Harvard Educational Review* 40, no. 1 (Winter 1970): 29-50.

4.   On structural rigidities of the market, see Dafne Greenwood, "The Institutional Inadequacy of the Market in Determining Comparable Worth: Implications for Value Theory," *Journal of Economic Issues* XVIII, no. 2 (June 1984): 457-64.

5.   The same analysis applies to other countries, although the United States will be the primary illustration in this context.

Bibliography

Abramson, Jill. "For Women Lawyers, an Uphill Struggle." *New York Times Magazine*, 6 March 1988.

Affirmative Action: The Unrealized Goal, Washington, D.C.: Potomac Institute, 1973.

Ajayi, J. F. A., and Michael Crowder, eds. *History of West Africa*. Vol. II. New York: Columbia University Press, 1972.

Altehar, A. S. *The Position of Women in Hindu Civilization*. Delhi: Motilal Banarsidass, 1956.

America, Richard F., ed. *The Wealth of Races: The Present Value of Benefits from Past Injuries*. New York: Greenwood Press, 1990.

Anderson, Bonnie S., and Judith P. Zinsser. *A History of Their Own: Women in Europe from Prehistory to the Present*. New York: Harper & Row, 1988.

Arrow, Kenneth. "Models of Job Discrimination." In Anthony H. Pascal, ed., *Racial Discrimination in Economic Life*. Lexington, Mass.: Lexington Books, 1972.

Babb, Florence A., "Andean Marketwomen in the Economy," in June Nash and Helen Safa. *Women and Change in Latin America: New Directions in Sex and Class*. South Hadley, Mass.: Bergin and Garvey Publishers, 1985.

Bacon, Alice Mabel. *Japanese Girls and Women*. Boston: Houghton Mifflin, 1892.

Badran, Margot. "Women and Production in the Middle East." *Trends in History* 2, no. 3 (1982): 59-88.

Badri, Balghis. "Women, Land Ownership and Development: The Case of Sudan." *The Ahfad Journal* 3, no. 2 (Dec. 1986).

Ballhatchet, Kenneth. *Race, Sex, and Class under the Raj: Imperial Attitudes and Policies and Their Critics, 1793-1905*. London: Weidenfeld and Nicolson, 1980.

Baratz, Stephan S., and Joan C. Baratz. "Early Childhood Intervention: The Social Science Institutional Racism." *Harvard Educational Review* 40, no. 1 (Winter 1970).

Barclay, William, Krishna Kumar, and Ruth P. Simms. *Racial Conflict, Discrimination and Power*. New York: AMS Press, 1976.

Bashan, Richard. "National Racial Policies and University Education in Malaysia," in William C. McCready, ed., *Culture, Ethnicity, and Identity: Current Issues in Research*. New York: Academic Press, 1983.

Beck, Lois, and Nikki Keddie, eds. *Women in the Muslim World*. Cambridge, Mass.: Harvard University Press, 1978.

Becker, Gary. *The Economics of Discrimination*. 2d ed. Chicago: University of Chicago Press, 1971.

Beller, A. H. "Occupational Segregation by Sex: Determinants and Changes." *Journal of Human Resources* 17, no. 3 (Summer 1982): 371-92.

Bergmann, Barbara. "The Effects on White Income of Discrimination in Employment." *Journal of Political Economy* 79 (March-April 1971).

Blake, W. O. *The History of Slavery and the Slave Trade, Ancient and Modern*. Columbus, Ohio: J. & H. Miller, 1857.

Bloch, Marc. *Slavery and Serfdom in the Middle Ages*. Translated by William R. Beer. Berkeley: University of California Press, 1975.

Böhning, W. R. "International Migration in Western Europe: Reflections on the Past Five Years." *International Labour Review* 118, no. 4 (July-August 1979).

Boserup, Ester. *Women's Role in Economic Development*. New York: St. Martin's Press, 1970.

Braun, Denn. *The Rich Get Richer: The Rise of Income Inequality in the United States*. Chicago: Nelson-Hall, 1991.

Bridenthal, Renate, and Claudia Koonz. *Becoming Visible: Women in European History*. Boston: Houghton Mifflin, 1977.

Browne, Robert S. "The Economic Case for Reparations to Black America." *American Economic Review* 62, no. 2 (May 1972): 39-46.

Cahn, Susan. *Industry of Devotion: The Transformation of Women's Work in England, 1500-1660*. New York: Columbia University Press, 1987.

Cambridge Economic History of Europe. Vol. I. Edited by. M. M. Postan. Cambridge: Cambridge University Press, 1966.

Carter, S. B. "Occupational Segregation, Teachers' Wages, and American Economic Growth." *Journal of Economic History* 46, no. 2 (June 1986): 373-83.

Cherry, Robert. *Discrimination: Its Economic Impact on Blacks, Women, and Jews*. Lexington, Mass.: Lexington Books, 1989.

Coleman, James. *Equality of Educational Opportunity*. Washington, D.C.: U.S. Department of Health, Education, and Welfare, 1966.

Connings, Kathy. "The Earnings of Female and Male Middle Managers: A Canadian Case Study." *Journal of Human Resources* 23, no. 1 (Winter 1988): 34-56.

Conway, D. A., and H. V. Roberts. "Reverse Regression, Fairness, and Employment Discrimination." *Journal of Business and Economic Statistics* 1, no. 1 (January 1983): 75-85.

Corcoran, Gervase O. S. A. *Saint Augustine on Slavery*. Rome: Institutum Patristicum, 1985.

Cotton, Jeremiah. "Discrimination and Favoritism in the U.S. Labor Market."
    American Journal of Economics and Sociology 47, no. 1 (January 1988).
Cox, Donald. "Inequality in the Lifetime Earnings of Women." *Review of
    Economics and Statistics* (August 1982).
Cox, Oliver C. "The Rise of Modern Race Relations." In William Barclay,
    Krishna Kumar, and Ruth P. Simms. *Racial Conflict, Discrimination and
    Power*. New York: AMS Press, 1976.
Current Population Survey. Ann Arbor, Mich.: Consortium for Political and Social
    Research, 1976.
Dandamaev, Muhammad A. *Slavery in Babylonia: From Nabopolassar to
    Alexander the Great (626-331 B.C.)*. Translated by Victoria A. Powell.
    DeKalb, Ill.: Northern Illinois University Press, 1984.
Danziger, Sheldon G., and Daniel E. Weinberg, eds. *Fighting Poverty: What
    Works and What Doesn't*. Cambridge, Mass.: Harvard University Press, 1986.
Devoud, Marcelle, and Martine Levy. "Women's Employment in France:
    Protection or Equality?" *International Labour Review* 119, no. 6 (Nov.-Dec.
    1980): 744.
Dinnerstein, Leonard, and Frederic Cople Jaher, eds.. *The Aliens: A History of
    Ethnic Minorities in America*. New York: Appleton-Century-Crofts, 1970.
Dotson, F., and L. Dotson. "Indians and Coloureds in Rhodesia and Nyasaland."
    In M. L. Barron, ed., *Minorities in a Changing World*. New York: Knopf, 1967.
Duff, John B., and Larry A. Green, eds. *Slavery: Its Origin and Legacy*. New
    York: Thomas Y. Crowell Company, 1975.
England, P. "Occupational Segregation Rejoined [The Failure of Human Capital
    Theory to Explain Occupational Sex Segregation]." *Journal of Human
    Resources* 20, no. 3 (Summer 1985): 441-43.
Esman, Milton J., and Itamar Rabinovitch, eds. *Ethnicity, Pluralism and the State
    in the Middle East*. Ithaca, N.Y.: Cornell University Press, 1988.
Faaland, Just, J. R. Parkinson, et al. *Growth and Ethnic Inequality: Malaysia's
    New Economic Policy*. New York: St. Martin's Press, 1990.
Fabohunda, Eleanor R. "Female and Male Work Profile." In Christine Oppong,
    ed., *Female and Male in West Africa*. London: George Allen and Unwin, 1983.
Finley, M. I., ed. *Classical Slavery*. London: Frank Carr, 1987.
Foster, Charles R. "The Underrepresented Nations." In Charles R. Foster, ed.,
    Nations Without a State: Ethnic Minorities in Western Europe. New York:
    Praeger, 1980.
Gallo, Patrick J. *Ethnic Alienation: The Italian American*. Cranbury, N.J.:
    Fairleigh Dickinson University Press, 1974.
Garlan, Yvon. "War, Piracy and Slavery in the Greek World." In M. I. Finley ed.,
    Classical Slavery. London: Frank Cass, 1987.
Gellner, E., and C. Micaud. *Arabs and Berbers*. London: Duckworth, 1973.
Genovese, Eugene D. *Roll, Jordan, Roll: The World the Slaves Made*. New York:
    Pantheon Books, 1975.
Glenn, E. N. "Racial Ethnic Women's Labor: The Intersection of Race, Gender,
    and Class Oppression." *Revolutionary Radical Political Economics* 17, no. 3
    (Fall 1985): 86-108.

Goldin, Claudia. *Understanding the Gender Gap: An Economic History of American Women*. New York: Oxford University Press, 1990.

Gordon, David M., ed. *Problems of Political Economy: An Urban Perspective*. 2d ed. Lexington, Mass.: Heath, 1977.

Green C. A., and M. A. Ferbe. "Employment Discrimination: An Empirical Test of Forward versus Reverse Regression." *Journal of Human Resources* 19, no. 4 (Fall 1984): 557-69.

Greenwood, Dafne "The Institutional Inadequacy of the Market in Determining Comparable Worth: Implications for Value Theory." *Journal of Economic Issues* XVIII, no. 2 (June 1984).

Gregory, Jeanne. *Sex, Race and the Law: Legislating for Equality*. London: Sage Publications, 1987.

Guy, Donna J. "Women, Peonage, and Industrialization: Argentina, 1810-1914." *Latin American Research Review* 16, no. 3 (1981): 65-89.

Halsey, Margaret. *Color Blind: A White Woman Looks at the Negro*. New York: Simon and Schuster, 1946.

Hammerman, Herbert. *A Decade of New Opportunity: Affirmative Action in the 1970's*. Washington, D.C.: Potomac Institute, 1984.

Hay, Margaret Jean, and Marcia Wright, eds. *African Women and the Law: Historical Perspectives*. Boston: Boston University African Studies Center, 1982.

Heidhues, Mary F. Somers. *Southeast Asia's Chinese Minorities*. Hawthorn, Victoria: Longman, 1974.

Hepburn, A. C., ed. *Minorities in History*. New York: Edward Arnold, 1978.

Hepple, Bob. *Race, Jobs and the Law in Britain*. London: Penguin Press, 1968.

Hibbert, A. B. "The Economic Policies of Towns." In M. M. Postan, E. E. Rich, and Edward Miller, eds. *Cambridge Economic History of Europe*. Vol. III. Cambridge: Cambridge University Press, 1963.

Hijab, Nadia. *Womenpower: The Arab Debate on Women at Work*, Cambridge: Cambridge University Press, 1988.

Hoffman, Joan. *Racial Discrimination and Economic Development*. Lexington, Mass.: Lexington Books, 1975.

Hourani, A. H. *Minorities in the Arab World*. London and New York: Oxford University Press, 1947.

Hundert, Gershon David. "The Role of the Jews in Commerce in Early Modern Poland and Lithuania." *Journal of European Economic History* 16, no. 2 (Fall 1987).

Huttman, Elizabeth, ed. *Urban Housing Segregation of Minorities in Western Europe and the United States*. Durham, N.C.: Duke University Press, 1991.

Jaynes, Gerald David, and Robin M. Williams, Jr., eds. *A Common Destiny: Blacks and American Society*. Washington, D.C.: National Academy Press, 1989.

Jensen, Willy. *Women Without Men: Gender and Marginality in an Algerian Town*. Leiden: E. J. Brill, 1987.

John, Sir Rupert. *Racism and Its Elimination*. New York: United Nations Institute for Training and Research, 1981.

Johnson, G., and G. Solon. "Estimates of the Direct Effects of Comparable Worth Policy." *American Economic Review* 17, no. 1 (Jan. 1985).

Jusenius, Carol L., and Richard M. Scheffler. "Earnings Differentials Among Academic Economists: Empirical Evidence on Race and Sex." *Journal of Economics and Business* 33, no. 2 (Winter 1981): 88-96.

"Justice Marshall's Constitutional Critique." *Focus* (June 1987).

Kain, John F., ed. *Race and Poverty: The Economics of Discrimination.* Englewood Cliffs, N.J.: Prentice-Hall, 1969.

Kamalich, Richard F., and Soloman W. Polacheck. "Discrimination: Fact or Fiction? An Examination Using an Alternative Approach." *Southern Economic Journal* 49, no.2 (October 1982).

Klinov, Ruth. "Ethnic Discrimination in the Israeli Labor Movement." Hebrew University (November 1991), mineo.

Krauss, Peter. *The Persistence of Patriarchy: Class, Gender, and Ideology in Twentieth Century Algeria.* New York: Praeger, 1987.

Kreps, Juanita M., ed. *Women and the American Economy: A Look to the 1980s.* Englewood Cliffs, N. J.: Prentice-Hall, 1976.

Krueger, Anne O. "The Economics of Discrimination." *Journal of Political Economy* 71 (October 1963).

Lange, D. "The Kingdoms and Peoples of Chad." In D. T. Niane, *General History of Africa*, IV, UNESCO. London: Heinemann.

Lavrin, Asunción, ed. *Latin American Women: Historical Perspectives.* Westport, Conn.: Greenwood Press, 1978.

Leahy, P. J. "Are Racial Factors Important for the Allocation of Mortgage Money? A Quasi-experimental Approach of an Aspect of Discrimination." *American Journal of Economic Sociology* 44, no. 2 (April 1985): 185-96.

Leonard, J. S. "Affirmative Action as Earning Redistribution: The Targeting of Compliance Reviews." *Journal of Labor Economics* 3, no. 3 (July 1985): 363-84.

Lescott-Leszczynski, John. *The History of U.S. Ethnic Policy and Its Impact on European Ethnics.* Boulder, Colo.: Westview Press, 1984.

Levine, Hillel. *Economic Origins of Anti-Semitism: Poland and Its Jews in Early Modern Period.* New Haven, Conn.: Yale University Press, 1991.

Liddle, Joanna, and Rama Joshi, eds. *Daughters of Independence: Gender, Caste and Class in India.* London: Zed Books, 1986.

Lieberson, Stanley, and Mary C. Waters. *From Many Strands: Ethnic and Racial Groups in Contemporary America.* New York: Russell Sage Foundation, 1988.

Lieberson, Stanley, and Mary C. Waters. "The Rise of a New Ethnic Group: The Unhyphenated American." *Items* 43. no. 1 (March 1989).

Lipton, Merle. *Capitalism and Apartheid, South Africa, 1910-1984.* Totowa, N.J.: Rowman and Allenheld, 1985.

Lopez, Robert. "The Trade of Medieval Europe: The South." In M.M. Postan and H. J. Habakkuk, eds., *Cambridge Economic History of Europe*, Vol. II. Cambridge: Cambridge University Press, 1952.

Low, S. A., and D. J. Villegas. "An Alternative Approach to the Analysis of Wage Differentials." *Southern Economic Journal* 54, no. 2 (October 1987).

Lundahl, Mats. "The Rationale of Apartheid." *American Economic Review* 72, no. 5 (December 1982): 1169-79.

―――, and Eskil Wadensjo. *Unequal Treatment: A Study in the Neoclassical Theory of Discrimination*. New York: New York University Press, 1984.

Mackie, J. A. C., and Charles A. Coppel. "A Preliminary Survey." In J. A. C. Mackie, ed., *The Chinese in Indonesia: Five Essays*. Melbourne: Nelson with the Australian Institute of International Affairs, 1976.

Mallier, A. T., and M. J. Rosser. *Women and the Economy: A Comparative Study of Britain and the USA*. Houndmills, Basinstoke, Hampshire: Macmillan, 1987.

Marcus, Alexis, George Haines, Jr., and Leonard S. Simon. *Black People's Profiles in the Inner City*. Ann Arbor: University of Michigan Press, 1980.

Margo, Robert A. "Race, Educational Attainment and the 1940 Census." *Journal of Economic History* XLVI, no. 1 (March 1986).

Marshall, Ray. "The Economics of Racial Discrimination: A Survey." *Journal of Economic Literature* XII, no. 3 (September 1974).

Masters, Stanley. *Black-White Income Differentials: Empirical Studies and Policy Implications*. New York: Academic Press, 1975.

McCready, William C., ed. *Culture, Ethnicity, and Identity: Current Issues in Research*. New York: Academic Press, 1983.

McLaurie, R.D. *The Political Role of Minority Groups in the Middle East*. New York: Praeger, 1979.

McMahon, Theresa Schmid. "Women and Economic Evolution or The Effects of Industrial Changes Upon the Status of Women." Dissertation, University of Wisconsin, 1912.

McNabb, Robert, and George Psacharonpoulos. "Racial Earnings Differentials in the U.K." *Oxford Economic Papers* 33, no. 3 (November 1981).

Minorities in Conflict: A World Guide. Chicago: St. James Press, 1989.

Morewedge, Rosemarie T., ed. *The Role of Women in the Middle Ages*. Albany: State University of New York Press, 1975.

Moskoff, William. "Women and Work in Israel and the Islamic Middle East." *Quarterly Review of Economics and Business* 22, no. 4 (Winter 1982).

Motroshilova, Nelya V.. "Soviet Women in the Life of Society: Achievements and Problems." *International Social Science Journal* 35, no. 4 (1983).

Myrdal, Gunnar. *An American Dilemma: The Negro Problem and Modern Democracy*. New York: Harper and Brothers, 1944.

Nagel, Joane. "The Conditions of Ethnic Separatism: The Kurds in Turkey, Iran, and Iraq." *Ethnicity* 7 (1980).

Nash, June, Helen Safa, and contributors, eds. *Sex and Class in Latin America*. New York: Praeger, 1976.

Oppong, Christine, ed. *Female and Male in West Africa*. London: George Allen and Unwin, 1983.

Organization of American Historians. *Restoring Women to History*. Bloomington, Ind.: Organization of American Historians, 1988.

Pascal, Anthony H., ed. *Racial Discrimination in Economic Life*. Lexington, Mass.: Heath, 1972.

Phelps, Edmund S. "The Statistical Theory of Racism and Sexism." *American Economic Review* 62, no. 4 (September 1972).

Piore, M. J. *Birds of Passage: Migrant Labor and Industrial Societies.* Cambridge: Cambridge University Press.

Polacheck, S. W. "Occupational Segregation: A Defense of Human Capital Predictions [The Failure of Human Capital Theory to Explain Occupational Sex Segregation]." *Journal of Human Resources* 20, no. 3 (Summer 1985): 437-40.

Price, Richard, and Edwin Mills. "Race and Residence in Earning Determination." *Journal of Urban Economics* 17, no. 1 (January 1985).

"Racism." *Encyclopaedia Britannica,* 15 (1974): 360-66.

Reich, Michael. *Racial Inequality.* Princeton: Princeton University Press, 1981.

Remick, Helen, ed. *Comparable Worth and Wage Discrimination.* Philadelphia: Temple University Press, 1984.

Roberts, Elizabeth, *Women's Work, 1840-1940.* [in Britain], Basingstoke: Macmillan Education Limited, 1988.

Robertson, Claire, and Martin Klein, eds. *Women and Slavery in Africa.* Madison: University of Wisconsin Press, 1983.

Romero, Patricia W., ed. *Life Histories of African Women.* London: Ashfield Press, 1988.

Rose, Jerome C. "Biological Consequences of Segregation and Economic Deprivation: A Post-Slavery Population from Southwest Arkansas." *Journal of Economic History* XLIX, no. 2 (June 1989).

Rueschemeyer, Marilyn. "The Demands of Work on Human Quality of Marriage: An Exploratory Study of Professionals in Two Socialist Societies." In George Kurian and Rafun Ghosh, *Women in the Family and the Economy.* Westport, Conn.: Greenwood Press, 1981.

Rule, Sheila. "Black Britons Describe a Motherland That Has Long Held Them As Inferior." *New York Times,* 31 March (1991).

Russell-Wood, A. J. R. "Female and Family in the Economy and Society of Colonial Brazil." In Asunción Lavrin, ed., *Latin American Women: Historical Perspectives.* Westport, Conn.: Greenwood Press, 1978.

Ryan, William. *Blaming the Victim.* New York: Pantheon Books, 1971.

Sandhu, Kernial Singh. *Indians in Malaya: Some Aspects of Their Immigration and Settlement, 1786-1957.* Cambridge: Cambridge University Press, 1969.

Sandmeyer, E. C. *The Anti-Chinese Movement in California.* Chicago: University of Illinois Press, 1973.

Scott, Margaret. "Where the Quota is King." *New York Times,* 17 (November 1991).

Shanin, Teodor. "Ethnicity in the Soviet Union: Analytical Perceptions and Political Strategies." *Comparative Studies in Society and History* 31, no. 3 (1989).

Sharp, Ansel M., Charles A. Register, and Richard H. Leftwich, eds. *Economics of Social Issues.* 8th ed. Plano, Tex.: Business Publications Inc., 1988.

Shepherd, George W., Jr., ed. *Effective Sanctions on South Africa: The Cutting Edge of Economic Intervention.* New York: Greenwood Press, 1991.

Shmink, Marianne. "Women and Urban Industrial Development in Brazil." In June Nash, Helen Safa, and contributors, *Women and Change in Latin America: New Directions in Sex and Class*. South Hadley, Mass.: Bergin and Garvey Publishers, 1985.

Shulman, Steven, and William Darity, eds. *The Question of Discrimination: Racial Inequality in the U.S. Labor Market*. Middletown, Conn.: Wesleyan University Press, 1989.

Smith, James P., and Finis R. Welch. "Black Economic Progress after Myrdal." *Journal of Economic Literature* XXVII, no. 2 (June 1989).

Sowell, Thomas. *Markets and Minorities*. New York: Basic Books, 1981.

Stevens, F. S., ed. *Racism. The Australian Experience: A Study of Race Prejudice in Australia*. Vols. 1-3. New York: Taplinger Publishing, 1972.

Swepston, Lee "Latin America's Approaches to the 'Indian Problem.'" *International Labour Review* 117, no. 2 (March-April 1978).

Taylor, P. A., and S. W. Shields. "Mexican Americans and Employment Inequality in the Federal Civil Services." *Social Science Quarterly* 65, no. 2 (June 1984): 381-91.

Thurow, Lester C. *Poverty and Discrimination*. Washington, D.C.: Brookings Institution, 1969.

Tinker, Irene, ed. *Persistent Inequalities: Women and World Development*. New York: Oxford University Press, 1990.

Tobin, James. "On Improving the Economic Status of the Negro." In Paul Samuelson, ed., *Readings in Economics*. New York: McGraw-Hill, 1973.

Treiman, Donald J., Heidi I. Hartman, and Patricia A. Roos. "Assessing Pay Discrimination Using National Data." In Helen Remick, ed., *Comparable Worth and Wage Discrimination*. Philadelphia: Temple University Press, 1984.

Tuma, E. H. "Economic Costs of Ethnic and Sex Discrimination in Middle Eastern Society: Exploration." Department of Economics, University of California, Davis, Working Paper 381, 1991.

———. "The Economic Impact of the Capitulations: The Middle East and Europe: A Reinterpretation." *Journal of European Economic History* 18, no. 3 (Winter 1989).

———. "Why Problems Do Not Go Away: The Problem of Inflation." *Journal of European Economic History* 11, no. 2 (Fall 1982).

———. *European Economic History: Tenth Century to the Present*. Palo Alto, Calif.: Pacific Books, 1979.

———, and Barry Haworth. *Cultural Diversity and Economic Education*. Palo Alto, Calif.: Pacific Books, 1993.

Turgeon, Lynn. *State and Discrimination: The Other Side of the Cold War*. New York: Sharppe, 1989.

Verdugo, Naomi T., and Richard R. Verdugo. "Earning Differentials Among Mexican Americans, Black and White Workers." *Social Science Quarterly* 64, no. 2 (June 1984).

Viane, D. T., ed. *General History of Africa*. IV. UNESCO. London: Heinemann, 1981.

von Furstenberg, G., et al.. *Patterns of Racial Discrimination.* Vol. II. Lexington, Mass.: Lexington Books, 1974.

Wagley, C., and M. Harris. *Minorities in the New World.* New York: Columbia University Press, 1958.

Wallbank, Frank W. "Trade and Industry Under the Later Roman Empire in the West." In M. M. Postan and H. J. Habakkuk, eds., *Cambridge Economic History of Europe*, Vol. II. Cambridge: Cambridge University Press, 1952.

Ward, W. Peter. *White Canada Forever.* Montreal: McGill-Queen's University Press, 1978.

Wiesner, Harry F. *Working Women in Renaissance Germany.* New Brunswick, N.J.: Rutgers University Press, 1986.

Williams, Walter E. *South Africa's War Against Capitalism.* New York: Praeger, 1989.

Williamson, Joel, ed. *The Origins of Segregation.* Boston: Heath, 1968.

Willis, David K. *Klass: How Russians Really Live.* New York: St. Martin's Press, 1985.

Wirsing, Robert G., ed. *Protection of Minorities.* New York: Pergamon Press, 1981.

Wolgast, Elizabeth. *Equality and the Rights of Women.* Ithaca, N.Y.: Cornell, 1980.

World Dictionary of Minorities. Minority Rights Group. Chicago: Longman, 1990.

Wyzan, Michael, ed. *The Political Economy of Ethnic Discrimination and Affirmative Action.* New York: Praeger, 1990.

Yetman, Norman R., ed. *Majority and Minority.* 4th ed. Boston: Allyn and Bacon, 1982.

Yinger, J. "Measuring Racial Discrimination with Fair Housing Audits: Caught in the Act." *American Economic Review* 76, no. 4 (December 1986).

Index